Climate of Capitulation

Climate of Capitulation

An Insider's Account of State Power in a Coal Nation

Vivian E. Thomson

The MIT Press
Cambridge, Massachusetts
London, England

Set in Stone Serif and Stone Sans by Toppan Best-set Premedia Limited. Printed and bound in the United States of America.

Library of Congress Cataloging-in-Publication Data

Names: Thomson, Vivian E., 1956- author.
Title: Climate of capitulation : an insider's account of state power in a
   coal nation / Vivian E. Thomson.
Description: Cambridge, MA : MIT Press, [2017] | Includes bibliographical
   references and index.
Identifiers: LCCN 2016040518 | ISBN 9780262036344 (hardcover : alk. paper)
Subjects: LCSH: Air pollution--Government policy--Virginia. | Energy
   industries--Political activity--Virginia. | Electric utilities--Virginia.
   | Coal-fired power plants--Virginia. | Energy policy--Virginia. | United
   States. Clean Air Act. | Virginia--Politics and government--21st century.
Classification: LCC HC107.V83 A465 2017 | DDC 363.738/7--dc23 LC record avail-
   able at https://lccn.loc.gov/2016040518

10 9 8 7 6 5 4 3 2 1

dedicated to Martha Derthick

Contents

Acknowledgments

The list of those who helped with this book is long. I must start with my fellow Virginia State Air Pollution Control Board members Hullie Moore and Bruce Buckheit, without whom the events related here never would have happened. They brought enormous professionalism, expertise, integrity, discipline, and humor to their work on the Board. I have the greatest respect and admiration for them. Hullie is also a professional photographer who studied with Ansel Adams. Hullie's exquisite photo of the moon over Shenandoah National Park graces the jacket of this book.

Board member Sterling Rives invariably listened carefully, spoke thoughtfully, and took seriously the Board's responsibility to protect the public good. Board Chair Richard Langford and member John Hanson often disagreed with Hullie, Bruce, and me. But John and Richard helped make the Board a place where respectful, informed debates were the order of the day. Carl Josephson, Virginia's former Senior Assistant Attorney General, capably defended the Board's permit decision on the Mirant power plant.

The citizens of Alexandria, Roda, and Wise spoke out, attended meeting after meeting, year after year, and insisted on their right to clean air. Their courage and resistance to the status quo are an example for us all.

Bob Burnley and W. Tayloe Murphy Jr. epitomized strong environmental leadership dedicated to the public good. When I left the Air Board in 2010, I told the staff of the Virginia Department of Environmental Quality that they matter, that their individual voices and actions are important. I still believe that, in spite of the conclusions I have drawn about the structural barriers to environmental policy making in Virginia.

The following individuals generously provided interviews, information or photos: Professor Viney Aneja, University of North Carolina, Raleigh; John Britton, former outside counsel for the City of Alexandria; Bob Burnley, former Director, Virginia Department of Environmental Quality;

Elizabeth Chimento, citizen activist and leader, Alexandria, Virginia; Bill Euille, former mayor, City of Alexandria; John Harbison, Sierra Club volunteer; Aaron Isherwood, Sierra Club; Cale Jaffe, Southern Environmental Law Center; Colleen McKaughan, US Environmental Protection Agency; Jerry McCarthy, former Executive Director of the Virginia Environmental Endowment; Cat McCue, formerly of the Southern Environmental Law Center; W. Tayloe Murphy Jr., former Virginia Secretary of Natural Resources and longtime member, Virginia House of Delegates; Del Pepper, City of Alexandria City Council member and former vice mayor; Ignacio Pessoa, former City Attorney for the City of Alexandria; Albert C. Pollard Jr., former member of the Virginia House of Delegates; Lalit Sharma, Division Chief, City of Alexandria Office of Environmental Quality; Bill Skrabak, Deputy Director of the City of Alexandria's Office of Environmental Quality; Paul Smedberg, City Council member, City of Alexandria; Valerie Thomson, Director of Administration, Virginia Department of Environmental Quality; Khoa Tran, Senior Environmental Specialist, City of Alexandria Office of Environmental Quality; Tisara Photography, Alexandria, Virginia; and Jeff Whitlow, US Environmental Protection Agency. Email messages from the Kaine administration made publicly available by the Library of Virginia were important sources.

I thank Elizabeth Chimento and Hullie Moore for taking the time to read and comment on the draft manuscript. I am grateful to Jean Thomson Black and Joe Calamia of Yale University Press for their invaluable assistance and advice. At the MIT Press, Paul Bethge, Beth Clevenger, Miranda Martin, William Strong, and Anthony Zannino were instrumental. I thank Pete Andrews, Alice Kaswan, and Barry Rabe for their insightful criticisms, which improved and strengthened the book.

My daughters, Amelia and Flora Thomson-DeVeaux, cheered from the sidelines and provided inspiration by means of their fine examples as young professionals and intellectuals. I thank my mother, Selma Thomson, for her curiosity about this book and for her ongoing encouragement of my writing. My husband, Patrick Roach, was a reliable sounding board during my eight years on the Air Board. He provided much valuable input and moral support as the cases documented here unfolded. Pat provided astute editorial and substantive comments on the manuscript. My many conversations with him about the book shaped its substance and style in countless important ways.

This book is dedicated to Martha Derthick, renowned scholar of federalism and public policy, who graciously offered to be my dissertation advisor many years ago. Martha launched me on my unexpected journey as an academic. She was always ready to provide criticism and feedback on this work, and she encouraged its development from the very start. She was my friend for over twenty years, even though we probably never voted for the same political candidate. Martha remains my model for how to undertake research and write about politics and policy. Her intellectual stamp is all over this book. She is sorely missed.

Introduction

In official documents submitted to the United Nations in 2015, President Barack Obama committed the United States to reducing emissions of greenhouse gases in 2025 by 26 to 28 percent below 2005 levels. This promise faces strong political headwinds because of Donald Trump's campaign threat to withdraw from international climate agreements. But meeting this obligation is an important piece of the world's struggle to ameliorate climate change. Despite China's status as the leading emitter of greenhouse gases, the United Nations emissions-reduction commitment of the United States represents a substantial fraction (5.8 percent) of 2014 global carbon dioxide emissions. By one estimate, the United States emitted 29.3 percent of cumulative global carbon dioxide emissions between 1850 and 2002, as compared with 7.6 percent for China. The United States owes a debt to the global community for its high-polluting path to wealth and power.[1]

A large piece of the United States' reductions in greenhouse-gas emissions must come from the electric utilities. In 2014 electricity generation was the source of 30 percent of the United States' overall greenhouse-gas emissions. For perspective, in 2013 total carbon dioxide emissions from electric utilities in the United States exceeded by 1.8 times those in the 28 European Union Member States combined.[2]

The states will play a central role in reducing carbon dioxide emissions from the electric utilities, because of the states' primacy in regulating stationary sources of air pollution. Using Clean Air Act authority, the federal US Environmental Protection Agency (EPA) has adopted regulations with state-specific goals for greenhouse-gas emissions from fossil-fuel-fired power plants. This particular state-federal partnership is called the Clean Power Plan, which Donald Trump promised while campaigning to overturn. As is the case with the Clean Air Act's regulations generally, no state may be forced to implement such measures. But if the Clean Power Plan survives, it seems likely that many of the states, if not all of them, will eventually accept delegated authority for undertaking these regulations, thereby retaining control over what happens to the electric utilities within their borders. Emission reductions expected under the Clean Power Plan constitute 40 percent of the US's overall United Nations commitment in 2025. Those reductions will come as electricity generation continues to move from coal-fired facilities to less polluting sources.[3]

Reducing carbon dioxide emissions from coal-fired power plants confers significant public health benefits from improved local and regional air quality. As coal-fired utilities' carbon dioxide emissions decrease, so do those facilities' sulfur dioxide and nitrogen oxides emissions, which degrade air quality and harm public health by contributing to elevated particulate matter and urban smog levels. African Americans and Latinos suffer from disproportionately high levels of asthma, which can be exacerbated by urban air pollution and by the high temperatures associated with climate change. To ensure that low-income and minority communities receive fair treatment as power plant emissions are reduced, the EPA has encouraged state agencies to emphasize environmental justice concerns.[4]

Although pundits have predicted that regulating carbon dioxide emissions from the electric utilities could cause coal's demise in the United States, the US is, and will remain, a coal nation—that is, a country that relies on coal for generating electricity even as coal-fired power plants shut down across the country. In 2015 coal consumption in the US fell by 29 percent relative to peak levels in 2007. But according to US government projections, even if the Clean Power Plan were fully implemented in 2030, Americans would still receive from one fifth to one fourth of their electricity from coal-fired power plants, as compared with one third in 2015. The Clean Power Plan would be a first important step in regulating the nation's carbon dioxide emissions from the electric utilities. The United States will remain dependent on coal for electric power for the foreseeable future.[5]

The Clean Power Plan rests on untested legal authority; as a result, the federal courts may alter the Plan's shape; so could Congress or the president. But under every scenario, even if the Clean Power Plan does not come into force, the states will continue to play an important part in reducing electric utility air pollution. Strong state-level political will and institutional capacity, especially in the forty states that produce or consume coal, are critical to the nation's success in reducing carbon dioxide emissions from electricity generation.[6]

Entrenched state-level cultural, institutional and economic biases threaten those efforts. By illuminating those forces and the ways in which important actors wield political power in the arena of state-level air pollution policy, we can adopt tools to help ensure that national emissions-reduction commitments and the associated public health improvements will be realized. This book provides insights into the expression of power in states' air pollution policy making through first-person, policy-participant case studies and through analysis that generalizes the cases.

Clean Air Policy Making at the State Level

Two important kinds of processes for making air pollution policy play out in the United States as state officials implement the Clean Air Act or state-specific air pollution laws to reduce emissions from stationary sources such as power plants and factories. State environmental agencies adopt regulations that apply across entire industry categories. Once those regulations are in place, each affected polluting facility receives source-specific permit limits. Permits become precedents for similar facilities elsewhere in the nation, because permit writers must often apply to a specific polluting source the limits determined to be "best" or "available" in a particular industry category.

Air pollution permits for stationary sources represent the point at which government mandates for reducing air pollution become reality. Thus permit writing is an especially potent form of environmental policy making. Legal phrases such as "best available control technology" have no meaning until translated into conditions that apply to a particular facility. Permits for large sources such as power plants are highly specific and technically detailed, and such permits can easily exceed a hundred pages. Affected companies lobby hard for special treatment at both the regulation and permitting phases, not only because they want to minimize costs at the facility covered, but also because every set of Clean Air Act limits for major sources becomes a benchmark for similar facilities elsewhere in the United States.

From 2002 to 2010, I was a member and vice chair of the Virginia State Air Pollution Control Board (known informally as the Air Board), which adopts air pollution regulations for the state. While I was on the Air Board, it could also choose to oversee permits for specific facilities. The Air Board is an independent citizen's (unpaid) regulatory entity, whose members have fixed terms, usually of four years. Board members are appointed by the governor and confirmed by Virginia's General Assembly. I was part of a three-person Board majority that some observers considered assertive.

Through three case studies, I recount overt and covert power struggles surrounding the Board's charged decisions concerning coal and air pollution in Virginia. Some officials in the state environment agency undermined and opposed us, as did some members of the state legislature and one governor (a Democrat). The Virginia General Assembly interfered directly with the Board's decisions and with the Board's makeup and authority. In two cases the Board's controversial Clean Air Act pollution limits held up in court. In the last case the Board lacked strong legal authority and could not assure protection for Appalachian residents exposed to locally high, unhealthy levels of coal dust. In straightforward terms I document the tools of power: economic strength, campaign finance contributions, information, technical-legal expertise, citizen voice, and agenda setting. I describe the actors who affected the Board's decisions and the ways in which they mattered. Publicly available email messages from Governor Tim Kaine's administration show that the Board's activities were watched closely at the highest levels of state government.

My insider's case studies illuminate how Clean Air Act policy processes work on the front lines, when state policy makers translate legal mandates into source-specific emission limits. On the one hand, these narratives reveal systemic obstacles to environmental and public health protection in Virginia. The state's political culture embraces easy relationships between state officials and electric utility and coal interests. Too often Virginia's regulators become seduced by, or lack the ability to resist, powerful companies and their resources. Inappropriately cozy relationships between regulators and the businesses they regulate corrupt Virginia's environmental policy-making processes. On the other hand, these case studies provide a useful corrective to observers who reduce environmental policy processes to unhelpful slogans ("Policymakers just need to understand science better") or to faulty abstractions ("Citizens don't matter"). Virginia's citizens thrust public health risks from coal-related air pollution into the spotlight and forced companies to meet their Clean Air Act obligations.

It is natural to wonder if Virginia's circumstances apply elsewhere. Virginia is considered centrist and a swing ("purple") state in national elections, with broad regional variations that mirror those in many other states. An understanding of political and economic factors affecting Virginia's policy processes regarding air pollution might reveal patterns repeated in other coal consuming or producing states.

Accordingly, this book also asks whether the circumstances fostering Virginia's climate of capitulation are found in other states. That analysis focuses first on six states with high coal production and consumption and whose electric utilities emit large amounts of carbon dioxide: Illinois, Indiana, Kentucky, Pennsylvania, Ohio, and Texas. In 2014 the electric utilities in these states emitted 773 million metric tons of carbon dioxide, which almost equals the 2014 carbon dioxide emissions from the entire country of Germany. These states include what now are called "red" and "blue" states—that is, states that have gone Republican ("red") and Democratic ("blue") in recent presidential elections. Also included is an analysis of eleven Southern states' potential vulnerability to a climate of capitulation. The Southern states are, by and large, not coal producers. But they are important coal consumers, and, as a result, their collective carbon dioxide emissions in 2014 amounted to 815 million metric tons. In 2014 the sixteen states examined in this book were responsible for 65 percent of carbon dioxide from all the electrical generating facilities in the United States.[7]

A Rationale for a Book About Air Pollution in the United States

Air pollution in the United States and in other industrialized nations formerly turned sunsets blood red, caused notorious episodes that killed and sickened hundreds of people, and killed non-human organisms. In the Pennsylvania borough of Donora, longtime residents recalled red sunsets caused by air pollution emitted by nearby steel manufacturing facilities. Art historians now believe that great masters' colorful depictions of sunsets over the centuries serve as indicators for air pollution and volcanic eruptions, with more "fiery" sunsets showing higher levels of airborne dust particles.[8]

Donora was the site of a three-day "motionless clot of smoke" in 1948 that killed twenty people. Two hundred New Yorkers died in a suffocating 1963 smog episode. An estimated 4,000 people died in a 1952 episode of air pollution in London caused by the widespread burning of coal by households and power plants. Around the turn of the twentieth century, some "smoke-blinded" Londoners perished by falling into the Thames. One study has linked 1950s infant mortality rates in Gary, Indiana, to air pollution from steel mills. Leaded gasoline caused elevated blood lead levels in urban dwellers generally, but inner city African American children were especially hard hit by lead poisoning. In the 1970s, forests across Europe succumbed to the combined stresses of air pollution, pests, and climatic factors; that phenomenon was dubbed *Waldsterben* (forest death).[9]

Air pollution is even thought to have driven natural selection. Schoolchildren studying biology learn about the peppered moth, whose predominant coloration patterns in England changed from light to dark and back to light as soot pollution waxed and waned. When levels of air pollution were high, birds could easily feed on white moths when they landed on tree trunks blackened by pollution. As soot levels declined, tree trunks lightened, dark moths became better targets, and the moth population turned whiter once again. Though some observers have raised hard questions about the peppered moth story, evolutionary biologists are once again convinced that air pollution, varied pigmentation in the moth, and predation are linked.[10]

In the United States we regard such dramatic stories as anecdotes from a distant, dirtier past. Since 1970, when a much-strengthened version of the federal Clean Air Act was passed, urban air quality has improved greatly in the United States as a result of combined national and state efforts. The public health benefits are substantial. Episodes of air pollution have decreased in severity and frequency, and air pollution has become less obvious to the general population. An estimated 160,000 fewer people in the US died in 2010 because of the Clean Air Act's programs. Reducing fine particulate matter levels has improved life expectancies across the nation. In a series of rulemakings that started in 1973, the EPA ordered a phasedown in gasoline lead, with a national leaded gasoline ban taking effect in 1996. As a result of the EPA's regulation of power plant sulfur dioxide emissions, which harm public health and cause ecosystem acidification, sulfur deposition in the eastern states has decreased by more than 70 percent since the early 1990s.[11]

But in 2016, 127 million Americans lived in areas that did not attain the National Ambient Air Quality Standards, which the EPA establishes to protect public health and welfare. An estimated 79,000 Americans died in 2013 because of fine particulate air pollution, as compared with 32,500 traffic deaths in that same year. Many ecosystems have not recovered from past levels of acid deposition or still experience excessive loads of incoming pollution. Even though levels of air pollution generally are much reduced, minority and low-income residents can be disproportionately affected by remaining amounts. For example, in Los Angeles estimated lifetime cancer risks associated with diffuse sources of air pollution, such as traffic, are higher for low-income and minority residents. Concentrations of particulate matter measured in 2008 in the Virginia community of Roda (the case examined in chapter 3) far exceeded the applicable national Clean Air Act standard and were comparable to levels seen near open mines in India. There remains much work to be done.[12]

States implement the Clean Air Act's provisions for stationary sources such as power plants and refineries. The first page of the federal Clean Air Act says that state agencies are fundamental in the struggle to provide every American with safe air to breathe. However, if the states are not doing their job, public health and environmental protection are at risk.

Climate change is perhaps our foremost environmental challenge, and the Clean Air Act has evolved into the nation's climate-change law. Federalism experts have emphasized the importance of maintaining state independence and autonomy in federal schemes for controlling greenhouse gases. Strong state roles allow for experimentation, foster policy learning from existing state renewable energy and climate change programs, and help ensure that states can maintain their "democratic prerogatives." But a critical question is whether the US states as a whole can muster the technical capacity and the political will to develop and enforce standards for all air pollution, including carbon dioxide emissions, coming from power plants. Resistance to regulation on the part of the electric utilities and the coal industry has always been especially fierce.[13]

Shotgun Marriage Federalism

In the 1970 version of the Clean Air Act, Congress created a forced political marriage between the states and the national government that persists to this day. Nevertheless, not all parts of the Clean Air Act rely on the states. Among the responsibilities the EPA bears are establishing emission standards for new vehicles and new, large stationary sources, regulating the use of chemicals that deplete the stratospheric ozone layer, setting standards for toxics in fuels such as lead and sulfur, and establishing—and regularly revisiting—the National Ambient Air Quality Standards. By centralizing authority with EPA for these regulatory programs, Congress aimed to provide guaranteed air quality protections for all Americans, ensure use of the best technology when businesses built new facilities, and avoid multiple sets of vehicle emission standards.[14]

Yet much of the Clean Air Act relies on the states for implementation of EPA's nationally set standards, with the possibility of EPA backup should a state fail to act. This partnership makes sense. The federal system in the United States places a premium on maintaining state-level authority, and it would be virtually impossible for EPA to establish and enforce emission standards for the nation's many thousands of large stationary sources of air pollution. But institutional capacity and political will vary greatly among the fifty states, and those variations sometimes create obstacles to the expression of legal mandates or the public will. In the environmental policy arena, weak institutions can inhibit the realization of forceful political will or intense public sentiment.[15]

Absolutely central to the notion of a democracy is citizen control. Environmental policy making presents one of the most formidable arenas for maintaining that control, because of specialized technical-legal language, because vaguely articulated public support for reducing emissions does not translate readily into precise policies, and because politicians are variably receptive to public opinion supportive of pollution control, as a function of political culture, ideology, and state-level economic circumstances. Regulating air pollution presents the additional complication that benefits and costs are distributed asymmetrically, with those bearing costs and benefits often separated in time or space. Politicians typically want to confer benefits, not burdens, on their constituents. Groups potentially bearing the economic burdens of complying with environmental regulations tend to be quite attentive to what politicians do, while many members of the general public, who reap the benefits of better air quality, are often politically inattentive, unless air pollution is immediately evident.[16]

Analysts who study government administrative processes make competing claims about the extent to which attentive groups capture public officials and extract regulatory favors at the expense of the general public. In the principal-agent school, some scholars assert that the regulated community (the "principals") controls legislators and executive agency officials (the "agents") with an iron grip. Others say that private interest control is not inevitable and that leadership can matter a great deal when governors, presidents, legislators, civil servants, or citizens act on behalf of ideas about the public good, as opposed to self-interested motives. Yet another view, which elevates institutional considerations over those of principals and agents, holds that administrative agencies are constantly "under stress" by virtue of being subject to conflicting demands from political executives, legislators, and the courts.[17]

Much of this literature applies to the national government. Researchers interested in illuminating the factors affecting environmental policy making at the state level have quantified the connection between environmental outcomes or program strength and variables such as partisan affiliation of the governor or the legislature, state per capita income, per capita spending on environmental programs, public opinion indicators, or levels of "good management." In the case of air pollution, such studies confront formidable methodological obstacles. Air pollution travels and is transformed chemically in the atmosphere. Thus, the quality of the air in a particular region is likely to be only partly attributable to state or local programs to control air pollution or state or local resources in that same geographic area.[18]

Collapsing entire state programs into summary indicators of strength or weakness, which is necessary for much quantitative analysis, is hardly straightforward. Per capita state income may not be a good indicator for absolute amount of government revenues collected and, therefore, may not be connected with a high willingness by citizens to support environmental programs. Individuals, ideas, and events can matter in environmental policy processes and outcomes, and no quantitative model can capture the ways in those factors might make a difference. Chapter 5 elaborates on the problems with trying to attribute environmental program features to the partisan affiliation of state-level politicians and or to public opinion indicators.[19]

Rather than trying to develop an overarching theory about the determinants of state-level environmental policy programs or outcomes, this book works bottom up and inside out, from case studies based on first-person experiences, to characterize state-level tendencies in the making of air pollution policy and the ways in which policy outcomes can vary as a function of those tendencies. The book's primary analytical objectives are to illuminate how power was expressed as state-level policy makers implemented the Clean Air Act in Virginia for coal-related air pollution, to describe the likely origins of power biases observed in those cases, and to ask whether those same forces might apply in fifteen other states that rely on coal. Those analyses rest on well-established theoretical and empirical work concerning the expression of power, regulatory capture, state-level political culture, state legislature professionalism, and the impacts of campaign finance on policy makers' behaviors and decisions.

The results of the analyses presented in the chapters that follow indicate varying degrees of vulnerability to industry favoritism, resistance to change, and insensitivity to public preferences. Such distortions threaten policy makers' ability to reduce the substantial carbon dioxide emissions from US coal-fired power plants. The final chapter proposes corresponding reforms to the Clean Air Act's shotgun marriage that Congress created in 1970. A well-functioning state-federal partnership is critical to fulfilling the United States' climate-change responsibilities to the global community and to meeting public health obligations to the nation's citizens at home.

The Air Board: A Citizen Regulatory Body

The Virginia State Air Pollution Control Board is a citizen regulatory board. Citizen boards are found throughout the United States at the state and local levels, with varying degrees and kinds of authority. One reason for establishing such boards is to create bodies with independence from direct control by politicians or career civil servants, such as agency directors. In theory, unsalaried board members should not be motivated by financial gain, but by the technical, legal, and policy dimensions of the questions at hand. Another goal of citizen boards is to ensure that decisions are clearly communicated to the public at large, since board meetings that occur in the public let board members query agency staffers and managers. Members of the general public may feel more at ease with testifying before citizen boards. The overall intention is to force agency managers to integrate information from many sources and to explain their recommendations coherently, in the public eye.[20]

One in-depth study of state environmental boards said that boards can act "as a higher, more deliberative body, removed from the bureaucracy" and that they can "take a long-range view of matters and represent the interests of the public at large." Because such boards are "composed of private citizens, they are meant to broaden the base of decision making by providing in put from all walks of life." Finally, such boards can "serve as a check on the power of any one governor or his [sic] departmental director." Citizen boards should "increase citizens' direct representation in, and access to governmental decision-making."[21]

Virginia is not unusual in having adopted state-level citizen environmental boards. According to one thorough count, seventeen states, including Virginia, had environmental regulatory boards made up of citizens as of 2000. But each state's boards are distinctive. The professional, fourteen-member California Air Resources Board (ARB) is the United States' best-known state environmental board. The ARB is justifiably renowned for leading the rest of the nation, including the national government, with progressive air pollution policies that stretch back to the 1970s. The ARB's executive director and approximately 1,300 staff report directly to the Board's full-time chair.[22]

Other than Virginia, four states examined in this book rely on citizen boards for environmental regulatory or policy decisions. Alabama's Environmental Management Commission consists of seven members appointed for six years. Their authority includes "developing the state's environmental policy, hearing administrative appeals, administrative orders, and variances issued by the Department [of Environmental Management], adopting regulations, and selecting an ADEM [Alabama Department of Environmental Management] Director." South Carolina's Board of Health and Environmental Control consists of eight members with four-year terms whose legal authority includes selecting the ADEM's staff director and fixing that person's salary. Environmental board members in Illinois and Texas receive professional salaries. Illinois's full-time five-member Pollution Control

Board has a 45-member staff and is charged with adopting regulations and adjudicating "contested cases" for all types of pollution. Board members may not hold any other salaried positions or "engage in any other business, employment, or vocation." Shortly after the Board's creation in 1970, one observer concluded that the Board's resources and independence had resulted in more and better informed regulations. The Texas Commission on Environmental Quality, which was preceded by the Texas Natural Resources Commission, oversees air, water, and waste programs. Three full-time commissioners manage the work of approximately 2,700 staff and management officials.[23]

The statutory authority of the Virginia State Air Pollution Control Board is broad. Among the Board's legal duties are: to adopt air pollution regulations for the "control and abatement of air pollution throughout the Commonwealth"; to ensure that the Board's regulations are enforced and to grant variances, where appropriate; to issue permits to specific facilities and to collect permit fees; and, to license vehicle inspection stations. Until 2008 the Board could choose to oversee facility-specific permits. The Board has the authority to initiate reports or investigations. The Board's seven members, increased in 2008 from five members, are nominated by the governor and confirmed by the state legislature, usually for terms of four years. They are to be "knowledgeable of air quality control and regulation" and "shall be fairly representative of conservation, public health, business, and agriculture." Since the Board is a part-time, unsalaried body that usually meets only a few times a year, many Board responsibilities are routinely delegated to the state Department of Environmental Quality (DEQ) management and staff. The Air Board is meant to be a citizen-expert partner of the professional staff and managers at the DEQ, thereby providing creative tension.[24]

I did not campaign to be on the Air Board. Rather, in 2002, while on a guest faculty appointment in Denmark, I received an email message from a friend to ask whether I might apply to serve on the Air Board, given my experience with air pollution policy at the EPA. She suggested I send my résumé to W. Tayloe Murphy Jr., Governor Mark Warner's Secretary of Natural Resources and one of Virginia's most eminent politicians and environmentalists. Mr. Murphy had earned a special reputation as a protector of the Chesapeake Bay during his 18 years as a member of the state's House of Delegates. He was renowned for his commitment to conservation and environmental protection and he had chaired the Chesapeake Bay Commission. Mr. Murphy had also overseen two General Assembly reports that criticized the DEQ for poor management, low staff morale, and for favoring the interests of businesses over those of public health and the environment.

As Secretary of Natural Resources he worried publicly about Virginia's status as last in conservation spending among the fifty states. For my part, I wondered if I could handle the Air Board commitment while meeting my responsibilities as a faculty member at the University of Virginia. Nonetheless, I accepted an Air Board appointment. What I could not anticipate was political tempests that would involve two governors and the state legislature.[25]

Secretary Murphy's continued doubts about the DEQ became evident to me early in my Air Board tenure. He felt the DEQ's Air Division "was too prone to give the regulated community what it wanted." My experience on the Air Board would vindicate Mr. Murphy's fears. The DEQ's management expected the Board to accept or, at most, fine-tune the Agency's proposals and to accept at face value the information presented as the basis for those proposals. Many Board members seemed content with a passively accepting role. One Board member even commented that it was our job to serve the regulated business community. My fellow Board members Hullie Moore, Bruce Buckheit, and I did not subscribe to that philosophy.[26]

Policy Firestorms

Between 2006 and 2010 the Board undertook three contentious, technically complicated decisions involving coal-fired power plants or coal dust from mining vehicles, because citizens clamored for our involvement. Our actions were unusual, since Air Board members generally lack the resources, time, and expertise to delve into the details of permits or regulations. Participants included thousands of citizens, the state Department of Environmental Quality, federal agencies, the courts, city governments, state agencies, two governors, and the General Assembly, the state's legislative body.

These high profile cases not only provide an extensive public record and rich narrative, they throw into relief the elements of power that are the central focus of this book. One case played out in northern Virginia and the other two took place in in Appalachia. Each situation involved highly technical, complicated legal and policy matters that consumed hundreds of hours of the Board's time.

In Alexandria, which lies in the northeast corner of Virginia across the Potomac River from Washington, the Board considered for almost two years the issue of sulfur dioxide limits for the nearly 60-year-old coal-fired Mirant power plant. The facility was located in the heart of urban Alexandria on the Potomac River, with houses and apartment complexes literally right

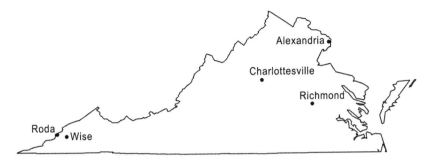

Figure I.1
A map of Virginia (courtesy of David Gist, GIS Specialist, University of Virginia Library). For perspective, the distance from Wise to Alexandria is 415 miles.

next door. This particular power plant was designed with unusually low stacks to avoid accidents with plane traffic at nearby Ronald Reagan Washington National Airport. Air pollution wafted from the facility directly onto its neighbors, who had complained since 2001 about soot and respiratory problems. The Board became involved in 2006, a year after Mirant's own analysis showed that the facility's emissions were causing violations of the National Ambient Air Quality Standards for sulfur dioxide, nitrogen dioxide, and particulate matter, and after the DEQ had failed to force the facility to reduce its emissions. Mirant's managers resisted strict regulatory limits and challenged the Board's credentials. Before the Board became involved, Mirant had paid a stiff fine for exceeding federal nitrogen oxide standards by almost two times at the Alexandria plant.

In Wise (located in Virginia's southwest tip, more than 400 miles from Alexandria), the Air Board wrote permit limits for the new, widely unpopular Dominion Virginia power plant fueled by waste coal, virgin coal, and wood. Many citizens thought the Board had the authority to deny the permit altogether. Rather, given overwhelming support from state and local politicians, the Board's choices were whether to adopt limits for the facility or wait until the new, seven-person Board was seated in July 2008. If the Board chose the latter route, the new appointees might simply defer to the DEQ's judgment and impose less stringent limits. Earlier that year the state legislature and Governor Tim Kaine, a Democrat who later became a US senator and then a candidate for vice president, had expressed openly their displeasure with the Board's actions in Alexandria by adopting legislation that weakened the Board's authority and expanded its numbers, a strong indication that the Board's new appointees would be selected for their willingness to rubber stamp the DEQ's suggestions.

The Wise case, which inspired the documentary film "The Electricity Fairy," necessitated extensive Board research on limits for sulfur dioxide, particulate matter, mercury, and nitrogen oxides, since DEQ staff members and managers seemed inclined to accept Dominion's recommendations for the facility's pollution limits. A two-day hearing at the end of June 2008, held in a high school auditorium not far from a mountaintop coal mine, attracted local politicians and hundreds of citizens. Governor Kaine wrote the Board a stern letter before the public hearing, thereby inserting himself into the decision-making process even though the Board is an independent body not subject to executive control.[27]

In Roda, also located in the state's southwest Appalachian corner, the Board confronted unusually high dust pollution thrown up by coal truck traffic in a country hollow. Local residents' complaints found no audience in the state Department of Mines, Minerals, and Energy. So they resorted to working with the Sierra Club. Careful measurements of the hollow's pollution by Viney Aneja, a professor of Air Quality and of Environmental Technology at North Carolina State University, showed particulate matter concentrations that far exceeded national standards established under the Clean Air Act and resembled levels in industrializing countries. Once again Board members were at odds with the DEQ's managers and staff, who criticized Dr. Aneja's measurements and balked at writing regulations involving mining trucks.[28]

Virginia's Air Pollution Control Board has a great deal of authority on paper, but in reality its members are hemmed in by dependence on others for information. A constant theme with the DEQ's leadership was constrained funding and hiring freezes. Thus the Board's demands for extra information and exacting, stringent standards were unwelcome. Nonetheless, the Board's decisions survived court challenge, with one exception in which a state judge nullified a provision for the Wise County facility that DEQ staff members had advocated on Dominion Power's behalf. Ultimately, Dominion seemed unbothered when that part of the permit was overturned.[29]

Despite the fact that the Board's decisions were not challenged by the regulated entity in Wise and passed judicial muster in Alexandria and in Wise, some observers regarded the Board's decisions as too tough on industry. In 2007, even before the Air Board made any decisions in Alexandria or Wise, Governor Kaine and the Virginia General Assembly proposed to eliminate the Air, Waste, and Water Boards and combine them into one megabody. Faced with stiff public resistance to that bill, the governor and the General Assembly instead constrained the Air Board's permitting authority and expanded the Board from five to seven members. Packing the Board eliminated the Board's slender three-person majority.[30]

In the end the Board could point to some important accomplishments. Dominion Virginia Power committed to reduce power plant carbon dioxide emissions, a rare concession when greenhouse gases were not yet formally recognized as pollution under the federal Clean Air Act. For Dominion's new coal-fired power plant in Wise, the Board adopted—and the company accepted—far stricter mercury and sulfur dioxide limits than DEQ staff members and managers had advocated. One environmental blogger said the Board had adopted the nation's most stringent standard for mercury. In a promotional video produced after the Wise facility was operating, Dominion bragged that the permit limits were "the strictest ever written into an air permit in the United States." The Board turned a spotlight on high dust levels stirred up by coal truck traffic in Roda and, as a result, the responsible companies instituted effective dust control practices. The limits the Board adopted for the Mirant power plant in Alexandria reduced sulfur dioxide emissions by over seventy percent, far more than DEQ staff members had proposed. The Board's work paved the way for an agreement between the City of Alexandria and Mirant promising approximately $34 million in capital equipment investments. In 2011 the facility's new owners decided to shutter it rather than make those expenditures.[31]

A Climate of Capitulation in Virginia and Elsewhere

The Air Board encountered a "climate of capitulation," a term adopted in this book to describe favoritism toward private interests and an inclination to maintain the status quo. In a climate of capitulation, elected politicians and civil servants tend to give in to the regulated community's desires for weak standards, whether those preferences are explicitly stated or merely anticipated. In Virginia, deeply embedded social, political, and economic factors contribute to these biases. Those factors include utility and coal industry donors that are especially dominant in campaign finance, an amateur legislature that relies heavily on outsiders for technical input and advice, and cultural understandings that elevate elite control, constrain public participation, and diminish public service. Partisan affiliation can matter in the environmental policy arena, but Virginia's climate of capitulation involves Democrats and Republicans alike. Members of both parties represented Virginia's coal country in the General Assembly, and they united across party lines in their rush to try to give Dominion Power what it wanted by way of weak air pollution permits.

Because of the Virginia's ideological contrasts, the politics of resistance and interest in Virginia could spill beyond the state's borders. Virginia's twenty-first-century mixture of views is reflected in its status as a swing state in presidential elections. Democrats and Republicans alike win state offices. Since 1990 four governors have been Democrats and three have been Republicans. Virginia is bound to conservative traditions such as coal mining, states' rights, and Southern gentility while also having a sizable immigrant population and one suburban county so progressive some call it the People's Republic of Arlington. US Representatives from the state's northern urban areas have scored high (the Democrat Gerry Connolly has a "lifetime" score of 97 percent) with the League of Conservation Voters, while Representatives from the Richmond area have scored poorly (Republican Eric Cantor had a "lifetime" score of 4 percent).[32]

The state's disparate regions include the rural mountainous Appalachian southwest, the former capital of the Confederacy (Richmond), the Shenandoah Valley, the Chesapeake Bay, and the Atlantic coast "Tidewater" area. Virginia is a regional amalgam with cultural elements of the Old South, New South, recent immigrants, and the northeast, with a strong dollop of nearby Washington. The state's most fundamental cultural fault line separates the more densely populated and more politically liberal north near Washington from the rest of the state, much of which is more conservative. One observer says of northern Virginia combined with the state's more southerly regions, "It's as if you grafted South Carolina onto the suburbs of New Jersey." Fine-grained local differences lent particular stamps to each Board decision, even as we encountered similar powerful political currents across the state.[33]

While state-level political processes, cultural traditions, and institutions vary quite a bit in the US federal system, the observations that emerge from the Virginia case studies point to patterns that are potentially generalizable to other states. The coal industry and electric utilities wield widespread influence across the United States at the state and national levels. Low natural gas prices have led to a widespread decline in coal consumption, but coal production and consumption are still important across the nation. Many states, especially in the South, share with Virginia a traditionalistic political culture whose hallmarks are resistance to change and a tendency toward closed-circle decision making. Part-time, amateur legislatures are found in many other states, and such bodies can become overly dependent on outside groups, especially powerful industries, for advice, technical input, and bill drafting.[34]

Using the findings in Virginia, we can widen our geographic scope with a look at six top coal consuming and coal producing states—Illinois, Indiana, Kentucky, Ohio, Pennsylvania, and Texas—and at the eleven states considered to constitute the South. Even without access to the inner workings of air pollution policy-making processes in these states, we can see whether we find political, institutional, and economic circumstances that might foster a climate of capitulation. Specifically, it is possible to examine whether these states show the cultural inclinations and institutional weaknesses found in Virginia that could make it hard for state officials to develop responsive, effective plans for reducing carbon dioxide from fossil-fuel-fired power plants. For each of the states mentioned above, relative susceptibility to imbalances in political power is gauged through an analysis that includes the same factors that have contributed to Virginia's climate of capitulation: patterns of coal and electric utility campaign contributions between 2001 and 2015, political culture, and legislative professionalism. That analysis includes a look at the potential effect of partisanship and state-level public salience on the making of policies regarding air pollution.

The Many Faces of Power

Successful exercise of governing power in the US environmental policy arena depends on the simultaneous alignment of sundry forces. Political inertia favors the status quo in US politics because of the well-known system of checks and balances. Further, the costs of controlling pollution are easy to quantify and experienced now, while the benefits of reduced pollution are often deferred, difficult to specify, or diffuse. Imposing near-term private costs with the promise of uncertain or future public benefits is always a difficult political task.[35]

To overcome these constraints, those who make environmental policy must possess at a minimum clear legal authority and procedures that facilitate rational, transparent decision making. They must decide to exercise their authority, bargain effectively with the regulated community, and strike compromises to build coalitions. Strong public demand for environmental protection is a necessary foundation for policy makers' action. Policy makers' hesitation in areas like climate change has been attributed variously to special interest influence, partisan divisions, weak political commitment, vacillating public opinion, and uncertain legal authority.[36]

In a climate of capitulation, powerful business interests constrain the political agenda and receive favored treatment. Civil servants shrink from taking actions that displease polluting companies. Those biases come about when companies exercise the "three faces of power," as they are termed in the political science literature. Especially dominant campaign donors exercise the first face of power when they push officials to do that which they would not otherwise do by withholding, threatening to withhold, or providing campaign finance funding. Through the "second face of power" companies advance their own interests by keeping certain options off of the policy agenda, and they can do so merely by reputation. In the second face of power it is not necessary to act, it is enough to be the "guerrilla in the closet." When officials' views and preferences are shaped by longstanding power relationships, the third face of power comes into play.[37]

One reason why companies can mold policy discussions in these disparate ways is that information is power in the environmental policy arena. Making defensible environmental policy decisions requires intelligible, detailed, and credible information about specific engineering processes, public health effects, legal authority, and environmental impacts. Because of its highly specialized, technical nature, such information can exclude the uninitiated and can prove confusing even to seasoned participants in the making of policy. Ordinary citizens often cannot penetrate the complicated jargon used in environmental policy decisions. Many laypersons undoubtedly give up rather than invest the time needed to participate meaningfully.

Possessing the expertise and funds to generate and understand such information is a basic requirement to participate effectively in the US environmental policy arena. Providing misleading information or refusing to provide relevant information constitute especially potent exercises of power in environmental policy decisions. The Board faced these problems many times and lacked its own staff, thus driving the Board members to undertake independent research.

An enduring complication with environmental policy making is that regulators depend on businesses for information to establish regulatory limits. While national regulators can remain at a distance from the regulated community by working through formalized communication channels and by using contractors as intermediaries, in Virginia officials and members of the regulated community meet in person repeatedly, over many years. At the Air Board's public hearings, which happened four to ten times yearly during my tenure, state environmental bureaucrats and managers mixed in the audience with lobbyists, predominantly composed of people representing private interests. As a result of these frequent interactions, close, sympathetic relationships can develop between regulators and the business community. Private interests are also a key source of information for Virginia's General Assembly, which is professionally weak because of short sessions, low pay for legislators, and few staff. The Air Board's independence from specific political constituencies or the regulated community allowed its members to be a disruptive force.

Sources of Information; Outline of the Book

The case-study narratives in chapters 1–3 rely on events documented in the public record, which consists of state and local government documents, public comments, court transcripts and decisions, newspaper articles, and publicly available email correspondence from Governor Tim Kaine's administration. Attached to those events is my understanding of how the Board's power affected, and was affected by, events, laws, information, individuals, and groups. It will be evident to the reader where my interpretations enter into the narrative. Discussions around influence politics, energy production and consumption, campaign finance patterns, citizen input, and political culture draw on government documents, on studies undertaken by non-governmental entities, and on the scholarly literature. Technical analyses with environmental and energy data are readily available through government agencies such as the EPA and the Energy Information Administration and in the published and gray expert literature. Law review articles provide interpretive and historical information on the Clean Air Act's structure and application. State-level campaign finance data are available through the National Institute on Money in State Politics. Important primary sources include EPA's regulations, Virginia administrative law, and the Clean Air Act itself. I use my own Air Board records.

Key framing ideas about the exercise of political power, the states and environmental issues, and political culture originate with scholars such as R. Douglas Arnold, Christopher Bosso, Matthew Crenson, Steven Croley, Martha Derthick, John Gaventa, David Konisky, Steven Lukes, Peter Morton, Morton S. Baratz, Joseph S. Nye Jr., Barry Rabe, and Peter Cleary Yeager. Public opinion indicators come from the work of Barry Rabe, Jon Krosnick, and the Yale University Project on Climate Change Communication. This book relies on the enduring work of Daniel Elazar, who classified all fifty states with respect to political culture, and the empirical studies of Peverill Squire and Gary Moncrief, who have studied and ranked the state legislatures' levels of professionalism.[38]

Chapters 1–3 describe the forces that constrained and enhanced the Air Board's actions in three different cases involving coal and two major electric utilities in Virginia's urban north and mountain southwest. These chapters illustrate the effects of legal authority, especially the federal Clean

Air Act, state political culture, interest group influence, policy-making procedures, citizen input, administrative resources, legislative professionalism, and availability of information on the Board's ability to make reasoned, supportable decisions.

Chapter 4 introduces the concept of a "climate of capitulation" that skews air pollution decision making in Virginia toward the coal and electric utility sectors. These interests wield substantial power in US politics generally, and one would expect coal interests to have more influence in states where coal mining and coal combustion both have long histories, as they do in Virginia. But the strength of the coal industry and one dominant utility in Virginia is magnified by contextual factors that set the political stage on which state policy makers act. Those factors are campaign finance laws that let coal and electric utility interests overwhelm other donors, thereby indebting politicians of all political stripes; a traditionalistic political culture, which tends toward inertia and elite control and encourages civil servants to capitulate to the regulated company; and a part-time legislature that depends on outside groups for information and bill drafting, especially in highly technical areas.

Chapter 5 provides details on the nature of state-federal partnerships created by the Clean Air Act's various programs. While "cooperative federalism" is often used to refer to those collaborations, "shotgun marriage federalism" better captures the often tense and discordant nature of EPA's relationship with the states. Chapter 5 sets forth the challenges involved with implementing the Clean Power Plan and underscores the importance of the carbon dioxide emission reductions that policy makers have hoped to realize from the Plan. This chapter also provides background information on six important coal-consuming and coal-producing states: Illinois, Indiana, Kentucky, Ohio, Pennsylvania, and Texas. Unclear partisanship patterns and a lack of predictable connections between public opinion and the actions of policy makers show that we must reach beyond partisanship and opinion surveys to anticipate how state-level policy makers might respond to the need to reduce carbon dioxide emissions from coal-fired power plants.

For those six important coal states and for the eleven states in the South, Chapter 6 analyzes the potential for power biases observed in the making of air pollution policy in Virginia. Included for each state are descriptions of political culture, legislative professionalism, coal dependence, campaign finance patterns, and state-level public opinion polls. Summary scores for each state gauge relative vulnerability to a climate of capitulation in the making of air pollution policy. Results indicate that Illinois, Indiana, Ohio, and Pennsylvania exhibit low to moderate vulnerability to a climate of capitulation, with Texas and Kentucky joining Virginia as the most vulnerable to a climate of capitulation. All eleven Southern states show high vulnerability to a climate of capitulation. Chapter 6 connects what one scholar calls the South's "defensive conservatism," which has its origins in longstanding race problems, with the environmental policy arena.[39]

The final chapter ties together chapters 1–6 by proposing state and national reforms intended to counteract state-level biases toward coal and electric utility interests and to augment the influence of citizens in the air pollution policy process. The first suggestion calls for Clean Air Act process changes to bolster citizen participation and effectiveness in the states. EPA grant support for citizen-sponsored studies and new citizen Clean Air Act oversight committees would broaden and strengthen citizen influence. These regional citizen committees would evaluate, and provide independent input to EPA on, Clean Air Act plans submitted by the states. The second reform suggestions calls for augmenting state legislature professionalism in states with citizen legislatures, with the objective of increasing legislator independence from regulated entities.

The third suggested reform recommends mitigating the corrosive influence of state-level campaign finance contributions through systems of public financing. The fourth suggested reform addresses environmental and economic injustices long visited upon the nation's coal regions. State-level carbon trading policies or federal pollution cleanup programs should channel funding to economically distressed areas, including those traditionally dependent on coal mining. Finally, national and state reforms should incentivize energy efficiency improvements and foster decentralized installation of renewable electrical power. Not only would such programs buttress the states' efforts to reduce emissions of greenhouse gases; incentive-based programs have flourished even in states with a wide variety of political-institutional settings. Further, decentralizing the generation of electrical power will help diffuse political power away from electric utilities and fossil-fuel interests.

1 Mirant: No Good Deed Goes Unpunished

In March 2008, my fellow State Air Pollution Control Board members and I faced a tense audience in Alexandria, Virginia. In ten long public meetings held over seventeen months we had struggled to set appropriate air pollution limits for the Mirant coal-fired power plant just across the Potomac River from Washington. A Department of Energy study estimated that twenty people were dying and thousands were being sickened every year because of that 60-year-old facility's air pollution. Meeting attendees often wore shirts or armbands signifying which side they were on. All eyes were on the Board. The audience seemingly believed the Board held all the cards when it came to making policy.[1]

The pollution limits the Board had adopted for Mirant had proved technologically feasible, had met the Clean Air Act's public health standards, and had withstood court challenge. Nonetheless, key staff members and managers in the state Department of Environmental Quality (DEQ) consistently opposed the Board's efforts, throwing procedural and substantive obstacles in the Board's way. Governor Tim Kaine and his staff undercut the Board, as did the Virginia General Assembly.

So the Air Board did not hold all of the cards. Rather, the Board's powers were contingent, constrained by deeply rooted political and economic understandings in Virginia.

This chapter tells the story of the Air Board's efforts to bring Mirant's air pollutant emissions into compliance with the Clean Air Act's requirements. Local, state and federal government agencies, including the federal Department of Energy and the US Environmental Protection Agency, became embroiled in this tense, high-stakes controversy.

Before beginning that narrative, some backtracking to another power plant permit is helpful. This case involved a power plant that threatened to degrade air quality in Shenandoah National Park. The Board exercised its authority to oversee directly that power plant's emission limits, and the

Board's close attention to that permit resulted in more stringent limits than DEQ staffers had originally contemplated. This modest precedent laid the foundation for the Board's eventual decision to take over the Mirant permitting process from the DEQ.

Prelude: Ozone and Shenandoah National Park

Shenandoah National Park is long and thin, snaking 80 miles along the spine of the Blue Ridge Mountains. Local lore holds that in 1935, when the Park was founded, it was possible to see the Washington Monument, 70 miles from the Park's northernmost point, from some points in it. Now the park's vistas are regularly impeded by air pollution consisting of fine particulate pollution, which is transported from local and regional sources of sulfur dioxide and nitrogen oxides. Those same pollutants occur in acidic forms ("acid deposition") that degrade ecosystems and cause a variety of adverse human health effects. Nitrogen oxides also contribute to elevated water pollution levels in the Chesapeake Bay and in other bodies of water, and they stimulate the formation of ground-level ozone (smog).[2]

In the United States we have made important strides in combating smog, which is formed when oxides of nitrogen (NOx) and volatile organic compounds combine in the presence of heat and sunlight. High ozone levels cause a variety of adverse respiratory symptoms that can lead to hospitalization, emergency room visits, lower productivity, and permanent lung damage. Despite three decades of increasingly intensive efforts to reduce NOx emissions from vehicles and from other combustion sources, emissions are higher than they might have been because of steady population growth, increased motor vehicle use, higher GDP, and climbing electricity demand. Our addiction to driving is a prime reason that national NOx emissions declined by only 54 percent between 1970 and 2014, even though NOx emission rates from new cars decreased by 98 percent in that same interval.[3]

Emissions of NOx can contribute to fine particulate pollution, acid deposition, and ozone formation hundreds of miles away. Winds move air pollution, and so air-quality problems often stem from a combination of nearby and faraway sources. As a result, Shenandoah National Park's air quality has been degraded. The Park's ozone levels have rivaled those in nearby urban areas. In fact, in 2004 the EPA designated the Park a "nonattainment," or dirty air, area for smog because air-quality concentrations exceeded national ozone standards. The Park joined population-dense northern Virginia and Richmond as officially dirty air areas, those violating the National Ambient Air Quality Standards (NAAQS).[4]

With the NAAQS program, which was enacted in the 1970 Clean Air Act Amendments, Congress established the principle that all Americans should breathe clean air. The EPA has established and repeatedly revised NAAQS for six pollutants: ambient ozone, carbon monoxide, lead, nitrogen dioxide, particulate matter, and sulfur dioxide. Under the Clean Air Act, a key goal is for every part of the country to attain the NAAQS.[5]

State officials are responsible for implementing the federal NAAQS program, and they must adopt air pollution controls so that all areas will comply with the NAAQS. New sources of air pollution in nonattainment areas are allowed, but they must apply stringent pollution control technology and offset their new pollution by lowering existing pollution in the area. The goal of this "New Source Review" program, which is required under the federal Clean Air Act, is to allow industrial growth while also fostering improvements in air quality.[6]

Against the backdrop of persistently high ozone levels in the Park and the Park's ozone nonattainment designation, Competitive Power Ventures, Inc. requested in 2004 a permit for a new natural-gas-fired power plant only a few miles away in rural Warren County. Citizens and National Park Service officials asked the Board to take a hard look at the facility's emissions, which included a considerable amount of nitrogen oxides. Some argued the power plant's emissions should meet the stringent Clean Air Act requirements for large sources in nonattainment areas rather than the less strict requirements applicable in Warren County. Because Warren County had no ozone monitoring data, it was not classified as a nonattainment area, even though it borders the Park, which was then an ozone nonattainment area, and even though Warren County was relatively close to urban areas suffering from elevated ozone levels.[7]

The Board attended carefully to these concerns. Competitive Power Ventures ultimately volunteered to exceed the pollution control requirements for clean air areas by purchasing NOx emission reductions ("offsets") elsewhere. On a 4–1 vote the Air Board accepted the company's offer to include those stricter-than-required limits in the permit. According to one news article, "even environmentalists conceded that the Competitive Power Ventures plant would be fairly clean." By 2006 Shenandoah National Park's air quality was attaining national ozone standards. Ultimately, that particular power plant was never built.[8]

Mirant Before the Air Board's Direct Oversight

State or federal permits specifying pollution limits are lengthy, technically complex documents that are specific to individual installations. At each meeting the Air Board received a list of the facilities across the state that were violating their legally permissible air pollution limits. Soon after I joined the Board in 2002, the Mirant facility in Alexandria appeared on the Board's "high priority violators" report.

Mirant's generating capacity was 482 megawatts, a moderate amount, but at the time it was one of three sources of electricity for much of Washington. Mirant was on the high priority violators' list because the facility had flouted its nitrogen oxides limit, emitting almost twice as much as allowed. During the summer of 2003 the plant had exceeded by 965 tons its summertime NOx limit of 1,065 tons. The US EPA, the Virginia DEQ, and the US Department of Justice took enforcement action. In 2004 the company paid a $500,000 fine and, in a settlement with the EPA, Maryland, and Virginia, agreed to install NOx control equipment at four power stations in the Washington region.[9]

As part of this agreement Virginia's DEQ was to examine Mirant's other major pollutants, sulfur dioxide and particulates, for which the DEQ had not yet set emissions limits. This particular power plant had unusually low exhaust smokestacks because of plane traffic to and from nearby Ronald Reagan Washington National airport. Mirant's squat light brown stacks are easily recognizable by airline passengers flying past Alexandria. Low stacks meant that the facility's substantial emissions did not travel far, especially on hot, still, stagnant summer days.

Alexandria citizens had complained about Mirant's soot pollution for years. They noticed light gray dust on their windowsills and cars. The DEQ had taken no action, even when faced with clear evidence that Mirant's particulate matter pollution was carpeting surrounding neighborhoods with fine particulate matter. In April 2003, DEQ staff members collected some dust samples near the plant at the urging of nearby residents. The DEQ's microscope analysis showed that "uncombusted coal dust constituted up to 50 percent of each sample." Mirant denied the validity of the DEQ's results. DEQ staffers decided not to pursue the matter any further, casting doubt on the link between adverse health effects and particulate matter emitted from Mirant's facility.[10]

DEQ staff members and managers were engaging in what one scholar has dubbed "anticipatory politics": they hesitated in the face of a recalcitrant, powerful company with ample resources. When anticipatory politics come into play, civil servants like the microscope technician learn that regulatory inaction is rewarded over action. Deeply entrenched patterns of anticipatory politics, or what I describe in chapter 4 as a climate of capitulation,

Figure 1.1
Mirant coal-fired power plant, Alexandria, Virginia (photo courtesy of Khoa Tran, Environmental Program Manager, City of Alexandria).

persisted at the DEQ throughout my time on the Board and spurred the Board's eventual involvement in the Mirant permit.[11]

The DEQ's light handling of the regulated community was not new. Rather, the agency's tendency to submit to business interests had been the subject of a legislative review in the 1990s. Reports released in 1996 and 1997 by the Joint Legislative Audit and Review Commission (JLARC), a review body of the Virginia General Assembly, criticized the DEQ on many grounds, including low morale, chaotic planning and management processes, and staff fear of management reprisal for acting contrary to the desires of a regulated entity. Specifically, the 1996 interim report said "DEQ technical employees fear retaliation for making a decision consistent with law and regulation but which upsets a member of the regulated community." In the 1997 final report, business representatives reported high satisfaction with the DEQ's "customer service orientation" while members of the environmental community agreed with DEQ staffers that economic considerations were winning over environmental ones. One DEQ staff member told the JLARC committee:

Few of my colleagues believe the agency is being steered toward environmental protection. Too many times we have been instructed to back down from a protective stance so that permittees will not be upset ... . Agency procedures have been tossed out when a permittee challenges them, simply to keep the permittee happy. There is no spine. So long as I do as I am instructed, I do not think my job is at risk.

Another section of the 1997 report indicated that staff trust in management was eroded by "being instructed to ignore regulations." Both reports emphasized that the DEQ had become an agency whose self-perceived mission was to serve the regulated community first and the general public second.[12]

Governor Mark Warner's Secretary of Natural Resources, W. Tayloe Murphy Jr., had chaired the Commission that authored the 1996 and 1997 oversight reports on the DEQ. When Mr. Murphy became state Secretary of Natural Resources in 2002, he remained concerned about the DEQ's performance. He worried that the DEQ's air division was capitulating to the regulated community. "That's why I recommended strong appointments to the Air Board," Mr. Murphy recalls. "Sometimes it's possible to accomplish through regulation what you can't do through legislation."[13]

After the DEQ's regional managers refused to pursue the results of their staff's dust analysis, Alexandria residents Elizabeth Chimento and Poul Hertel completed a careful, thorough 85-page report in which they documented unequivocally, based on lab analysis conducted at Penn State University, that coal particles and partially combusted coal dust constituted a "significant amount" of samples collected on windowsills near the Mirant facility. Their report also summarized a Harvard University health study estimating that installing "Best Available Control Technology" at the Mirant facility would avoid about 40 deaths, 43 hospital admissions, 560 emergency room visits, and 3,000 asthma attacks per year. Ms. Chimento and Mr. Hertel paid for the Penn State analysis and undertook the research necessary to write a convincing document, even though they were not trained as environmental experts.[14]

In 2004 the City of Alexandria established the Mirant Community Monitoring Group, consisting of two city council members and interested citizens. The group followed closely Mirant's activities and air pollution, served as a conduit for disseminating information to interested citizens, provided technical comments and suggestions for studies, and gave feedback to the City Council. This group bridged the gap between the public at large and their elected politicians. Elizabeth Chimento was a leader in the monitoring group's efforts.

Figure 1.2
Elizabeth Chimento, Alexandria activist (photo courtesy of Living Legends of Alexandria).

Ms. Chimento and Mr. Hertel paid $3,000 to Sullivan Environmental Consulting, Inc., to perform an atmospheric modeling study, which showed that Mirant's emissions were washing down onto Marina Towers, a nearby high-rise condominium building. In 2004, armed with these results, City officials and residents pressured the DEQ to take the situation more seriously.[15]

The City's environmental staff, Bill Skrabak, Khoa Tran, and Lalit Sharma, with the help of contractor Malay Jindal, compiled the City's technical-scientific case with respect to the effects of Mirant's emissions and the facility's technical capacity to lower those emissions. John Britton was the City's outside counsel, and he coordinated the team's technical-legal work. All told the City would eventually spend $1 million on counsel and consultants for the Mirant case. At key points after the Board became more actively involved, the City's team would wait for Air Board meeting materials, which DEQ staffers sometimes sent only the night before the meeting was to happen. Then the City's staff stayed up late to compile their comments and organize a presentation. On one such occasion City staff members had to awaken early to drive to from Alexandria to the Board's meeting, which was happening at some distance.[16]

The DEQ ordered Mirant to model air quality in order to assess the plant's effects on local levels of sulfur dioxide and particulate matter. On 19 August 2005 Mirant was to deliver the results of that modeling. DEQ Director Robert Burnley ordered his staff to stay late so they could evaluate the Mirant report even if it arrived after the Agency's usual close-of-business time. The study's alarming conclusions indicated that, under the conditions modeled, the facility's emissions were causing violations of NAAQS for sulfur dioxide, fine particulate matter, and nitrogen dioxide. More specifically, the report said that modeled values exceeded short-term standards for these pollutants by five to eighteen times, with "widespread" and "severe" areas of noncompliance, and exceeded the long-term NAAQS by three to twelve times. Modeled levels at the facility's fence line and beyond exceeded worker protection standards, "indicating the potential for OSHA violations within the plant boundaries."[17]

The very evening Director Burnley received the report, he instructed Mirant by letter to "immediately undertake such action as is necessary to ensure protection of human health and the environment." Mirant shut down five days later. Elizabeth Chimento recalls that Robert Burnley called her to say, "You were right all along." "At least one high-ranking Warner administration official," Mr. Burnley said, "disagreed with [my] approach and did not support it. The governor, however, was an enthusiastic supporter

Figure 1.3
Robert Burnley, former Director, Virginia Department of Environmental Quality, and W. Tayloe Murphy Jr., former Virginia Secretary of Natural Resources and former Delegate, Virginia House of Delegates (photo courtesy of Robert Burnley).

who closely followed the activities over the next few weeks and became personally involved." Secretary of Natural Resources W. Tayloe Murphy Jr. praised Mr. Burnley's efforts, saying, "Good work, Bob. Thanks for your fine work regarding air quality in the National Capital Area."[18]

After only a few weeks Mirant abruptly reopened the facility, without a warning to state officials. Governor Warner took Mirant to task, writing on 21 September 2005: "I expect better cooperation from Virginia's corporate citizens … . I will not tolerate any assault on the health, safety and welfare of Virginia's citizens or the environment, and I insist on compliance with environmental laws and regulations. This matter must be brought to a swift and responsible conclusion … . The bottom line is you need to either fully comply with environmental laws and regulations or shut down. There is no middle ground here."[19]

Two powerful federal agencies weighed in. In December 2005 the federal Department of Energy ordered the plant to keep running because it was a key supplier of electricity to the District of Columbia and to the local sewage treatment facility. The DOE based this decision on authority to act during an emergency. The Southern Environmental Law Center challenged the DOE's decision on the grounds that no emergency existed. DEQ Director Burnley also questioned the DOE's order, arguing that electricity reliability could not form the basis for overriding the Clean Air Act's requirements. In January 2006, Mr. Burnley wrote to the DOE when the local electricity supplier took transmission lines out of service, which Burnley believed would "force the plant to operate at or near full capacity" without having installed pollution control measures: "DEQ demands DOE order a postponement of PEPCO's planned outage of the 230kV transmission lines serving the Potomac River Substation until such time as the Potomac River Generating Station has installed and is able to operate pollution control equipment essential to assure that emissions from the plant do not injure the health and safety of the citizens of Virginia." Director Burnley also reported to Secretary of Natural Resources W. Tayloe Murphy Jr. of resisting pressure from the US EPA and the Department of Energy to allow Mirant to operate at levels that might cause violations of the NAAQS: "We will continue to hold the high ground until we go broke paying lawyer's fees." [20]

Mr. Burnley retired from government service in early 2006. Governor Warner's term ended in January 2006. His successor was Tim Kaine, who had served as Mr. Warner's lieutenant governor.

In May 2006 the US EPA intervened, ordering that Mirant take all reasonable steps to limit its emissions, perform daily "predictive modeling" that would specify the plant's permissible operating level for the anticipated weather conditions, place sulfur dioxide monitors at the plant's periphery to ensure that the national ambient standards for sulfur dioxide would not be violated, and install alarms that would sound if monitored levels reached 80 percent of the sulfur dioxide NAAQS. The EPA's Administrative Compliance Order would expire on 1 June 2007, by which time the state was supposed to set a permanent sulfur dioxide limit for the facility. Under orders from PJM, the electricity transmission grid operator, Pepco, the regional electricity supplier, began upgrading the transmission grid to make Mirant redundant.[21]

In the summer of 2006 Alexandria residents continued to observe disturbing instances of strangely colored smoke issuing from the Mirant facility. DEQ staffers agreed initially that these incidents constituted violations of the Mirant's permit conditions and that Mirant should have reported them right away. But then DEQ staffers waffled, saying these episodes were "exceedances," not "violations." According to Elizabeth Chimento's detailed notes, DEQ staffers asked Mirant "why they shouldn't get a violation." Although it is not unusual for regulatory agencies to negotiate solutions with polluters when they violate their permit conditions, DEQ's reactions hint at an unwillingness to enforce the law.[22]

The Air Board Joins the Mirant Fray

The Air Board decided unanimously in September 2006 to take over the Mirant permitting process. At that meeting, City of Alexandria officials and residents packed the Board's meeting room in a Richmond suburb to ask for the Board's intervention. Those attending and pleading for the Board's oversight included State Senator Patsy Ticer, State Delegates Brian Moran and David Englin, Alexandria Vice-Mayor Redella "Del" Pepper, Alexandria's deputy environmental director Bill Skrabak, and Tim Aiken, a staff member for US Congressman Jim Moran. Mr. Burnley was no longer the DEQ's Director. The Board felt that the DEQ's leadership had not made sufficient progress in the year since the plant's 2005 emergency shutdown.[23]

The Board members were aware of the challenges that lay ahead because of our extensive collective experience in the air pollution and electric utility arenas. Bruce Buckheit, an energy and environmental consultant, had directed air pollution enforcement at the EPA, where he oversaw enforcement efforts against many electric utilities that had flouted the Clean Air Act's requirements. The Honorable Hullihen ("Hullie") Williams Moore had been member and Chair of the State Corporation Commission for twelve years, during which he had gained extensive knowledge of the electric utility industry in Virginia. For my part, I am trained as a natural scientist, a political scientist, and an environmental policy expert. My first career was at the EPA, implementing the Clean Air Act. Our colleagues Richard Langford, a chemical engineer and former environmental manager for Celanese Corporation, and John Hanson, an environmental attorney in private practice, were knowledgeable about air pollution policy, technical analysis, and law.

In one public meeting after another for the next twenty months, the Board explored the best course for reducing the facility's air pollution. Many citizens and local politicians, including Alexandria's Mayor Bill Euille, Vice Mayor Del Pepper, and City Council member Paul Smedberg, urged the Board to impose stringent limits. Representatives for Mirant attacked the Board's decisions and professional qualifications in public and in the courts. Mirant's managers and outside attorneys tried to paint the Board as technically lacking. But because of the Board's collective expertise it was clear, as they say in the South, "that dog won't hunt."

New information came to light with respect to the facility's effects on public health. A study commissioned by the City of Alexandria confirmed that Mirant's emissions "contributed to widespread and serious violations of the NAAQS for fine particulate matter." An extensive November 2006

Department of Energy analysis indicated that Mirant's emissions had caused 37 premature deaths, 50 heart attacks, and thousands of other less serious but adverse respiratory illnesses in the year before the plant was shut down in August 2005. The DOE's analysis estimated that, even after the EPA order went into effect, 14 people suffered premature death and 18 were the victims of heart attacks over a nine-month period as a result of Mirant's emissions. Using accepted methods for converting adverse health impacts into social costs, I estimated that, for only three of the many adverse health consequences realized, Mirant's pre-shutdown emissions imposed more than $200 million in social costs yearly.[24]

DEQ staffers and managers objected to the Board's requests for information, saying they were overburdened and understaffed. Between 2003 and 2007, the size of the DEQ's staff had risen from 786 to 843. Still, in 1992, when the DEQ was established, an implementation plan envisioned that 883 employees would be needed to fulfill the Agency's mission. The number of programs and tasks needed to implement federal environmental programs had grown since the DEQ's establishment. Former DEQ Director Robert Burnley saw only tepid commitment to the environment in Virginia's budget.[25]

Nonetheless, the DEQ's weak proposals for Mirant's emissions indicated more than a simple lack of resources and time. From 1994 to 1998, Governor George Allen's administration forced early retirements and layoffs. DEQ staff members were deeply unhappy, and they admitted to the General Assembly's Audit and Review Commission their fear of demanding anything from the regulated community.[26]

The DEQ's resistance to the Board's involvement took procedural forms. Board members often received Board meeting materials with inadequate time to prepare. DEQ staffers and managers tried to cut this Board member out of a meeting. The Board's April 2007 meeting was scheduled on a day when I had teaching obligations at the University of Virginia. Less than two weeks before the meeting, a DEQ staff member said I could not participate remotely because audio conferencing might involve technical interruptions that could interfere with the Board's deliberations. I was not allowed to participate from my public University of Virginia office because the public would supposedly not have access to my location, even though the University of Virginia is a public entity. Nonetheless, I volunteered to join the meeting through a landline phone at a local state forestry department office. When I arrived at the forestry department no one knew about the arrangement. The staff located a small office with a landline phone and I participated in the meeting. No member of the public attended and, in fact, it would have been hard to find the office where I was squirreled away.[27]

At its April 2007 meeting the Board voted to solicit public comment on the DEQ's proposed limits and a second set of more stringent limits, since the Board was concerned that the DEQ's proposal might not protect against violations of the NAAQS for sulfur dioxide. The Board also requested comment on Mirant's proposal to undertake a "stack merge" that would combine exhaust streams, thereby increasing the height of the facility's pollution plume, dispersing emissions over a wider area, and reducing emissions close to the facility. Mirant and the DEQ's management contended that the stack merge did not require a permit. Hullie, Bruce, and I felt the company might increase its overall emissions in conjunction with the merge. The three of us wanted to make a decision in May, before the EPA's Administrative Compliance Order expired on the first of June.[28]

Before the Board's next meeting, Mirant's attorneys and the CEO of Pepco, the regional electricity supplier, complained about the Board to Governor Tim Kaine. Both letters were dated May 16. Pepco and Mirant's attorneys asked that DEQ Director David Paylor be empowered to overrule the Board and issue the more lenient limits favored by DEQ staff. Governor Kaine did not weigh in at this point. But his aides would do so after the Board made its permit decision in May.[29]

In May 2007, on a 3–2 vote, the Board found DEQ's proposed agreement with Mirant to reduce emissions of sulfur dioxide to 8,359 tons per year from a high of 13,946 tons in 2004 inadequate. Rather, the Board followed the dictates of the company's own study, which indicated that, to avoid violations of the national sulfur dioxide standards, sulfur dioxide emissions should be no more than 3,813 tons per year—less than half the level in the DEQ-Mirant proposal. The company sued in June 2007 to have the permit overturned. Mirant asserted that we did not follow proper procedure, that the Board acted outside its authority, that the Board's members did not have the technical capacity to decide the permit's limits, and that the Board ignored the advice of DEQ staffers and management. One Mirant official claimed that the Board acted out of "personal bias against coal-burning power plants."[30]

Even as Senior Assistant Attorney General Carl Josephson prepared to defend the permit decision in court, the governor's office intervened. An aide to Governor Kaine, Mark Rubin, convened a series of meetings in Richmond involving representatives from the DEQ, the City of Alexandria, and Mirant. According to one participant in these meetings, fifteen to twenty people attended. Air Board member Bruce Buckheit was an observer. He had to take care not to violate administrative procedures that might prevent his voting at future Board meetings.

The City of Alexandria's staff and attorneys eventually broke off the meetings in frustration. Ignacio Pessoa, who was then the City of Alexandria's attorney, recalls:

It was the consensus of the Alexandria team that the governor's office became directly involved with the Mirant permit application at the company's behest and for the purpose of helping Mirant obtain a permit from the state on terms the company desired. While discussions with the governor's office were underway, the City received an anonymous tip that Mirant and DEQ had reached an agreement in secret, and that the DEQ director would soon issue the permit sought by the company. The information warning the City about this impending deal proved to be correct. Fortunately, the Air Board had previously voted to take direct jurisdiction over the Mirant permit application process, and the City argued that this board action divested the DEQ director of any jurisdiction to issue such a permit. To his credit, Mark Rubin agreed with the City's argument; the deal between Mirant and DEQ was derailed.[31]

Meanwhile, Mr. Josephson defended the Board's actions in court as well reasoned, lawful and supported by "substantial evidence." Mr. Josephson noted that the Board had full authority to decide permit limits and did not have to defer to the DEQ. He observed that "even if the Board's decision were not supported by substantial evidence, the Board may also reasonably adopt a risk averse or environmentally conservative position in regulating a profit-oriented power-generating facility, whose production results in emissions of harmful pollutants that can contribute to premature mortality and cause other adverse public health and environmental consequences, especially when its electricity generation is no longer essential to electric reliability in the District of Columbia." He pointed out that the public health costs of Mirant's air pollution far exceeded the company's estimated lost revenue from operational limits that might result from the 3,813-ton limit. The DEQ's air-quality modeler, Michael Kiss, confirmed that if Mirant emitted more than 3,813 tons per year the facility would violate the three-hour NAAQS for sulfur dioxide.[32]

During the same hot summer of 2007, the DEQ's management decided to grant Mirant's request to "merge" the emissions streams from its five stacks into two stacks, thereby sending the facility's air pollution farther up into the air, so that Alexandria citizens would be exposed to lower concentrations of the facility's air pollution. But a stack merge might also increase the facility's overall emissions, as a result of engineering changes. The City of Alexandria requested that the DEQ delay its approval of the decision until the City could respond. DEQ Director Paylor consulted with

Secretary of Natural Resources Preston Bryant, who said, "Giving them more time is akin to giving them a bat to beat us with." In August 2007 Mirant started construction on the stack merge, without waiting for the Board's authorization.[33]

The City of Alexandria objected, claiming that the stack merge required a permit from the Air Board because of the potential for an overall emissions increase. Mirant asserted that the facility's emissions would not increase, and DEQ staffers agreed with Mirant's assessment. In a contentious five-hour meeting held in the basement of an Alexandria recreation center, the Board met in September and decided on a 3–1 vote that the stack merge project could not proceed without a permit.[34]

The Board's work continued in public meetings held between October 2007 and March 2008. The Board's goal was to write a comprehensive permit that included all air pollutants of concern, not just sulfur dioxide. The Board considered whether to issue a "two stack" or "five stack" permit for Mirant. In so doing the Board examined information presented by the DEQ and the public, including the City of Alexandria, on the appropriate emission limits under both the two stack and five stack scenarios.

Levels of acrimony and mistrust remained high. The City of Alexandria wrote to DEQ Director David Paylor in November 2007 of "deep dissatisfaction and frustration" with the "eleventh hour and surreptitious manipulation of the November 20, 2007 State Air Pollution Control Board meeting agenda to include a discussion of an operating permit for the Mirant Potomac River power plant that would allow emissions from two merged stacks instead of five." The City accused the DEQ's management of backroom decision making that constituted "behavior [that] shattered all pretense of transparency, fair play and public involvement—an absolute subversion of the public trust."[35]

Even as the Board focused intently on overseeing the Mirant permitting process, it conducted its usual business, which consisted of public meetings on various regulatory actions and a conference on mercury emissions from power plants. A new issue arose on the horizon: Dominion Power's request for an air pollution permit for a new power plant in Wise County, in southwest Virginia. That facility would burn a mix of waste coal, virgin coal, and waste wood.[36]

Governor Kaine's staff continued to follow what the Board was doing. Mirant appealed the Board's decision to require a permit for the stack merge. Soon thereafter gubernatorial aide Mark Rubin signaled to DEQ Director David Paylor and Secretary of Natural Resources Preston Bryant the need to "brainstorm possible solutions to the problem." A staff report to Governor

Kaine in September 2007 flagged the Mirant issue and its connection with Dominion's plans for the new power plant in southwest Virginia, saying, "the Air Board's actions are attracting the attention of a number of legislators, especially Senator Wampler, who fears how an 'out-of-control' Board might treat the proposed coal-fired Dominion plant in Wise County."[37]

In March 2008 the Circuit Court of Richmond upheld the Board's May 2007 permit for Mirant. Judge Melvin Hughes found the Board's requirements lawful and justifiable on the basis of "ample" evidence. "The authority for the Board to act as it did is there," he said.[38]

Mirant's management seemed to see the writing on the wall. At the Board's seven-hour meeting in March 2008, which opened this chapter, a negotiated solution was just around the corner. The Board voted to delay any decision on the Mirant permit until DEQ staffers had addressed a number of important questions, including ensuring that the permit's fine particulate limits were adequately protective. Within a matter of weeks, the City of Alexandria and Mirant entered into a settlement agreement that allowed the company to undertake a stack merge, accepted the Board's limit for sulfur dioxide, and required the company to invest $34 million to reduce particulate matter emissions from the facility. In July 2008 the Board unanimously approved that agreement.[39]

Three years later, GenOn, the power plant's new owner and later a part of NRG, decided to close the facility before undertaking the improvements required by the settlement agreement. Michael Bloomberg, New York's mayor, emphasized the national importance of that announcement: "There are millions of people across America committed to putting our country on a new energy path and communities like Alexandria are on the front lines." GenOn said the closure was a "market-driven decision." Lower natural gas prices, which made coal-fired facilities less competitive, and the potential cost of complying with new EPA regulations may have convinced GenOn that the facility had served its useful life. Mayor Bill Euille offered to help Mirant employees find other jobs, and by September 2012, just before the plant shut down, almost all workers had accepted transfers or decided to retire. Total emission reductions from closing the plant amounted to 2 million tons of carbon dioxide, 3,813 tons of sulfur dioxide (5 percent of the total 2011 sulfur dioxide emissions from Virginia's electric utilities), and 1,867 tons of nitrogen oxides per year.[40]

By July 2008 the Board's exhausting work with Mirant was largely finished. But in politics no good deed goes unpunished. Our activities had not gone unnoticed in the state capital. In fact, the governor's office and the

Figure 1.4
City of Alexandria elected officials and staff involved in the Mirant case. From left
to right: Councilman Paul Smedberg; William Skrabak, Deputy Director of the Office
of Environmental Quality; Vice-Mayor Redella Pepper; Lalit Sharma, Division Chief,
Environmental Quality; Mayor William D. Euille; Khoa Tran, Senior Environmental
Specialist (photo courtesy of Khoa Tran, Environmental Program Manager, City of
Alexandria).

DEQ had undertaken to undermine the Board starting in October 2006, just
after we took over responsibility for the Mirant permit.

Backlash in Richmond

In March 2007, only a few months after the Board's decision to take over
the permitting process for Mirant, Virginia's General Assembly considered and almost passed a bill that would eliminate the state Air, Water,
and Waste Boards, replace them with a mega-board, and strip the boards
of their permitting powers. The state Water Board had also angered some
powerful constituents. As a result, the Boards and their powers were on the
chopping block. The "Board bill" would have combined the Air, Water, and
Waste Boards into an eleven-member body and transferred all permitting
functions to the DEQ's Director.

Email correspondence indicates that, with Governor Kaine's knowledge, his top staff and the DEQ's Director drafted the Board bill and pushed for its passage. In October 2006, barely after the Air Board had assumed authority for the Mirant permit and months before the Board had acted to set emission limits, Governor Kaine's senior aide Mark Rubin emailed other staff in the governor's office, copying Secretary of Resources Preston Bryant. Mr. Rubin described the "considerable consternation with both the air and water board [*sic*] in the business community resulting from recent decisions. There are rumors that legislation is being considered that would affect how they do their work." He indicated that the Air Board had attracted the attention of the Virginia Chamber of Commerce and of Frank Wagner, a Republican state senator from Virginia Beach. By December, top-level officials from the DEQ and from the governor's office were discussing how to draft a Board consolidation bill. Mr. Bryant remarked, "the single most important component in the bill to its proponents is removing permitting authority from the boards and placing it into the DEQ director's hands." A working paper described how to accomplish that end, and Mr. Bryant said "We'd prefer to work on drafting this bill in-house at DEQ."[41]

In January 2007, Mr. Bryant sent a detailed email message to Governor Kaine, who had requested updates on the Board bill. Mr. Bryant said that some proponents of the bill in the General Assembly might be motivated by "retribution from industry for recent past votes (i.e., King William Reservoir, Mirant, Galleria project in Chesterfield County)." He worried about Board members who might testify against the bill and said he had "done my best to "tamp down board members" making such statements.[42]

City of Alexandria leaders and residents denounced the Board bill as an "emasculation" of the Air Board when, in their view, the DEQ had "become a captive of industry, particularly of power companies." Shelton Miles, Chair of the State Water Pollution Control Board, reacted bluntly in an email message to Secretary of Natural Resources Preston Bryant:

All permit decisions will become subject to bureaucratic & administration 'fiat' without an independent review from a panel of ordinary citizens that spans administrations. ... The clear signal of this bill, in the context of recent events, is that a Board that does not instantly suspend its own judgment and accept political direction without regard to law, regulations, the record before it, and the merits of the case will be replaced by one means or another. This is politics @ its worst caricature in a system where those with money & power rule the day without regard to individual rights, the public interest, or the merits of the case.[43]

The purported rationale for the proposed consolidation was that a mega-board overseeing air, water, and waste would make wise decisions on the basis of multimedia assessments. The practical problem with this theoretically worthy goal is that federal environmental laws involving state-level action are medium-specific, e.g., the Clean Air Act, the Clean Water Act, the Resource Conservation and Recovery Act. Those laws can limit room for considering overall environmental impacts. Each law is technically complicated and legally intricate and requires specialized expertise.

In a letter to various legislators, former Secretary of Natural Resources and House of Delegates member W. Tayloe Murphy Jr. found the bill "an inappropriate reaction to a few high profile decisions made by the current Boards." Mr. Murphy criticized the legislature for introducing the bill "without any prior opportunity for thoughtful study by the members and former members of the affected Boards, by the conservation organizations of Virginia and the citizens they represent." Mr. Murphy continued:

The bill does more than consolidate the three existing boards into a single board. I believe that this alone is a mistake because the water, air and waste programs are quite different and call for separate divisions within the Department of Environmental Quality to administer them. It is vitally important that all board members understand the details of the program they administer ... . In addition, the transfer or permitting authority from the water and air boards to the DEQ Director would eliminate meaningful public participation in the permitting process...[44]

Another ostensible reason for concentrating permitting authority in the DEQ Director's hands was to prevent unqualified Board members from making technically complex decisions. However, at the time Air Board members had considerable technical, legal, and policy background. In a February 2008 opinion editorial published in the *Virginian-Pilot*, the main newspaper for the Hampton Roads–Norfolk area, former DEQ Director Robert Burnley underscored the five-member Air Board's estimated "125 years" of collective experience and emphasized that, by contrast, several DEQ Directors had had no scientific training. "The real issue," Mr. Burnley said, "is very simple. A few special interests want more control over environmental permitting. They believe, and they are probably right, that they can more easily influence a single bureaucrat than they can multi-member boards."[45]

The Air Board members' qualifications were not the problem. Rather, the business community and some officials (including, apparently, the governor's staff, the DEQ's Director, and the Secretary of Natural Resources) were unhappy with the ends to which we applied our considerable knowledge. Alexandria's citizens and officials lobbied hard against the Board consolidation bill. Poul Hertel, one of the Mirant Monitoring Group's leaders, said, "I'm thoroughly surprised that a Democratic governor would do what he has accused the Bush administration of doing—having industry lobbyists write legislation to benefit themselves at the cost of the people he is supposed to support." Elizabeth Chimento, another of the Monitoring Group's leaders, remarked that, "DEQ has really degenerated since Kaine became governor. It has allowed Mirant to use faux science. It nit picks everything the residents and City suggest and practically gives Mirant a blank check to do what they want." Alexandria City Attorney Ignacio Pessoa blasted the bill: "This legislation is not only ill advised, it is an insult to the Virginia tradition of citizen input and participation. It makes no sense to take away authority from citizen boards and put it into the hands of the bureaucracy." Southern Environmental Law Center attorney Cale Jaffe asserted, "Taking the existing citizen boards out of the permitting process would be a grave mistake. It would mean that decisions with serious public health and environmental consequences would be made behind closed doors."[46]

The Board bill did not pass in 2007, in the face of protests from citizens' groups, members of Congress from northern Virginia, and Alexandria officials. Rather, the bill was held over for consideration in the 2008 General Assembly. The DEQ formed a stakeholder group to discuss changes to the Board bill for the 2008 General Assembly session. As this process was underway, Secretary of Natural Resources Preston Bryant summoned the chairs and vice chairs of the three Boards to Richmond. Since I was vice chair of the Air Board, I attended that meeting. It was evident that the governor who had appointed many of us now wanted to diminish our authority because we were holding the regulated community to the Clean Air Act's requirements. Preston Bryant and Kathy Frahm, an aide to DEQ Director David Paylor, claimed that the bill was not an administration initiative. However, the contemporaneous email messages cited above indicate that the DEQ's Director and members of Governor Kaine's staff were involved in drafting and promoting the bill.

Ultimately, the General Assembly enacted in March 2008 a law that transferred Air and Water Board permitting authority to the DEQ Director and staff, with the possibility of Board oversight if enough citizens requested it. The current five-member Air Board retained authority over the Mirant Alexandria facility. However, the Air Board would be expanded to seven members in July 2008, making the Board's size "consistent with" that of the Water and Waste Boards. The effect of that change would be to allow the governor to appoint new members, who would likely be chosen for their willingness to cede authority to the DEQ's management and staff. Former DEQ Director Burnley saw the new law as part of a pattern in which most new environmental laws in Virginia "have weakened environmental protection for the sake of various special interests."[47]

Not coincidentally, Governor Kaine and local politicians, Democratic and Republican alike, supported the new, intensely controversial coal-fired power plant in Wise County that Dominion Virginia Power had proposed and whose air pollution permits were pending before the DEQ and the Board. It seemed likely that Governor Kaine's July 2008 Air Board appointees would defer to the DEQ's judgment on the Wise County facility's permits. In 2004 the General Assembly and Governor Mark Warner had blessed Dominion's plans for this generating station, to be powered by virgin coal, waste coal, and wood.[48]

After its work in Alexandria had been completed, the Board turned its attention to Dominion's permit application for the Wise County power plant, the subject of the next chapter. Permits written by the Board's three-person majority would be the best shot at tough restrictions for a facility that was a political fait accompli. At the end of June 2008 the Board would face another anxious crowd, this time in a hot high school auditorium in Wise. Rural, mountainous Wise would seem a world away from suburban Alexandria. But Mirant was fresh in mind.

2   Wise: "Rogue Board"

Wise County, Virginia, a rural area of magnificent natural beauty, nestles in the far southwest corner of Virginia in the Appalachian Mountains. Kentucky and Tennessee lie only a stone's throw away. Spectacular mountain vistas dazzle the eye and entice tourists who want to enjoy the out-of-doors. Richmond, the state capitol, and the state's other population centers lie hundreds of miles distant. In many ways southwest Virginia's political and cultural affinities are more Appalachian than Virginian.

In June 2008 I was headed to Wise County for the State Air Pollution Control Board's hearing on Dominion Power's proposed new coal-fired electrical generation plant. When I checked into a bed and breakfast and mentioned that I was from Charlottesville, a mid-size central Virginia city that is home to the University of Virginia and Thomas Jefferson's home, Monticello, the innkeeper replied, "Oh, I've been to North Carolina!" He was confusing Charlotte, North Carolina, with Charlottesville, which might seem a world away for some residents of southwest Virginia.

Wise County is geographically isolated from the state's major urban areas by mountains and distance. But southwest Virginia is intimately bound to the state's history, cultural heritage, and political-economic identity. The Virginia Mountain Boys, an important early bluegrass band, came from southwest Virginia. According to Wise County's website, this remote section of the state was a "site of constant conflict during the Civil War."[1]

Battles continue in Wise County, but they concern coal, not slavery. Open mines have devoured whole mountaintops, leaving them wasted and scoured of vegetation and burying or contaminating nearby waterways. Detritus from deep mines has long been problematic. Hundreds of piles of waste coal mar the landscape and pollute water through sedimentation and leaching of acidic contaminants. Such mounds can combust spontaneously. The devastation wrought by mining practices has stimulated sustained political resistance to what Kathy Selvage, a prominent Wise County activist, has called "strip mining on steroids." Ms. Selvage, a Wise County native whose father once worked the deep mines, asked in 2005, "Are we rushing to flatten the whole county?"[2]

Coal reserves originally attracted thousands to the area in the late nineteenth century. The hope was that exporting coal would bring affluence to the area. But according to Ron Heller, a University of Kentucky historian, "that kind of development generated wealth for the few, but an often difficult and challenging life for the many." Ms. Selvage perceives a web of connections among environmental destruction, concentration of political and economic power in the coal companies, and poverty in Wise. The writer John Gaventa observed that "Central Appalachia is a region of poverty amidst riches; a place of glaring inequalities" because its residents were poor while absentee coal company owners extracted great wealth from the area's coal reserves. Those undertaking the hard labor of extracting coal from the region's mines included African Americans, who made up a sizeable fraction of Virginia's coal miners until the 1940s.[3]

Mining now accounts for only about 3,500 jobs in southwest Virginia, a small number in comparison with the 3.9 million employees in the state as a whole but significant in view of the region's relatively small population. Local officials estimated that, as of 2015, 46 percent of Wise County's economy depended on the coal industry. The local newspaper is called *The Coalfield Progress*. Southwest Virginia lies in the crosshairs of conflicts over destructive mining practices and the United States' dependence on coal for generating electricity.[4]

Wise County struggles to attract economic development and its population suffers from health problems. The county's poverty rate in 2014 was 21.9 percent, far exceeding the statewide rate of 11.8 percent. Median household income in 2014 was 59 percent of the statewide median. The well educated tend to leave for more promising job markets, and those who stay may succumb to disproportionately high rates of drug abuse. Coal miners are susceptible to injury, and some become addicted to painkillers. According to a Harvard University health study, the women of Wise County saw a slight decrease in life expectancy between the mid 1980s and 1999. This "reversal of fortune," as the Harvard researchers dubbed it, runs counter to the overall nationwide trend of increasing life expectancy. In 1999 life expectancy for women in Wise County was 76 years, as compared with 80 years nationally. Wise County's men have fared somewhat better, with a life expectancy in 1999 of 73.4, about seven months shy of the national life expectancy.[5]

The region's troubles made a new coal-fired power plant in Wise County seem like an answer to local politicians' prayers. Two Democratic governors and the Virginia General Assembly provided sustained bipartisan political support for the power plant. In 2004, Governor Mark Warner signed legislation enabling the construction of "a coal-fueled generation facility that utilizes Virginia coal and is located in the coalfield region of the Commonwealth." The 2004 legislation declared the unplanned, unpermitted, hypothetical facility to be "in the public interest." The actual facility, a 668-megawatt generating station proposed in 2006 by Dominion Virginia Power, would be expensive, costing an estimated $1.8 billion, and at least one credible analysis projected that its construction would increase electricity rates statewide.[6]

Governor Tim Kaine, a Democrat who was elected in 2005, supported Dominion's proposal, which would involve a power plant that would burn virgin coal, waste coal, and waste wood—a "hybrid" energy facility. In 2006, Governor Kaine's Secretary of Commerce and Trade testified in hearings before the State Corporation Commission as follows: "I can't stress enough Governor Kaine's and my and the administration's support for this project." Projected economic benefits to the region included 800 construction jobs, 75 post-construction jobs at the power plant, 300 coal mining jobs, and $5 million yearly in new tax revenues for a county whose budget was $44 million. The facility would consume waste coal that was polluting regional streams and rivers. Members of the Wise County Board of Supervisors raised the specter of brownouts if the power plant was not built and promised confidently that "the power plant when it comes on line will be the cleanest in the world."[7]

But local and state citizens' groups took issue with these claims and saw the plant as a public health, environmental, and economic liability. Not only would it justify continued mountaintop mining and contribute to global warming; it might create huge amounts of air pollution that could harm people and nearby forests, which were already suffering from years of acid deposition. One of the plant's opponents said it would "savagely blow up entire mountains, feed the resulting exposed coal to a proposed power plant that is unnecessary, create lots more greenhouse gases, and doom the good people of southwest Virginia to living with a brutal extraction industry that has no future." Cale Jaffe, a lawyer with the Southern Environmental Law Center, asserted that "clean coal is a misnomer" and recommended improvements in energy efficiency as the cheapest solution to obtaining more electrical power. In the eyes of these observers, the facility should not be built.[8]

When asked in a March 2008 radio interview why he supported Dominion's proposal, Governor Kaine asserted the need for reliable, low-cost energy. He claimed that the Air Board and the State Corporation Commission would decide whether or not the Wise power plant would be built. But the latter comment was disingenuous, as the General Assembly had already declared the facility to be "in the public interest." The facility's longstanding bipartisan support guaranteed that it would be built, one way or another. The Virginia State Corporation Commission, whose approval is needed for new power plants, initially balked at Dominion's proposed high rate of return on the Wise County power plant. But state lawmakers testified in support of the facility. Ultimately, Dominion received a guaranteed, handsome return on its investment.[9]

These were the political dynamics that culminated in the Air Board's June 2008 public hearing in Wise. If the five-member Air Board refused to issue air pollution permits, Dominion would have a much easier time after the Board's configuration changed on 1 July as a result of 2008 state legislation. At that point, the Board's enlarged seven-member body would undoubtedly defer to the DEQ's decisions. The lenient permit limits proposed by the DEQ indicated that its management was willing to appease Dominion at the expense of public health and environmental protection. The central question in Wise for my fellow Air Board members and me was not whether the air pollution permits would be issued but, rather, how strict they would be.

The story that follows describes the events and decisions that led to the Board's two-day June 2008 hearing in Wise County. Publicly available email messages reveal the extent of behind-the-scenes efforts to undercut the Board's efforts by the DEQ's Director, the Secretary of Natural Resources, Governor Kaine, and his aides. In one agitated email message from Secretary of Natural Resources Preston Bryant to Governor Kaine, Mr. Bryant called us a "rogue Board."[10]

Waiting for Godot

Dominion submitted the first part of its application for air pollution permits in the summer of 2006, with other portions (e.g., air quality modeling) following in early 2007. Until early 2008 the Board sat on the sidelines as the DEQ evaluated Dominion's application, without which the company could not construct and operate the Wise County facility. We listened to testimony on the facility's possible impacts, including claims of adverse impacts on Great Smoky Mountains National Park in neighboring North Carolina.

The Board asked Dominion and DEQ staff members to work together to propose a facility that would be highly protective of public health and the environment. We waited to see the DEQ propose permit limits that complied with the Clean Air Act's strict requirements.[11]

The Clean Air Act required two distinct permits for the Wise County power plant. The first was the "Prevention of Significant Deterioration" (PSD) permit, which mandated the application of "Best Available Control Technology" to limit the power plant's emissions of conventional air pollutants such as sulfur dioxide and particulate matter. PSD permits apply in the relatively clean-air areas meeting the EPA's National Ambient Air Quality Standards. The Clean Air Act also restricts the amount by which air quality in these clean-air areas can be degraded, requiring permit applicants to demonstrate through modeling that their proposed emissions will not exceed allowable impacts on air quality or harm nearby national parks or wilderness areas. The source's emissions may not cause violations of the National Ambient Air Quality Standards.[12]

The second permit required application of "Maximum Available Control Technology" (MACT) to reduce the facility's "hazardous air pollutants" or "toxics." In Clean Air Act parlance, these terms refer to pollutants, such as mercury and arsenic, that are emitted in much smaller amounts than the conventional pollutants but whose serious effects—including cancer and neurotoxicity—are felt at low concentrations. Mercury is a neurotoxin that persists in the environment and bio-accumulates up the food chain. Infants are at special risk of developing mercury poisoning. Because of mercury's well-known serious adverse health and environmental effects, it was one of the first substances to be designated a hazardous air pollutant under the federal Clean Air Act. Once emitted into the atmosphere, mercury falls to the surface and contaminates land and water. Birds exposed to mercury can develop reproductive problems. Many streams and rivers in Virginia, including several in the southwestern part of the state, have been deemed dangerous for fishing because of mercury buildup in fish tissues. Coal-fired power plants have been the most significant source of mercury air pollution in the United States, contributing an estimated 50 percent of national mercury emissions.[13]

Although mercury was a special focus of the MACT permit, dozens of other air toxics, including arsenic, dioxin, chromium, and acid gases, are also emitted from coal-fired power plants. When Dominion submitted its original permit request in 2006, federal law did not require facility-specific mercury emissions reductions. In 2005 the EPA had decided to exempt power plants from the Clean Air Act's strong MACT provisions and to establish instead a mercury emissions cap-and-trade program for coal-fired power plants. That program would set a national cap on mercury emissions from coal-fired power plants and would let affected facilities buy and sell emission allowances rather than meet individually fixed emissions targets. Among the many concerns over the trading program was that the ecosystems most in need of reduced mercury deposition might receive even more mercury, because trading allows emission reductions to happen where they are most cost-effective, not where they are most needed environmentally.[14]

The Air Board's response to the EPA's proposed mercury emissions trading program for power plants prompted a sharp reaction from the Virginia General Assembly. In 2006 the Board was faced with adopting the EPA's mercury emissions trading program, which seemed weak and insufficiently protective—especially for a state with many mercury-contaminated waterways. As one scientific expert explained, the trading program might exacerbate "hot spots" of mercury contamination. The EPA seemed to have illegally exempted power plants from stringent mercury emission reductions. The Board's concerns were shared by officials in other states, many of whom decided not to join EPA's trading program and opted instead for a more stringent, technology-based approach that would result in mercury emission reductions at every power plant covered by the rule. The Air Board proposed for public comment two approaches to deal with mercury emissions from power plants: the EPA's cap-and-trade approach and one that required the control technology that had been adopted in many other states. Within a few weeks of the Board's decision, and well before the Board could receive public comments on the two approaches, the Virginia General Assembly and Governor Tim Kaine removed the decision from the Board's hands and passed a law instructing the Air Board to adopt the EPA's mercury cap-and-trade program.[15]

That program was overturned in court. In February 2008 a federal appeals court ruled that the EPA's decision to exempt power plants from maximum available technology requirements for mercury violated the Clean Air Act. From that point forward, the act's Maximum Available Control Technology requirement applied to the Wise County facility. Eventually the EPA would develop national technology-based standards for mercury pollution from coal-fired power plants. But in the spring of 2008, in the wake of the court's decision, the DEQ and the Board were suddenly faced with writing a toxics permit with no benchmark standards. The Clean Air Act required case-by-case MACT determinations if no national rule was in place.[16]

Dominion's final permit application, which was submitted in August 2007, called for allowable emissions of 744 tons of fine particulate matter,

3,369 tons of sulfur dioxide, 1,930 tons of nitrogen oxides, and 72 pounds of mercury per year. Those levels were far too high. After all, the Board had required that the much older, slightly smaller Mirant power plant in Alexandria reduce its sulfur dioxide emissions to 3,813 tons per year. New facilities are always expected to emit much less pollution than old facilities because new facilities can build pollution controls into their design. A key issue was the Wise County facility's 5.37 million tons of carbon dioxide emissions. In 2008 greenhouse gases were not regulated under the Clean Air Act. Since the permits at issue were Clean Air Act permits, whether the Board had the authority to require technologies that would reduce carbon dioxide emissions was not clear.[17]

The DEQ's first draft of permissible emission limits, published in January 2008, differed little from the pollution amounts proposed by Dominion, with the exception of reductions in allowable emissions of fine particulate matter. In January 2008 the DEQ proposed limits of 3,292 tons of sulfur dioxide, 1,920 tons of nitrogen oxides, 329 tons of fine particulate matter, and 72 pounds of mercury per year. Commenters pointed out that even these somewhat tighter limits were unacceptably weak when considered against known applicable technologies. After the February 2008 judicial decision to invalidate the EPA's mercury trading program, the DEQ reduced allowable mercury emissions from 72 to 49 pounds per year.[18]

A growing public chorus accused the DEQ of failing to abide by the Clean Air Act. Fifteen hundred citizens asked the Board to take over the permit because of concerns over mercury and carbon dioxide emissions, sulfate and nitrate pollution loads in Great Smoky Mountains National Park, mountaintop mining, and environmental justice. A documentary filmmaker was following the heated controversy. We considered exercising our authority to oversee yet another facility's air pollution permits.[19]

In January 2008 matters began to come to a head. DEQ staffers and managers were frustrated with the Board's continued insistence on revising downward the emissions levels proposed in the permit and with watching the Board members work through these complicated issues in public. Virginia law specified that no Board member could speak with more than one other Board member outside of the Board's formally announced public meetings. The goal of that prohibition was to ensure that the public had full access to the Board's deliberations.

The Board members knew that overseeing the permit would be a contentious and labor-intensive process. But Hullie, Bruce, and I said repeatedly in public Board meetings that the limits contemplated by the DEQ did not meet the Clean Air Act's requirements. In 1997 an audit commission of the

Virginia General Assembly had criticized the DEQ for kowtowing to the regulated community and for relegating to the back seat the department's responsibility to protect human health and the environment. The commission's report said that DEQ employees feared for their jobs if they "upset" regulated entities. Those tendencies had persisted. The DEQ's willingness to accede to the regulated community had been on full public display during the Board's struggle to reduce the Mirant power plant's air pollution.[20]

At the Board's March 2008 meeting, Hullie Moore led the charge to take over the permit. Hullie said the proposed permits failed to comply with the Clean Air Act's requirements. He elaborated his conclusion in a long prepared statement in which he set forth the results of his detailed analysis of fuel content and emission rates at other Virginia power plants. He indicated that proper analysis of Best Available Control Technology for sulfur dioxide emissions, as required under the Clean Air Act, would include consideration of cleaner fuels. Several much older coal-fired power plants in Virginia, permitted in the early 1990s, showed sulfur dioxide emission rates lower than those proposed by DEQ for the Wise County facility. Hullie's research with respect to mercury emission controls showed that a much older facility achieved a mercury emission rate eight times lower than that proposed by the DEQ for the new Wise facility, and that five existing power plants in Virginia emitted mercury at lower rates than proposed by Dominion. Mercury emissions for eight existing Virginia power plants with total generating capacity over three times that of Wise would, in 2010, have together mercury emissions equal to that proposed for the Wise facility.[21]

After presenting his lengthy analysis, Hullie concluded that the DEQ's proposed limits did not meet the letter of the Clean Air Act:

It appears to me highly unlikely that the proposed permits could survive appellate scrutiny at either the state or federal level. I do not know what the final decision should be with respect to the Wise County project. I do know that cleaner coal must be considered. I know that alternatives must be considered. For months I have asked questions and consulted with DEQ staff and asked the Company to expand their analysis and rethink their proposal. I have refrained from acting, hoping that the Company's proposal would be changed or fully analyzed as required by law. This has not happened.

The Board must now assume the authority and responsibility for the Dominion Wise County applications. In the long run I believe this action will save time compared to starting over after an appeal. Accordingly, I move that the Board assume authority and control of the permits for the Dominion Wise County project.[22]

Board member Bruce Buckheit urged Dominion to consider building a facility that would use Integrated Gasification Combined Cycle (IGCC) technology, which would emit far fewer greenhouse gases. He explained that he was not necessarily advocating IGCC, which at the time had not been widely applied and was expensive, but that he thought the IGCC technology should be explicitly considered. He criticized Dominion for proposing a facility with an inefficiently high heat rate, pointing out that the facility that would burn roughly the same amount fuel of to produce a unit of electricity as the 60-year old Mirant facility in Alexandria. "We're talking about two plants that get 15 miles per gallon," he said, likening heat rate to a vehicle's fuel economy.[23]

My comments justified a decision to oversee the permit by underscoring the extraordinary public controversy over the draft permits, as evidenced by the estimated 5,000–6,000 comments received on substantive issues. Many people disputed the DEQ's determination of the lowest achievable emission rates. The National Park Service warned of potential damage to vegetation in nearby wilderness and park areas from the emission levels proposed by Dominion and the DEQ. Such areas receive protection from adverse impacts under the Clean Air Act. Decades of acid deposition, whose origins were with sulfur dioxide and nitrogen oxides emissions from coal-fired power plants near and far, had taken their toll on Virginia's streams and forests. Although the National Ambient Air Quality Standards were not violated in the area, regional air quality was far from pristine because of nearby sources, such as the coal-fired Clinch River power plant, and because of long-distance transport. Park Service comments also pointed to the large amounts of solid waste that would be generated by the limestone used to reduce sulfur dioxide emissions. I pointed out that Governor Kaine had convened a task force to consider how to reduce emissions of greenhouse gases in the state, even as this permit proposed to increase those emissions substantially.[24]

Our colleagues Richard Langford and John Hanson wanted to handle the issues Hullie, Bruce and I had raised while letting the DEQ write the permit. Richard and John voted against the Board's assuming responsibility for the permits, even though they had voted with us in 2006 to assume control over the Mirant permit. The final vote was 3–2 in favor of taking over the permits.[25]

After that meeting, Bruce, Hullie, and I had only three months to collect information and consider new permit limits. Dominion had requested final permits by 1 July 2008, and we were under pressure to make a good faith effort to meet the company's request. Further, on 1 July the Board would become a seven-person body. In light of Governor Kaine's support for an enlarged Board, his outspoken support of the Wise power plant, and his office's disapproval of how we handled the Mirant permit, it seemed likely that he would appoint new members who would be inclined to side with the DEQ and Dominion.

We could not have guessed just how anxious Governor Kaine and his staff had become about the Board's potential involvement with the Wise permit. Email messages that have since become public reveal the nature of the many conversations that happened over our heads and behind our backs. In January 2008, before the Board took over the permitting process for the Wise facility, Governor Kaine asked Secretary of Natural Resources Preston Bryant about the Board's legal authority to require carbon dioxide controls and to discourage the use of Virginia coal. The governor pointed to the 2004 Virginia law specifying that the facility should be built in the coal-field region of the state and should use Virginia coal. Mr. Bryant responded that, although some Board members might not interpret the law as the governor preferred, the 2004 law declaring the power plant to be in the public interest "arguably does not tie any of the environmental boards' hands as long as they are arguably acting within their authority." A March 2008 email message indicates that Governor Kaine was laboring under the mistaken impression that the DEQ's proposed permit limits would make the Wise County power plant much cleaner than other coal-fired power plants in Virginia.[26]

In February 2008, Governor Kaine seemed surprised when the *Bristol Herald-Courier*, the major newspaper closest to Wise, published editorials opposing the Wise County power plant. The governor asked his staff if there was any reason to sound a "cautionary note" about mountaintop coal mining. Secretary of Natural Resources Bryant replied that the DEQ was "wrapping up" public hearings on the air permits, that greenhouse-gas limitations "do not exist now," and that, in southwest Virginia, "coal is a whopping $2 billion industry." Steve Walz, who headed Virginia's Department of Mines, Minerals and Energy, emphasized the General Assembly's 2004 declaration that the power plant was in the public interest. But Mr. Walz admitted that 25 percent of Wise County had been surface-mined and that Virginia had not done well with energy conservation, which many power plant opponents said could obviate the need for new generating capacity. He reported that Dominion blamed consumers for increasing energy demand by purchasing "energy hogging plasma TVs." Mr. Walz speculated that many people were ignorant about the impact of "their gung-ho consumerist lifestyle," which he said, "points out the need to educate consumers."[27]

As the Air Board's 20 March meeting approached, agitated email exchanges among members of the governor's staff anticipated that the Board might vote to take over the Wise permit and overreacted to a Board-initiated suggestion for a policy change. On 19 March, Governor Kaine's scheduling director indicated that Dominion's CEO and president, Tom Farrell, and two top Dominion executives, Bob Blue and Eva Teig Hardy, wanted to meet with the governor to talk about the Wise facility "and possible legislative initiatives." A counselor to the governor responded, "I would prefer that it not be an in person meeting." Secretary of Natural Resources Preston Bryant warned that if the Air Board decided to deny air pollution permits for the Wise County facility, attempting to reverse that decision "would reflect negatively on the Governor." At about the same time, Board members Hullie Moore and Bruce Buckheit circulated proposed changes to the DEQ's "Suitability Policy," because, in their view, the existing policy appeared to delegate unlawfully to local zoning authorities power to decide whether an air pollution source was "suitable" for the area. Hullie and Bruce felt that local authorities could not have the information and expertise to make such decisions and that such decisions rested legally within the Board's purview. They wanted to solicit public comment on their suggested modifications to the Suitability Policy. Mr. Bryant responded testily:

Mr. Buckheit and Mr. Moore have prepared this document, and they've sprung it on Dave Paylor just a few days before the meeting.

This is insulting and is an affront to DEQ management and staff. But that's the least of its effect.

In short, this policy, if adopted, upends DEQ's air division. The Air Board will, in effect, become the air division. (See #5).

This Air Board is out of control—I am saying it for the umpteenth time. It is time for intervention, as much as we may have wanted to avoid it. When this hits the streets, the business community will be up in arms—and, in my opinion, rightfully so. If the board is going to act on this, it tells me that the proposed Dominion plant is caput.[28]

In the weeks after 20 March 2008, when the Board assumed responsibility for deciding the Wise County facility's permit limits, emails among the DEQ's management, the governor's staff, and Governor Kaine emphasized Dominion's interests. In the exchanges that have been made publicly available, environmental quality and public health protection took a back seat. Four days after the Board assumed responsibility for issuing the Wise County permit, Democratic and Republican members of the General Assembly from southwest Virginia suggested that the governor block the Board's action. On 24 March Mark Rubin told Governor Kaine,

"[Republican] Senator [William] Wampler called today to advise that he, [Democratic Senator Phil] Puckett, [Democratic Delegate Bud] Phillips and [Republican Delegate Terry] Kilgore will be sending you a letter asking you to send down an amendment ... to put the permitting authority for the Wise County plant in the agency instead of the Board. He cannot imagine why you would not do that. The letter will not come quickly because they do not want to tip off anyone that this is their strategy."[29]

Less than a week after the Board had taken over the permitting process, DEQ Director Paylor and Secretary of Natural Resources Bryant discussed the possibility of having Governor Kaine intervene in the Board's decision making. Mr. Paylor suggested that the governor could excuse his action by claiming that the Board was "completely ignoring the actions of the GA [General Assembly] in 2004." In April, Governor Kaine and his aides began to talk about the three new Air Board appointees, who would not be seated until 1 July 2008.[30]

More email messages reveal the extent to which the Air Board's independence continued to worry DEQ Director Paylor and the governor's staff, especially when Dominion raised concerns. In early 2008, negotiations continued on the bill that would move permitting authority from the Air Board to the DEQ's Director (a battle that was detailed in chapter 1). Mr. Paylor agreed with Dominion about the need to make it difficult for the Board to oversee the permitting process:

Essentially Dominion is rightly worried that anyone can get 25 signatures and game the system to send it to the Board for permit review. Heretofore, that has not been a problem for the water permits, and with a higher bar (25 signatures vs. 1) we have assumed that there will be fewer permits going to the water control board. There would be more going to air and there is nothing that precludes getting a bunch of signatures. Dominion is trying to figure a way around that.[31]

The 1997 General Assembly report's scorching criticism of the DEQ management's efforts to satisfy the regulated community comes to mind.

While these conversations were underway, public agitation over the Wise power plant continued. In May, activists presented to Dominion a petition, with 42,000 signatures, asking the company not to build the Wise County facility.[32]

The Process Matters

After taking over responsibility for setting permit limits for the Wise County power plant, Board members agreed to send detailed questions to the DEQ

Figure 2.1
Kathy Selvage and Kayti Wingfield with 42,000-signature petition opposing Dominion's Wise County power plant (photo courtesy of Cat McCue).

as soon as was reasonably possible. Within three weeks Bruce Buckheit delivered a detailed engineering analysis (28 pages, single-spaced) that displayed various scenarios about the known effectiveness of pollution-control techniques that could be used at the Wise facility. With cleaner coal and higher pollution-control efficiencies than assumed by Dominion or the DEQ, Bruce's analysis indicated that emissions would decrease substantially relative to the DEQ's latest proposal. Bruce spoke with special authority because of his extensive experience with power plants when he headed the EPA's air enforcement team.[33]

A casual observer might wonder why ascertaining the "best" or "maximum available" control technology is so complicated. Under the Clean Air Act, Best Available Control Technology (BACT), determinations are made case by case, considering the circumstances of each particular facility. BACT is the maximum degree of control that can be achieved, considering environmental and energy impacts. The EPA indicates that BACT may include "fuel cleaning or treatment and innovative fuel combustion techniques" and that "BACT may be a design, equipment, work practice, or operational standard if imposition of an emissions standard is infeasible." In making a BACT determination one must examine comparable kinds of facilities and choose the system that achieves the lowest emissions.[34]

In mid April I submitted seventeen detailed questions to the DEQ. I asked about the impacts of the facility's emissions on regional ozone and particulate-matter concentrations and about how the mercury emitted from the facility would affect mercury levels in nearby waterways, including a part of the Holston River in which the DEQ prohibited fish consumption because of high mercury and PCB levels. I asked what information led the Wise County Board of Supervisors to conclude (erroneously) that "Dominion has committed to utilize Carbon Capture Capable (CCC) equipment on the proposed facility to limit and reduce Green House Gases [sic] (GHG) thereby either eliminating or reducing the 'carbon footprint' of the state-of-the-art Virginia City Hybrid Energy Center." To emphasize the sheer scale of the facility's carbon dioxide emissions, I presented an ecologist's estimate that 5 percent of the state's area would have to be planted in pine trees to offset the Wise facility's carbon dioxide emissions.[35]

Hullie sent his questions to the DEQ in mid April, too. He asked for spreadsheets with details about the energy (BTUs), the mercury content, and the sulfur content of coal burned by electrical generating units in Virginia. He inquired about the costs of delivering, washing, and treating coal burned in Virginia's power plants and about the costs of alternative coals. He requested matrices that would display sulfur dioxide and mercury emissions as a function of energy content, the percent content of the pollutant in the coal, and the percent removal rate by pollution-control devices. He sought comparisons of sulfur dioxide and mercury emissions from Virginia's existing power plants.[36]

An enormous question was whether the Board could write permit restrictions that would reduce the facility's 5.3 million tons (4.8 million metric tons) of carbon dioxide emissions, which are huge in both absolute and relative terms. In 2008 Virginia's total energy-related carbon dioxide emissions, including transportation sources, amounted to 115 million metric tons.[37]

The legal basis for a decision to regulate carbon dioxide was at issue. In 2007 the US Supreme Court had decided that greenhouse gases qualified as air pollutants under the Clean Air Act because their environmental harms were "serious and well recognized." But in 2008 the US EPA had not yet declared carbon dioxide a pollutant under the Clean Air Act. A student at the University of Virginia School of Law concluded that Virginia law was broad enough to justify regulating carbon dioxide. His analysis showed that "Virginia's statutory definition of 'air pollution … is necessarily broad, open-ended, and not explicitly limited to criteria or hazardous air pollutants traditionally regulated by [the EPA]. Air pollution, as defined in the Virginia Code, 'means the presence in the outdoor atmosphere of one or more substances which are or may be harmful or injurious to human health, welfare or safety, to animal or plant life, or to property, or which unreasonably interfere with the enjoyment by the people of life or property.'"[38]

But doubts about the legal and technical viability of requiring carbon capture and control arose from other directions. At about the time we were submitting our detailed questions to the DEQ, the Virginia State Corporation Commission turned down Appalachian Power Company's request to construct a power plant that would use carbon capture technologies on the grounds of excessive expense and risk to ratepayers. The State Corporation Commission also questioned the lack of explicit procedures in Appalachian Power's plans for sequestering captured carbon.[39]

Further, it seemed unlikely that Virginia's Attorney General, Robert McDonnell, would defend in court a permit with carbon dioxide limits. McDonnell's staff had advised the Board that greenhouse-gas controls could be imposed on specific facilities only after the Board had "duly adopted regulations" that would apply to entire source categories. Environmental groups argued that the Supreme Court's 2007 decision provided a sufficient basis to subject carbon dioxide to the Clean Air Act's BACT requirements. Even if that logic held, there was little operational precedent for what constituted "BACT" for carbon dioxide emissions at the Wise power plant. If the Board ventured onto thin legal ice, the rest of the permit might be invalidated in court. Without the strong backing of the Attorney General's office, the Board risked having no counsel willing to defend the permit.[40]

As we wrestled with the thorny engineering, legal, and policy choices at hand, we faced important procedural questions about how to collect information. The Board expected to assemble in Wise County at the end of June for what might be a multi-day public meeting involving public comments and a series of votes. But somehow the Board members had to solicit and digest public comments in accordance with the legally prescribed administrative procedures, which were convoluted and opaque. Anyone who has been involved in making policy can appreciate former Representative John Dingell's famous claim: "I'll let you write the substance on a statute and you let me write the procedure, and I'll screw you every time." Eventually the Board members posted questions and answers on a specially created DEQ website, so the world could see what we were asking and how the DEQ and Dominion responded.[41]

Board members had to avoid "ex parte communications," the appearance of favoring one party in the Wise County case over another. When we visited the power plant's proposed site, no more than two of us walked around together and we were escorted by DEQ staff, not Dominion representatives. We were advised not to accept transportation of any kind from members of environmental groups. Board members could not exchange email or speak with more than one other member at a time, because to do so would constitute holding an unannounced meeting under Virginia law. Considerable email traffic among the Board members and DEQ staffers in April 2008 concerned the basic question of how to collect and consider publicly the information needed to ascertain the appropriate permit limits, without making the Board's decisions vulnerable to attack in court on the basis of administratively inappropriate decision making.[42]

Back-room political efforts to constrain the Board's decisions continued throughout the permitting and public comment process. In early June 2008 Senior aide Mark Rubin suggested to Governor Kaine that he might dismiss Board members for unlawful decisions, even though all we had done at that point was to take over the permit, a perfectly legal action. In mid-May DEQ Director David Paylor and Secretary of Natural Resources Preston Bryant crafted for the governor's office suggestions for how to proceed on the Wise permit. That document indicated that the Attorney General's office had told the Board that we could not regulate greenhouse gases "through a case decision" but, rather, would have to go through the standard regulation-setting process. Mr. Paylor and Mr. Bryant claimed that Hullie Moore and Bruce Buckheit were inclined to "insist on a CO_2 component. They take an expansive reading of their authority that likely the EPA doesn't even recognize." Among the options set forth in this document were meeting in private with Hullie and Bruce to "discuss their views of an acceptable permit."

In other words, the DEQ's director and the Virginia Secretary of Natural Resources were suggesting a meeting behind closed doors, out of the public eye, to negotiate with two of five Board members. Other options suggested were to have the General Assembly "direct that this decision be under the jurisdiction of the Department [of Environmental Quality]" or a "gubernatorial directive" to the Board. Finally, Mr. Paylor and Mr. Bryant raised the possibility that Bruce Buckheit could "negotiate directly" with Dominion, but that "he could only do this if he accepts that he cannot vote on the final permit."[43]

The idea of having Bruce meet privately with the permit applicant seems curiously at odds with repeated admonishments to the Board to avoid ex parte communications and with the Board's legal obligation to undertake its deliberations in public. Mr. Paylor suggested "indirect discussion with the applicant [Dominion], using DEQ as an intermediary." Bruce rejected the notion of participating even in indirect private discussions with Dominion and refused to "engage in any procedural matter that suggests a bias toward the applicant." "My goal in this permitting process," he continued, "is to ensure a fair, unbiased consideration of the issues. ... [The] suggestion (that meetings with Dominion are fine, but not meetings with opponents) is inconsistent with that goal. ... Use of an intermediary suggests that the contact is inappropriate and raises important considerations re 'circumvention.'" Mr. Paylor forwarded Bruce's indignant email message to Preston Bryant and to Mark Rubin, who remarked, "That should be the end of that idea. On to plan b."[44]

"Strictest Permit Limits Ever Written"

The Board and the DEQ scheduled a two-day meeting in the town of Wise for 24 and 25 June 2008. The Board received reams of information from the DEQ, Dominion, the National Park Service, the National Forest Service, environmental groups, and the public at large. The DEQ and the Board extended the comment period to allow ample time for public input. As the Clean Air Act required, the Forest Service and the Park Service were offered early opportunities to assess the possible effects on nearby federal public lands.

In late May, with only a few weeks to go before the public hearing, the DEQ tried to postpone the meeting. The excuse was that one Board member, John Hanson, had a business commitment in Ohio and thus could not be physically present. Behind the scenes, Secretary of Natural Resources Preston Bryant, DEQ Director David Paylor, and members of the governor's staff were trying to appease Dominion's top management by ensuring that John could participate. Previously, DEQ staffers had told me that Board members could participate in public meetings electronically only if they were physically in Virginia and if they were in a public place that was accessible to anyone who wanted to listen. But Dominion wanted John Hanson at the meeting. In a 22 May email to Governor Kaine, Preston Bryant elaborated on how to make Dominion happy and work around the "rogue" Air Board:

DEQ employees are feeling increasingly hung out to dry—not just by this rogue Air Board but, frankly by the Administration. It truly pained David to relay that message. ... The longer this thing goes on, the more "collateral damage" there will be. Frankly, the collateral damage reaches beyond just DEQ—it actually hits Dominion, and in a very $ignificant [sic] way ... . As you know, we have three appointments to make—two new ones (per the new law) and one to replace a member, John Hanson, who is resigning to move into DC.

We have been hopeful of having the Board act in June. Now, it turns out that Hanson has a court date in Ohio and cannot be excused. That reduces the June board meeting to 4 members. If a vote were taken in June, the Wise C. plant likely would be denied 1–3, or possibly 2–2.

Dominion has been told of this unfortunately wrinkly [sic] (Hanson's absence). Bob Blue [a senior vice president at Dominion] is not a happy camper. He has asked that every mountain be moved to have Hanson participate by phone from Ohio. This is not realistic. It'd be difficult from a FOIA perspective, from his court case obligations, and it would be awful looking politically. Dave Paylor is likely to reject Bob Blue's plea ... .

A Way Out? Push for a vote in July. ... The preferred way out ... is to appoint 2 new members and keep Hanson on the board through July (that is legally possible, I am told, his pending move to DC notwithstanding). The 2 new members would sit but recuse themselves, given the complexity of the matter and their being new to the board.

Governor Kaine responded, "I would appreciate the 3 [sic] of you talking about this email and then let's talk about it in person soon."[45]

Only a few days after this email exchange, Cindy Berndt, the Board's secretary, told the Board that the June meeting would have to be rescheduled. I responded to Cindy:

We cannot move the June meeting date. Members of the public and Dominion expect us to hold that public hearing ... . Two members of the Board could always call a special meeting, under the provisions of [State Administrative Code] 10.1-1304. And I am sure that two members would call for us to meet on June 24 and 25, as scheduled.

David Paylor wrote Preston Bryant and Mark Rubin on 16 June to say, "John can now not make any part of the air board meeting because the judges have shuffled the schedule. Bob Blue [a senior vice president at Dominion] will be calling you (perhaps as I write this) to ask you to put pressure on him to be available."[46]

Ultimately, John participated electronically from Ohio in the decision-making portion of our public hearing. Somehow Mr. Paylor had overcome his reluctance to have a Board member attend from a place that clearly wasn't available to the public in Virginia. I asked how it was legal under Virginia's FOIA laws for John to participate in this fashion. My email records do not show that I received a response.[47]

In early June, Mark Rubin, Preston Bryant, David Paylor, and Wayne Turnage scheduled a meeting with Governor Kaine to discuss the possibility of a gubernatorial "directive" to the Air Board, even though the Board is an independent body that does not report to the governor. Mr. Rubin also suggested to Governor Kaine that he might dismiss members of the Board summarily, despite our fixed terms, because we had "failed to follow a legal directive." But at that point the Board had not taken any action. DEQ Director Paylor had drafted a letter from the governor to the Board in mid May, even before the public comment period had closed. That first draft urges the Board to act on the Wise County permit before the end of June and to follow the Attorney General's advice, which appears to refer to the opinion that the Board did not have legal authority to regulate carbon dioxide from the Wise facility.[48]

Governor Kaine intervened in early June 2008, just before the Board would meet in public to write the Wise facility's permits. The final version of the governor's letter did not refer explicitly to the Dominion's Wise County facility. Instead, the letter cautioned the Board to "stay within the existing regulatory framework," which appeared to mean, at a minimum, "Don't regulate carbon dioxide." Governor Kaine also told us "not to consider any media other than air quality." Email messages indicate that Mark Rubin and David Paylor crafted the letter.[49]

Local and national news media quickly picked up the story. The *Bristol Herald-Courier* reported that "the governor is knee-deep in the muck" and "the implications of his letter are clear. The five-member citizen panel had better not stand in Dominion's way." According to a story titled "Calamity Kaine" on the website Huffington Post, "Virginia governor Tim Kaine set a new standard for politician mealy-mouthedness with a letter to his Virginia Air Board ... . The situation is clear to most Virginia watchers: Kaine is terrified of Big Coal, personified (or rather, corporatified) here by the Chicago-based Dominion Power."[50]

In late June 2008 the Board sat behind a table on a stage facing a packed high school auditorium. For eight hours on the first day we simply listened, as a parade of elected officials implored us to issue the needed permits for the facility, which promised jobs and revenue for the area, and as a stream of citizens variously begged us to deny or grant the permits. The DEQ had structured the comments so that opponents of the plant would alternate with supporters. By mid afternoon there were no more supporters in line, only opponents.

The public dialogue on the Air Board's actions had turned into a permit-vs.-no-permit debate. Environmental and citizens' groups helped frame the issue in this manner. But the Board had no power to stop the construction of the Wise power plant. If we voted to deny the facility's air pollution permits, it was likely that state politicians, including Governor Kaine and members of the General Assembly, would ensure another hearing for Dominion before a newly constituted Board under newly legislated procedures that were favorable to a more lenient permit. It was not clear that the Board had the legal authority to deny the permits.

On the second day of public hearings, the Board finalized the permits, pollutant by pollutant, over a nine-hour period in the auditorium of Wise's high school. The DEQ had revised the facility's proposed limits downward once again, to 2,469 tons per year for sulfur dioxide and eight pounds per year for mercury. Discussions among Board members, DEQ staffers, and Dominion representatives concerned the impacts of the facility's sulfur dioxide emissions on forests and streams already degraded by acid deposition; the fact that southeast streams and soils were not recovering as quickly as those in the northeast, even as sulfur deposition was reduced through the EPA's Acid Rain Program; the results of emission tests at comparable facilities; and, the legality and feasibility of using cleaner coal to reduce air pollution emissions. Board members pointed to indications that ambient levels of fine particulate in rural Wise County were close to violating the National Ambient Air Quality Standard, an unexpected finding in light of the fact that the NAAQS for fine particulate matter was attained in the Northern Virginia metropolitan area.

The Board's research, combined with information obtained from public comments, showed the facility could be far cleaner than the DEQ was proposing, based on the use of clean coal. The Board set the final limits at 604 tons per year for sulfur dioxide and four pounds per year for mercury—82 percent and 94 percent lower, respectively, than in the DEQ's original draft permits. Those limits would still allow Dominion to burn waste coal and thereby help reduce water pollution caused by piles of waste coal. Dominion agreed to concessions on carbon dioxide at a time when carbon dioxide was not an officially designated air pollutant under federal or state law. The Board adopted most of these restrictions unanimously.[51]

In a memorandum to the DEQ crafted after the meeting, I set forth my understanding of how the Board arrived at the final permit restrictions. The PSD permit limits reflected the "top-down" approach required by the Clean Air Act: available controls are ranked in descending order of stringency and the most stringent should be chosen unless the applicant can demonstrate convincingly that the technology is not achievable. Thus the Board considered stringent removal efficiencies, using an analysis of comparable facilities, and based the permit decision on the use of coals typically used by Dominion in other power plants. The Prevention of Significant Deterioration program also aims to ensure that clean air stays clean. Thus the Board gave special attention to comments from the federal land managers. The Park Service's comments indicated a need for limits lower than those suggested by the DEQ, to avoid new adverse impacts on acidified areas already degraded by decades of sulfur deposition. When setting the standard for the facility's toxics emissions, the Board sought the lowest mercury emission rate achieved by a similar power plant. The other air toxics emitted from the facility would be emitted in forms that were captured by the pollution-control equipment for particulate matter or volatile organic compounds that would be installed on the power plant.

With respect to the facility's considerable carbon dioxide emissions, the Board decided that it lacked regulatory authority under federal or state law to require application of Best Available Control Technology. But Dominion agreed to burn specified percentages of wood waste that would eventually reduce the facility's carbon dioxide emissions by 530,000 tons per year. The Board wrote those provisions into the Wise County permit, as well as Dominion's commitment to convert another power plant to natural gas, thereby avoiding additional yearly emissions of 300,000 tons of carbon dioxide.[52]

Board member Bruce Buckheit addressed the Board's choice not to set carbon dioxide standards in the permit. While voicing his support for climate change legislation, he said he saw no political consensus to regulate emissions of greenhouse gases and he feared a backlash if the Board denied the permit because of "carbon issues." Bruce emphasized the political backing the facility had received from two governors and the General Assembly alike. He said, "We need power in this country, and if we start having brownouts we will quickly lose any support we might need to get effective carbon legislation."[53]

My statement of the Board's rationale also addressed environmental justice considerations. At that time southwest Virginia had a relatively low per capita income and a high proportion of the population in poverty, compared with Virginia as a whole. Pollutants emitted by coal-fired power plants cause premature mortality, respiratory disease, and cardiovascular problems. The stringent air pollution standards the Board established would help to minimize the additional health risks imposed on the area's residents. Through the public comment process the Board established, including several days of hearings when any individual could speak, local residents had an opportunity to be heard. The widespread concern over the facility was one reason, although certainly not the only one, that the Board took over the permitting process. Meaningful involvement is key to realizing environmental justice.[54]

Dominion never challenged the permits in court. Company officials plainly knew they could achieve much more by way of emission reductions than they had indicated to DEQ staffers. As I walked out of the high school where we had held the hearing, an attorney for a leading environmentalist organization expressed gratitude for the stringent limits we had set, which could now serve as examples of BACT and MACT for other facilities around the nation during the permitting process.

Figure 2.2
Cale Jaffe and John Suttles, Southern Environmental Law Center attorneys, who argued successfully against the mercury "safety valve" clause (photo courtesy of Cat McCue).

But the Southern Environmental Law Center and other environmental groups challenged several aspects of the permits in court, including our decision not to regulate the facility's carbon dioxide emissions. The court granted that lawsuit on one point. On the advice of the DEQ, the Board had agreed that Dominion could petition later to have the MACT mercury limit changed. The Board was told that this "safety valve" provision simply duplicated existing state regulations and that any changes would be subject to the usual public notice and comment process. DEQ staffers assured the Board that the provision did not weaken the permit's mercury limits. The Southern Environmental Law Center asserted otherwise, indicating that Dominion officials were saying publicly "What the clause they're referring to says is that if we can't reach that level we will still be in compliance if we're between 49 and 72 pounds." The court agreed with the environmental groups and eliminated the mercury safety valve clause. Dominion officials seemed unbothered, and the DEQ and the Board promptly changed the permit to comply with the judge's decision. All other provisions of the PSD and MACT permits, including the emission limits the Board established as BACT and MACT, held up under judicial scrutiny.[55]

As of 10 July 2012, the $1.8 billion Wise power plant was up and running. In early 2013 the facility was meeting the emission limits the Board wrote into the facility's permits. In a promotional video for the facility, Dominion boasted that the limits are "the strictest ever written into a permit in the United States."[56]

3 Roda: Coal, Dust, and Inequality

Another Board matter had to do with a small rural hollow in the unincorporated Appalachian town of Roda, Virginia, not far from Wise. Coal trucks were traveling along Roda Road, a narrow, steep-sided road leading to and from the area's surface mines, which have scarred the landscape in every direction. Streams of trucks were raising clouds of dirt in their wake, as coal dust in their beds and mud caked on the trucks flew into the air. Residents counted ten trucks per hour, twenty hours a day, on weekdays. In 2009, when the Air Board became involved, there were nine active surface mining permits near Roda Road. A 2016 satellite view of the local area showed extensive mountaintop removal and a smattering of houses along Roda Road's four-mile stretch.[1]

The dust made outside activities intolerable and penetrated inside people's homes, which are located only 10 to 20 feet from the road. Nell Campbell, 91 years old, said she could not sit on her porch or work in her garden because of the dust. Her grandchildren couldn't play in the yard. Former coal miner Ronnie Willis, 70 years old, said he was forced to power wash his porch several times a year and that he had to change his furnace filter every month. He could not open the windows or take walks on the road. Mr. Willis suffered from emphysema and black lung disease and he worried about the impacts of the dust on his already degraded health. Mr. Willis spoke of the intimidation friends had experienced at the hands of coal companies: "Ever since Carl Ramey … challenged a coal company for conducting mining too close to his home and was told to stop harassing the coal company and ordered to pay their attorney fees, a lot of people in the community are afraid to challenge the companies that are harming our health and well being. But I am not afraid to stand up for myself and my community." Both Mr. Willis and Mrs. Campbell said their homes had become unmarketable because of the airborne filth.[2]

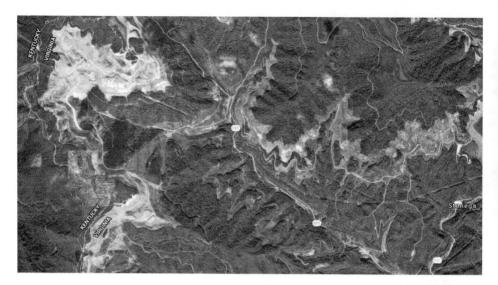

Figure 3.1
A Google Earth view of Roda Road (in center of photo) and surrounding surface mines.

In 2004, Mr. Willis, Mrs. Campbell and others had begun to complain to the Virginia Department of Mines, Minerals and Energy, the state agency that oversees mining operations, about the clouds of particulate matter raised by the trucks. Mr. Willis thought it would be a simple, inexpensive matter to reroute the trucks or wash them before sending them away from the mine. The Department of Mines, Minerals and Energy responded by saying it had no authority over dust stirred up by trucks on public roads.[3]

Roda's problems with fugitive dust came before the Air Board in 2009, soon after the Board's numbers increased from five to seven members because of a 2008 state law. Under those new provisions, the Board's members were to be "fairly representative of conservation, public health, business, and agriculture." The selection of three new Board appointees in the summer of 2008 was the subject of intense discussions in Governor Tim Kaine's office. Robert Burnley, Director of the state Department of Environmental Quality (DEQ) under Governor Mark Warner, was a candidate. Mr. Burnley's professional credentials were impressive, and his experience at the DEQ stretched back to the 1990s. It is hard to imagine anyone more qualified to sit on the state's Air Pollution Control Board.[4]

Figure 3.2
Coal trucks on Roda Road (photo courtesy of John Harbison).

But DEQ Director David Paylor attempted to dissuade the Secretary of Natural Resources, Preston Bryant, and a senior aide to the governor, Mark Rubin, from advancing Mr. Burnley's name, because Mr. Burnley had publicly opposed efforts to transfer power from the state's citizen environmental boards to the DEQ Director:

His actions in that process appear to me and staff to have created an alliance with the environmental sector that was not entirely consistent with his past. It has left some of us confused and unsure that he can operate independently in the future. My additional concern is that he would be set up as the final aribtor [sic] between the three environmental appointments and the others for issues in question. It would put too much power in one persons [sic] hands. In the past I may have trusted him in that role; I'm now unsure and don't relish that presure [sic] from my immediate predecessor in this environment.

Mr. Paylor indicated that, under state law, the Board should be composed of "reps from agriculture (a bit of a stretch for air), health, environment, and business." He said "the current board has 3 strong environmental reps" and thus the environmental sector was "fully represented." Among Mr. Paylor's top picks were "Ted," a "business advocate," and "Randy" (Gordon), who had been the state's health commissioner under Governor George Allen. As Governor Kaine's staff wrote and rewrote the announcement of Mr. Gordon's appointment to the Board, the governor's Conflict of Interest Director referred to him as "a token Republican."[5]

The Board's dynamics changed with its increased numbers. New member Sterling Rives was attentive and involved. Sterling was the attorney for Hanover County, a populous jurisdiction that lies to the north of Richmond, the state capital. Sterling labored with great good humor to find a middle ground between the Board's two three-member factions. Bernadette Reese had been a senior environmental engineer at BASF Corporation. Bernadette left the Board quickly, in August 2008. Her replacement was Marina Phillips, a private attorney who attended two Board meetings. Marina resigned from the Board because of conflict of interest concerns. After Marina came Manning "Chip" Gasch, a partner at Hunton and Williams, a Richmond-based law firm that had represented Mirant in its suits against the Air Board. Hullie Moore, Bruce Buckheit, Richard Langford and I remained on the Board. After Mirant and the City of Alexandria reached a settlement agreement in the summer of 2008, the most pressing issue on the Board's agenda was fugitive dust in Roda.

Why Worry About Dust?

Clouds of dust unquestionably constitute a nuisance, but they can also harm public health and non-human organisms as well. Particulate matter causes the most adverse human health effects when it consists of small-diameter particles known as fine particulate matter. Since the 1980s the US Environmental Protection Agency and other public health authorities have focused on reducing ambient (outdoor) air levels of particulate matter that can penetrate into people's lungs.[6]

The list of serious health effects from inhalable particulate exposure is long and growing. Ambient fine particulate matter is now recognized as a human carcinogen. Other adverse effects from exposure to particulate matter include respiratory illnesses (e.g., asthma and bronchitis), cardiovascular effects (e.g., heart attacks), and premature mortality. One reputable study estimated that 200,400 people died prematurely in the United States in 2005 because of exposure to fine particulate matter emitted from combustion sources. Of those deaths, 52,200 were attributable to emissions from coal-fired electric utilities and 52,800 were attributable to road transportation emissions. Another estimate holds that, worldwide, 3.2 million people died in 2010 because of outdoor exposures to fine particulate pollution. One expert has concluded that air pollution is "by far the leading environmental risk factor for disease."[7]

Particulate matter is especially harmful to sensitive populations—children, people with respiratory problems (like Mr. Willis), and elderly people (like Ms. Campbell). Poor and minority children are particularly susceptible to asthma. Recent research indicates that pregnant women exposed to high levels of fine particulate matter during their pregnancies are more likely to have children with autism. Particulate matter also reduces the clarity of the air. Depending on their chemical composition, airborne particles can harm ecosystems and damage manmade materials by contributing to acid deposition and high nutrient levels in water systems. Acidified particles adversely affect streams and forests, and high nutrient levels in waterways can lead to algae blooms, which, in turn, cause a variety of harms, such as depleted oxygen levels.[8]

Under legal authority granted by the Clean Air Act, the US Environmental Protection Agency has worked with state agencies for decades to reduce public exposure to unsafe levels of particulate matter. In successive waves of standard setting that started in 1971, the EPA has established and then revised the National Ambient Air Quality Standards (NAAQS) for particulate-matter standards. The first particulate-matter NAAQS was for "total suspended particulate matter," which applied to particles 25 to 45 micrometers in diameter. In 1987 the EPA revised the standard to focus on particles 10 micrometers in diameter or smaller. This "PM10" standard was supplemented in 1997 by the fine particulate "PM2.5" standards, which aim to protect public health and welfare against unsafe levels of particulate matter 2.5 micrometers in diameter or smaller. "Welfare" in this context means visibility, animals, vegetation, crops, and buildings. Particulate matter may be directly emitted or it may be formed in the atmosphere when other, precursor pollutants are transformed physically or chemically.[9]

The goal of the NAAQS program is that all Americans breathe healthy outdoor air. In an intensive, multi-year process the EPA has established and periodically revised the NAAQS, which by statute must provide an adequate margin of safety to the public from adverse health effects and protect public welfare against known or anticipated adverse effects. The EPA's emphasis on improving ambient (outdoor) air quality follows from the Clean Air Act's focus. The states submit implementation plans to the EPA showing how they will attain the standards. States can and do consider costs of control when they design their plans, and the states may choose which pollution sources to regulate.[10]

This federal-state partnership, which aims to reduce the public's exposure to unhealthy levels of particulate matter, has yielded substantial progress. Average PM2.5 levels in 217 US counties between the periods 1979–1983 and 1999–2000 declined by 32 percent, increasing average life expectancy by an estimated 0.4 years. These improvements took place even as the nation's population and economy grew. When Roda's particulate-matter problems came to the Board's attention, all areas of Virginia complied with the EPA's PM10 and PM2.5 air-quality standards.[11]

Unfortunately, the fact of statewide compliance in 2008 with the particulate matter NAAQS did not mean that Mr. Willis and Mrs. Campbell were breathing safe levels of particulate matter when the coal trucks sped by their homes. In the first place, the air pollution that people breathe is a function of their daily routines, and no fixed air pollution monitoring equipment can capture that variation. Scientists have long known that personal exposures to air pollutants vary substantially from those measured by federal and state air-quality monitors, which are stationary and placed in locations where they will remain for years, measuring trends in local air quality and assessing compliance with the NAAQS.

Variations in personal exposure to air pollution can happen because of differences in personal habits or in where people live. For example, people who commute in cars often experience elevated levels of particulate-matter air pollution. People living near busy roads show higher rates of respiratory and cardiovascular illness because of elevated exposures to fine particulate matter and other air pollutants. Many people spend a large portion of their days indoors, and levels of particulate matter inside homes and workplaces (from smoking or where fuels are burned indoors) can be high.[12]

The gap between actual exposures and those measured by air-quality monitors goes beyond the variability inherent in everyday living habits. Monitors that measure whether air quality attains the NAAQS do not necessarily detect high air pollution exposures. For example, coal-fired power plants can cause locally elevated levels of sulfur dioxide. Sometimes those facilities must place special monitors nearby to measure the source's impact on nearby peak concentrations, as was the case with the Mirant facility in Alexandria. The Virginia DEQ is required to locate its permanent air quality monitors, those measuring compliance with the NAAQS, in accordance with the EPA's guidelines. The EPA emphasizes the importance of gauging exposure in high-population areas. However, the EPA's guidance allows for the possibility of monitoring near "hot spots" or monitoring for "special purposes."[13]

Improving air-quality trends and the expense of monitoring for PM2.5 also affect where air-quality monitors are placed. Declining levels of particulate matter have helped to bring areas into compliance with the NAAQS, even though the EPA has increased the stringency of the NAAQS for fine particulate matter. Cleaner air makes it difficult to justify expenditures for additional monitoring stations. The nation's monitoring network for PM2.5 costs an estimated $50 million a year to operate. Such equipment is expensive to purchase and to maintain, and it's not easy to find public places for the monitors where they will be secure and represent local air quality.[14]

In Virginia the state Department of Environmental Quality gauges compliance with the National Ambient Air Quality Standards for particulate matter with approximately twenty monitoring sites around the state. Those monitors are concentrated in urban areas. The National Park Service operates particulate-matter monitors in Shenandoah National Park, and the City of Alexandria, in collaboration with the DEQ, maintains a particulate-matter monitor in Alexandria. The EPA considers those areas lacking monitors—and, thus, any data on particulate matter whatsoever—to be "attainment" (that is, meeting the NAAQS) or "unclassifiable."[15]

Because the DEQ locates its air-quality monitors in population-dense areas, air-quality problems in rural areas can be missed. In 2004, the DEQ and the Air Board knew that ozone levels exceeded the National Ambient Air Quality Standards in Shenandoah National Park only because the National Park Service had established its own monitors. Because of the state's emphasis on collecting data in urban areas, it was entirely possible that the dust thrown up by the coal trucks was creating a public health problem in Roda that had gone undetected by the closest DEQ monitor, which was 60 miles away, in Bristol. But that question could be settled only with local air-quality data gathered in Roda.[16]

Air Quality Typical of Industrializing Countries

In 2008 the Sierra Club and a local community organization, the Southern Appalachian Mountain Stewards, sponsored a study to document fugitive dust levels on Roda Road, directly in front of the Campbell and Willis homes. Dr. Viney Aneja, a professor at North Carolina State University in Raleigh, conducted the study. Two PM10 samplers collected data for two weeks in August 2008, with one sampler in Mrs. Campbell's front yard, not far from the entrance to the mines, and one sampler in Mr. Willis's yard, farther away from the surface mines. Dr. Aneja ensured proper quality control throughout the study and he collected the data in accordance with the EPA's reference methods.

Dr. Aneja's findings indicated that levels of PM10 on Roda Road regularly exceeded the EPA's 24-hour PM10 standard for air quality. Specifically, results for 16 of 24 sample days (twelve days for each sampler) on this four-mile stretch of road showed PM10 levels higher than the EPA's standard. Two samples exceeded the EPA's standard by three times. The EPA's 24-hour PM10 standard was exceeded 83 percent of the time at Mrs. Campbell's house and 50 percent of the time at Mr. Willis's house. Such high levels of particulate matter are unusual in the United States, where only a few parts of the country show measurements exceeding the EPA's 24-hour PM10 standard. Dr. Aneja said that, in almost forty years of conducting research on air quality, he had never seen such elevated measurements, which he compared with levels found in industrializing nations. Levels of particulate matter in Roda fell to acceptable levels on the weekends, when the coal trucks were not on the road. Dr. Aneja's results were published in a well-regarded scientific journal.[17]

Figure 3.3
Viney Aneja (center) and his monitoring team in Roda (photo courtesy of Viney Aneja).

Dr. Aneja reported his results to the Air Board in April 2009. His results hinted at the possibility of an extensive problem with truck-related fugitive dust in Appalachian communities near surface mines. The fact that levels of particulate matter were lower farther away from the mine suggested a connection with truck travel. A group of residents from Roda and nearby areas traveled almost 400 miles to Richmond to plead with the Board for appropriate regulatory action. On a unanimous vote the Board directed DEQ staffers to gather monitoring data in Roda and to take measures to address the excessive levels of particulate matter. The Board solicited health assessments from the Virginia Department of Health and from the federal Agency for Toxic Substances and Disease Registry (ATSDR).[18]

Soon after the Board's April 2009 meeting, two mining companies, Cumberland Resources and A & G Coal Company, instituted voluntarily in Roda a number of straightforward, low-tech dust-control measures, such as washing trucks before they left the mine sites, paving mine access roads, sweeping roads clear of dust, and adding gravel to an access road. DEQ staffers undertook an air monitoring study in Roda in the summer of 2009.[19]

The DEQ's air monitoring study showed substantially lower dust levels after institution of the dust-control measures, with only one reading above the EPA's PM-10 standard for air quality. DEQ staffers criticized Dr. Aneja's work, saying he had mistakenly included particulates larger than PM-10 in his analysis. However, Dr. Aneja put these concerns to rest because he had relied on the EPA's approved monitoring and analysis methods for measuring PM10. Further, Dr. Aneja found errors in the DEQ's analysis of his data. Specifically, the DEQ relied on light microscopy, which is not an approved method for determining the diameter of fine particles. DEQ staffers had mistaken agglomerations of small particles for individual large particles.[20]

DEQ staffers attributed the high levels of particulate matter observed in Roda to the lack of adequate drainage on the road, thereby implying that the coal company trucks were not to blame. But the results of monitoring conducted before and after the companies instituted dust controls pointed in another direction. The conclusion seemed inescapable: the mine operators' voluntary dust-control measures were reducing levels of fine particulate matter in Roda.[21]

Despite the success of the control measures in reducing the levels of particulate matter in Roda, there was no guarantee the companies would maintain these voluntary measures or that truck traffic would diminish in the future. Furthermore, it was possible that similar problems were occurring in other communities near Virginia's surface mines. In November 2009, Southern Appalachian Mountain Stewards and the Sierra Club petitioned the Board to establish fugitive dust regulations that would require mine operators to use "reasonable precautions to prevent particulate matter from becoming airborne." The petition listed the low technology actions that might constitute "reasonable precautions," such as washing and covering coal trucks and watering roads to reduce dust. The coal mining companies that had adopted these kinds of controls in Roda never indicated to the Board that the measures were especially costly. According to the petition, the DEQ and the Board were the appropriate regulatory entities, not the Department of Mines, Minerals and Energy (DMME).[22]

However, the DEQ preferred that DMME oversee remedies for Roda's dust problems. DEQ managers and staffers protested that they did not have the resources to develop a statewide regulation or to oversee the permitting process. DEQ staffers said that the regional air-quality monitors indicated good regional air quality that complied with the EPA's NAAQS and that Dr. Aneja's short-term study could not be used to classify an area as out of compliance with the NAAQS for particulate matter. A draft Memorandum of Agreement presented to the Board in November 2009 aimed to cede to DMME all responsibility for regulating mine-related fugitive dust, even though DMME showed no inclination to set forth restrictions at the Roda mines or anywhere else in southwest Virginia.

Several Board members felt it was the Air Board's responsibility to ensure that, in Roda and in Virginia's other coal mining communities, residents were protected from experiencing the extraordinarily high levels of particulate matter documented in Roda. The Board asked for advice on legal authority to develop a regulation that would ensure widespread adoption of the modest measures that Roda's coal mining companies had adopted voluntarily. The Board also requested that DMME expedite changes to the Roda mine permits to ensure that the voluntary dust-control measures stayed in place permanently.[23]

Federal and state public health experts weighed in with their assessments. The federal Agency for Toxic Substances and Disease Registry (ATSDR) reported on the potential health impacts of the levels of particulate matter that Dr. Aneja had measured. The Agency relayed its report to the DEQ's Director and the DEQ's southwest Virginia regional staff in March 2010. In understated fashion, the ATSDR concluded that the exposures reported were "likely to be of health concern, especially for sensitive individuals," assuming that "an important portion" of the PM10 monitored consisted of PM2.5. The report recommended that government authorities continue to implement measures to reduce the levels of particulate matter on the road passing by the Campbell and Willis homes.[24]

At the Board's March 2010 meeting two health officials offered opinions on the dust problem in Roda. ATSDR representative Lora Siegmann Werner summarized her agency's report. She emphasized the potential public health risks of the levels Dr. Aneja had documented and emphasized that the DEQ's existing air-quality monitoring network for assessing NAAQS compliance would not detect localized air-quality problems. Dwight Flammia, a Virginia Department of Health official, used simple but reasonable methods to infer PM2.5 levels from the PM10 air-quality data Dr. Aneja had collected. Mr. Flammia concluded that the EPA's 24-hour PM2.5 standard was exceeded in Roda in 2008 and 2009, with the highest monitored level exceeding the EPA's standard by almost three times.[25]

The Board decided to vote on the Sierra Club's petition in June 2010. Since the Board's numbers had increased to seven in 2008, scheduling meetings had become more complicated, especially since one member insisted he could meet only on Fridays. In the end Bruce Buckheit could not attend the June meeting. A tie vote on the Sierra Club's petition meant that the DEQ would not adopt regulations to ensure control of particular-matter levels near coal mines in Roda and elsewhere around Virginia.

"Them That's Got Shall Get, Them That's Not Shall Lose"

The June 2010 Board meeting was my last, since my term expired at the end of the month. At that meeting I felt much sympathy for the Roda residents who had once again spent a day driving to Richmond to plead their case. I was especially concerned over the potential health impacts of fugitive dust in Virginia's Appalachian communities generally, where the population already suffers from a host of illnesses. Billie Holiday's famous song "God Bless the Child" echoed in my head: "The strong gets more, while the weak ones fade."[26]

As far as I know, no General Assembly members or high-level gubernatorial counselors expressed concern over the air-quality problems on Roda Road. Had the Air Board voted in favor of establishing statewide fugitive dust regulations for truck traffic associated with surface coal mining operations, perhaps we would have drawn the attention of southwest Virginia's local politicians and Governor Robert McDonnell. Coal companies or their chief executives were among Governor McDonnell's steadfast campaign donors. Just four companies and two coal company executives gave Mr. McDonnell amounts totaling $1.3 million for his various statewide campaigns.[27]

The citizens of Roda who were breathing unacceptable levels of coal dust seemed to have little political voice or influence. No politician testified or wrote on their behalf, in stark contrast to the consistent and strong involvement of state and local politicians in Wise and Alexandria. The DEQ's management refused to undertake analysis or entertain regulatory action, no matter how modest, that would have guaranteed relief from the unacceptably high PM10 levels experienced by Mrs. Campbell, Mr. Willis, and their neighbors on Roda Road.

DEQ managers pointed to their scarce resources as a prime reason for not undertaking regulatory action or further analysis. According to former DEQ Director Robert Burnley, the DEQ is constantly overworked and underfinanced. But a state air-pollution-control agency suffering from a shortfall in resources can turn to others for advice and counsel. Excessive fugitive dust is not unique to Virginia. DEQ managers might have directed that staffers examine rules in other states that might serve as a model or consult with the US EPA's experts on fugitive dust regulations. I do not recall that the EPA's regional staff members in Philadelphia were consulted on the subject of Roda's air-quality problems. The EPA's regional offices are the Agency's points of contact for the states, and they assist with grants and program oversight, among other responsibilities.[28]

For example, in undertaking the research for this book, I found that Arizona air-pollution-control officials worked with the EPA's regional staff on a similar kind of problem. Western Pinal County, Arizona, has had high levels of particulate matter because of fugitive dust. After undertaking a multi-year monitoring study, EPA officials declared the area "nonattainment" in 2010 for the PM10 and the PM 2.5 National Ambient Air Quality Standards. The EPA's regulatory actions set in motion a state responsibility to implement control measures to protect public health and welfare from excessive exposure to particulate matter.[29]

By contrast, Roda's residents had no guarantee that the high, unhealthful particulate-matter levels they had breathed would be abated over the long term. The DEQ's responses were resistance to regulatory action, a willingness to hand over responsibility to the Department of Mines, Minerals and Energy, which had ignored the Roda residents' complaints for years, and skepticism over the results of Dr. Aneja's study. It was not only that members of the DEQ's monitoring staff refused to believe Dr. Aneja's results. They also said that, because his monitors were not sited in the required fashion and because his data were short-term, his study could not be used to indicate nonattainment with the NAAQS for fine particulate matter.

This latter claim is narrowly true, because the EPA requires three years of monitoring data from particular kinds of sites to determine whether an area attains the NAAQS. But a stubborn refusal to use Dr. Aneja's data showed little willingness to shine an investigative light outside the confines of the state's existing monitoring network, despite indications of serious air-quality problems in areas lacking permanent monitors.

That levels of fine particulate matter can be unexpectedly high in areas with relatively low populations is confirmed by the EPA's list of "design values" for levels of fine particulate matter. Design values are the air-quality concentrations the EPA uses to determine whether a particular area attains the National Ambient Air Quality Standards. At the time the Board was considering air pollution in Roda, Bristol, a small city of approximately 44,000 located only 60 miles from Roda, showed higher concentrations for fine particulate matter than Fairfax County, which has 1.1 million residents and is located in the Washington metropolitan area.[30]

In 2011, when I was no longer a member of the Air Pollution Control Board, the Board agreed that the DEQ should issue a guidance document that would transfer to DMME the responsibility for overseeing fugitive dust resulting from mining activities. But under Virginia law the Air Pollution Control Board, not DMME, is responsible for protecting public health and welfare from air pollution. There is no indication in DMME's statutory charge that the Department can or should write air pollution regulations into the permits issued to mining companies. A cynical observer might interpret the DEQ's insistence on transferring responsibility as tantamount to sweeping dust under the rug: out of sight, out of mind.[31]

Advocates of environmental justice often focus on the unequal protections afforded to minority communities. But environmental injustice also happens when policy makers slight the concerns and pollution exposures of those of modest means. The scholar Edwardo Rhodes defines environmental justice as "the fair treatment of all races, cultures, incomes, and educational levels with respect to the development, implementation, and enforcement of environmental laws, regulations, and policies." Rhodes says "fair treatment implies that no population of people should be forced to shoulder a disproportionate share of the negative environmental impacts of pollution or environmental hazards due to lack of political or economic strength." In his definition, which echoes that used by the US Environmental Protection Agency, Rhodes combines an outcomes-based test with a process-based test in gauging whether a community has been treated justly.[32]

Other leading environmental justice scholars agree that allowing room for citizen voice in policy-making processes is just as important as accomplishing fair public health and environmental outcomes. Kristin Shrader-Frechette is a leading proponent of procedural justice that ensures that vulnerable communities can give "free, informed consent" to polluting facilities. Shrader-Frechette's goal is hard to achieve. The barriers to meaningful citizen participation in the making of environmental policy include coded technical language that is difficult to penetrate and camouflages important uncertainties. Ordinary citizens routinely encounter institutional resistance to the credence of their observations—even in affluent urban areas, such as Alexandria, where community members have resources and can buy expertise. In Alexandria, DEQ staffers repeatedly downplayed citizen concerns over visible emissions from the Mirant power plants, and those same staff members sometimes employed opaque terminology. Other research on environmental justice in Appalachian coal communities highlights the special difficulty of ensuring procedural justice where residents can be marginalized because of their socioeconomic status and educational background.[33]

"Fair" treatment does not imply that all people should experience the same environmental outcomes but, rather, that no one should carry the burden of disproportionate impacts because s/he lacks political power. But in the case of the Clean Air Act's National Ambient Air Quality Standards,

Figure 3.4
Citizens' plea to Governor Tim Kaine (photo courtesy of Aaron Isherwood; photographer unknown). (Stonega is close to Roda Road.)

fair treatment means that all Americans should breathe air that attains those standards, because that is the act's statutory goal. Fair treatment also implies empowering communities with the procedural tools that give them full access to, and legitimacy in, policy making. Roda's residents complained for years to the Department of Mine, Minerals and Energy before their concerns came before the Air Board. Roda's coal mining companies changed their practices only after environmental groups sponsored Dr. Aneja's monitoring study and only after those data came before the Air Board.

There has been no real closure or lasting environmental justice for Roda's residents. It would be natural for them to worry about whether they will suffer again from unsafe levels of particulate matter stirred up by coal trucks and then have state air pollution policy makers write off their concerns as fabricated or insufficiently documented. Chapter 2 describes Southwest Virginia's problems with poverty and poor health outcomes. Unsafe air quality would contribute to a "triple jeopardy for health" that, in one scholar's words, "means that consequences are all the more severe and accumulative for some people than others." African Americans living in the coal mining areas of Kentucky, Virginia and West Virginia show even worse health and poverty than their White counterparts.[34]

Residents of coal mining areas in Virginia and elsewhere have borne economic and health burdens so that Americans could build prosperous lives based on electricity fueled by coal. Even as the United States turns away from coal and toward other sources of energy, we should not forget what the people of Appalachia have given us. We should remedy democratic institutions that, to paraphrase scholar John Gaventa, work reliably at the top but not at the bottom. The reforms suggested in chapter 7 return to this topic.[35]

4 A Climate of Capitulation

When the Virginia General Assembly proposed in 2007 to transfer power from the independent, citizen expert Air Board to the Director of the Department of Environmental Quality, one Alexandria resident denounced the proposal as evidence that the DEQ and the General Assembly had been captured by industry. Shelton Miles, chair of the State Water Pollution Control Board, whose permitting authority would be concentrated in the DEQ's Director under the same legislative proposal, remarked cynically, "Money and power rule the day without regard to individual rights, the public interest, or the merits of the case." Mr. Miles indicated to Secretary of Natural Resources Preston Bryant that the full membership of the Water Pollution Control Board thought the bill was being rushed through "without adequate review," that an eleven-person Board would be ineffective and members could not be knowledgeable on air, water, and solid waste matters, and that both the public and the permitted entities would suffer from reduced access to the permitting process. Mr. Bryant responded to the long list of substantive concerns that Mr. Miles related by, in effect, asking him to be quiet: "However, it still remains the administration's desire to avoid executive branch 'representatives,'—which I define broadly as you, me, and anyone else—from airing differing opinions on matters where the governor has made his opinion known." In his statement Mr. Bryant failed to recognize that the Virginia Air, Water and Waste Boards are independent citizens' bodies that do not report to the governor or the legislature. The Secretary of Natural Resources has no management authority over members of those boards.[1]

The starkly political exchange of views between Mr. Miles and Mr. Bryant undermines the notion of administrative decision making as a rational process. Under the Clean Air Act and under the nation's many public health and environmental laws, including the Clean Water Act and the Endangered Species Act, the making of environmental policy is supposed to be grounded in objective facts. Scientific, engineering and economic considerations lie at the heart of determinations over what pollution levels are appropriate and safe.

Yet Mr. Miles, along with others who objected to the Virginia General Assembly's attempts to transfer power away from the citizen-expert Boards, claimed that the General Assembly's lawmaking process was irrational in that the legislature's decision was not justified by studies or analytical work. Critics predicted that if the "Board bill" were to succeed, Virginia's environmental policy processes would become less transparent and more prone to favoring the regulated community. The latter claim rested on the fact that Virginia's citizen boards must deliberate and act in public, whereas the DEQ's Director can make decisions out of the public eye. Former DEQ Director Robert Burnley observed that many DEQ directors had no scientific training and, therefore, "The bills in question would transfer authority for issuing environmental permits from the boards to the DEQ director, who is likely to be an untrained and unqualified political appointee."[2]

In the late nineteenth century and the early twentieth century, political reformers optimistically envisioned public administrators as seekers of truth, uncorrupted by politics. Decision making informed by scientific tools promised an objective means of realizing the public interest. Through a "science of administration" expert civil servants could remove themselves from purely partisan considerations and provide a factual foundation for making difficult policy choices. The idea was that we should be able to trust technocrats, whether they are state, local or national officials, to illuminate the public interest through a reasoned, neutral process that rises above crassly political considerations. In the Progressive era the federal government reformed around the idea of "technical professionals and politically neutral administrators working toward the efficient realization of an overall public interest." But well before the Progressive era Woodrow Wilson, as a college professor, asserted in 1887 that politics should be separate from administration: "Administrative questions are not political questions. Although politics sets the tasks for administration, it should not be suffered to manipulate its offices."[3]

In keeping with the notion of objective administrative decision making, modern environmental laws involve complicated technical prescriptions. Some legal mandates involve economic efficiency while others involve safety, which is the principle embodied in the National Ambient Air Quality Standards, or best technology, which provided the basis for the permits the Air Board wrote for the Wise power plant. No matter the statutory goal, the "policy as science" vision holds that policy makers should rely on quantitative tests and information concerning emissions, risks, health effects, exposures, costs, and feasibility. Calculations that would have stymied experts of previous generations, involving enormous quantities of data and a bewildering variety of contingencies, can now be incorporated into spreadsheet algorithms. The rational process ideal holds that the making of environmental policy can become a kind of sophisticated puzzle solving in which technical and scientific information informs policy and legal judgments.

This utopian vision might hearten some while frightening others. Who exactly are these experts? Why have we devolved authority to them to protect public health and the environment? How can we trust them to act always for the greater good and not for narrow interests? How can we have faith in a discourse that is so opaque as to discourage public scrutiny? The experiences of the past fifty-odd years have taught us hard lessons about the limits to promises of environmental safety, lessons that can be telegraphed in a litany of disasters: DDT, Love Canal, Bhopal, Chernobyl, Fukushima, and Deepwater Horizon. Granted, sometimes policy makers must act on incomplete information that is later refined and points in different directions. But each of these disasters leaves us with discomfiting suspicions. Perhaps the experts are incompetent: they have deceived themselves as well as us. Or perhaps the deception has been deliberate. Neither encourages confidence in the decisions made above ordinary citizens' heads.

Incompetence is the less damaging of these conclusions. Everyone makes mistakes, after all, and the upward spiral of technology suggests that tomorrow's success will be built on the failures of today. The charge of deception, on the other hand, poisons the political atmosphere, undermining the very notion of objective evidence. What use is a scientific study to a political debate if one is deeply suspicious of the motives of those who enter it into the public record? Some observers of policy-making processes accuse policy makers of using deceitful discourses that disguise arguments in the form of data and merely validate previously decided positions. The most cynical observers claim that business interests invariably capture agency officials and use them to obtain regulatory "rents," that is, financial advantages or special treatment, and that legislators, eager for campaign financing, write public laws that favor private interests. Although the "rational" and "capture" schools spring from very different lines of thought, both write ordinary citizens out of the policy-making equation: citizens have neither voice (because they are not experts) nor power (because they are not moneyed interests).[4]

This chapter examines how we should interpret the policy processes and decisions outlined for the cases of Mirant, Wise and Roda in light of these disparate views about how public policy-making processes should or do work. After exploring whether state officials succumbed to regulatory capture, this chapter introduces the notion of a "climate of capitulation." Then the chapter locates the origins of Virginia's climate of capitulation in the state's political culture, part-time legislature, and patterns of campaign financing.

The Law Does Not Speak for Itself

Virginia's Department of Environmental Quality sponsored in April 2008 a public hearing to accept public comment on the DEQ's draft permit limits for Dominion's proposed coal-fired power plant in Wise County. At that point the Air Board had just assumed responsibility for the power plant's permitting process. Eventually the Board would strengthen substantially the permit limits the DEQ had proposed. State legislators testifying at the hearing criticized the Air Board, which at that time had barely begun the permitting process and had not yet proposed alternatives to the relatively weak emission limits set forth by the DEQ.

Democratic State Delegate Bud Phillips, one of many opposing the Board's involvement, asserted that "the law is the law." He went on at length, claiming, "Some people on that Air Board are anti-coal" and that the Board should "put this feeling aside and apply the law." Many witnesses at that hearing asserted that Dominion would use the latest, most stringent pollution-control technologies and praised the company's corporate citizenship. They claimed that the DEQ would write emission limits that would comply with the Clean Air Act's requirements. Those witnesses urged the Board to move quickly and embrace the DEQ's proposals.[5]

To pretend that environmental law mandates point to obvious, off-the-rack solutions and that companies will do the right thing voluntarily by way of pollution control is to cede political responsibility for protecting the public good. The DEQ's first set of permit proposals contained a sulfur dioxide limit more than five times as high and a mercury emissions limit ten times as high as those eventually adopted by the Board. Dominion's proposed permit limits were even higher than the DEQ's. In the end, "the law" in the form of a state judge affirmed the Board's limits.

The Clean Air Act does not speak for itself. Rather, all of the act's provisions require careful, informed interpretation and, for new source permits, thorough analysis of the kinds of techniques used to reduce emissions at comparable facilities. The DEQ and Dominion were not willing to adopt appropriately stringent limits without the extra scrutiny exercised by the Board. As fellow Board member Hullie Moore put it, Dominion proposed using such low quality coal they "may as well have been burning dirt." The DEQ did not question the assumption that Dominion would burn dirty coal. Deciding on emission limits that correspond to those achievable with "best" or "maximum" available technology and considering how best to protect air quality in accordance with the Clean Air Act's mandates demand careful analysis and much research.[6]

Business representatives from the regulated community have great disincentives to provide thorough assessments of regulatory options. When push comes to shove, companies will interpret the law in ways favorable to their bottom line. Corporations are responsible to their shareholders first, and those shareholders expect to make money. Minimizing the costs of pollution-control equipment increases profits.

In one example of the ways in which electric utilities have violated pollution-control requirements to save money, in the 1990s US Environmental Protection Agency officials found that 70–80 percent of electric utility companies did not comply with the Clean Air Act's New Source Review provisions, which require installation of pollution controls when companies undertake major modifications to their plants. The EPA's top enforcement official at the time, Sylvia Lowrance, called widespread electric utility violations of New Source Review the "most significant noncompliance EPA had ever found." She said the utilities simply flouted federal regulations: "companies understood what was going on, and they evaded the law." "It is surprisingly naïve," one legal scholar has noted, "to believe that most corporations are maximal compliers who are anxious to comply with the law … . Shareholder demands for greater returns on their investments will ensure that most companies will remain minimal compliers."[7]

Some observers might apply the term "regulatory capture" to explain the extensive misplaced confidence among legislators and state regulatory officials in Dominion's willingness to voluntarily embrace emission limits that met the Clean Air Act's standards. Perhaps we should ascribe to regulatory capture the huge gap between final emission limits set by the Board in Wise and Alexandria and those proposed by the DEQ's management and staff. Some might conclude that regulatory capture best describes the behavior of Virginia's Governor Tim Kaine, Secretary of Natural Resources Preston Bryant, and DEQ Director David Paylor, as they conversed behind closed doors about ways to undermine the Air Board. Perhaps one might make the case that coal mining interests captured the DEQ staff members who repeatedly denied the validity of air-quality data showing dangerous levels of fugitive dust in Roda and who refused to explore whether comparable problems existed near other surface mines. The DEQ's staff members and managers seemed to be wearing blinders and, as a result, apparently could not even begin to imagine that Roda's residents had been experiencing for years dangerous levels of particulate matter caused by the coal mining industry. But before concluding that regulatory capture applies in these instances, we should explore what the academic literature has to say on this subject.

Regulatory Capture vs. Climate of Capitulation

The regulatory capture literature is substantial and it is impossible to do it justice here. But we can extract some key points. Regulatory capture means that powerful interest groups receive regulatory favors, either because of complicity between those who write the laws and the agency administrators who implement them or because those administrators choose to bestow favored treatment. The capture literature by critics and proponents alike involves detailed speculation about whether and how groups can form and why administrators or legislators would respond to group pressures. That literature is important and fascinating, but for present purposes what matters is having an overview of what happens under a regulatory capture scenario.[8]

In a nutshell, regulatory capture happens when "regulation, in law or application, is consistently or repeatedly directed away from the public interest and toward the interest of the regulated industry, by the intent and action of the industry itself." On its face, this definition requires that we prove "intent and action of the industry" and that we connect those intents and actions with policy makers' responses. Actions must have occurred "consistently and repeatedly." We must be able to define that famously slippery concept "the public interest," and know that it has been violated. Industries must possess sustained power to manipulate to selfish ends legislative bodies such as the Virginia General Assembly and executive agencies such as the Virginia Department of Environmental Quality. Many theories of regulatory capture assume that elected politicians cave to business interests in exchange for campaign donations, but it is generally difficult to prove a quid pro quo, in part because many donors simply seek politicians with voting records they like. In sum, there is a high empirical bar to proving that regulatory capture—or something approaching it—has happened. One must document and connect intent, action, and reaction over a sustained period of time.[9]

These problems aside, several important aspects of the cases narrated in chapters 1–3 indicate that regulatory capture is not universally applicable to air pollution policy processes in Virginia. Leadership and ideas about protecting the public good and implementing the Clean Air Act's mandates mattered. DEQ Director Robert Burnley fought to accomplish emission reductions at Mirant that would guarantee compliance with the National Ambient Air Quality Standards. Governor Mark Warner appointed W. Tayloe Murphy Jr., a leading legislator-environmentalist, as Secretary of Natural Resources, and the governor was willing to take Mirant to task for riding roughshod over the Clean Air Act's standards. David Englin, Patsy Ticer, and Brian Moran, who represented Alexandria and nearby jurisdictions in the Virginia General Assembly, called for stringent pollution controls at Mirant, as did Alexandria's City Council and environmental staff. Despite encountering sustained resistance from the General Assembly, the DEQ's staff members and managers, and some of Governor Kaine's staff, the State Air Pollution Control Board successfully reduced power plant emissions at the Alexandria and Wise facilities far below those advocated by the DEQ and the regulated companies. Until July 2008 Virginia law allowed for the Board's direct intervention with the Mirant and Wise permits and anticipated through the Board's creation the possibility of a creative tension between the Board and the DEQ. My eight years of interacting with DEQ staff members and managers showed many of them to be truly committed to public health and environmental protection. I met state legislators and local politicians who evinced the same kind of dedication.

Mirant's and Dominion's managers were forced to accept protective but achievable emission limits, albeit after many months of public hearings and after a state court validated the Air Board's actions. The final emission limits the Board set for Mirant and for the Wise power plant resulted from information gathered and submitted by members of the general public, by state and local politicians, by the business community, and by environmental and legal professionals. In the Mirant case the Assistant Attorney General successfully defended the Board's actions in court. The City of Alexandria's outside counsel and the City's Deputy Director of Environmental Quality coordinated technical and legal analyses that illuminated the consequences of the Board's choices. Alexandria's mayor, vice mayor, and City Council were willing to spend a great deal of money on those analyses.

The Air Board debated and made decisions in public hearings. The Board scheduled most of its meetings on the Mirant facility in Alexandria, even when DEQ staffers wanted to schedule them closer to the DEQ's headquarters in Richmond, 100 miles away. The Board's decisions held up under challenge. Courts found the Board's decisions legal and appropriate, with the narrow exception noted in chapter 2 for the Wise case. The EPA's emissions trading scheme for power plant mercury emissions was overturned in federal court, vindicating the Board's doubts about the legality of that framework.

Still, at many turns Virginia's political and regulatory systems favored the electric utility and coal industries. DEQ staffers and managers were consistently reluctant to press coal and electric power interests to achieve emissions levels that met the applicable legal, technological, and safety standards. The official who opposed DEQ Director Robert Burnley's demand that Mirant lower its emissions, even when the company's own modeling showed flagrant violations of the National Ambient Air Quality Standards, remains in a high-ranking leadership position.

Despite the Air Board members' extensive experience with air pollution and environmental matters, Governor Kaine, members of his administration, and Democrats and Republicans in the General Assembly questioned the Board's judgment and undermined the Board publicly and privately. Email messages reveal that Governor Kaine's staff seemed eager to placate Dominion's executives. In an apparent attempt to ensure that Dominion's Wise County facility would receive its air pollution permits, without which the facility could not be built, Governor Kaine issued a gubernatorial directive to the Board, even though its members are independent of executive control. The governor's staff suggested dismissing Board members even before the Board had set permit limits for the Wise facility. Within a few weeks after the Air Board took over the permitting process for Mirant, and well before the Board proposed any emission limits for that power plant, the DEQ's Director became involved in writing legislation that transferred authority to him from the Air Board. The General Assembly instructed the Board to adopt the EPA's mercury emissions trading scheme, with no analysis to support that decision, despite widespread skepticism about the legality of the scheme, which was ultimately struck down in court. The General Assembly and Governor Kaine's administration proposed changing the Board's structure and diminishing the Board's authority without waiting to see what the Board would do by way of pollution-reduction requirements for the Mirant facility.

The mixed bag of observations presented in chapters 1–3 does not dovetail neatly with the concept of "regulatory capture," which presumes an administrative and legislative apparatus that lies wholly in the thrall of the regulated community. That result does not describe all aspects of the cases described in chapters 1–3, which also involved ideas about the public good. To their credit, scholars have attempted to introduce subtleties into regulatory capture theory. For example, some have proposed distinguishing between "strong" and "weak" capture, with the latter involving incomplete, limited industry influence that diminishes, but does not eliminate, social benefits. "Corrosive" capture is a term adopted for situations in which the regulated community manages to weaken or "reduce the scope" of regulation.

But capture theory as a whole invariably centers on the actions and intentions of the regulated entities and those entities' impact on the public interest, as opposed to those of the private sector. Defining those interests and ascertaining whether they have been advanced or retarded is hardly straightforward. Even those who believe regulatory capture is likely an important problem admit that supportive empirical evidence is lacking. Many studies have highlighted examples of policy making, especially at the federal level, that fail to comport with regulatory capture's predictions. Public officials can and do seek to serve the public interest, that is, they can be motivated by what scholars have called "the politics of ideas."[10]

Even if regulatory capture theory fails to apply to the cases presented in this book, persistent biases cannot be wished away. Some environmental regulators and enforcers describe their interactions with the regulated community as "positive." Unfortunately, such descriptors tell us nothing about the power dynamics animating those relationships. Environmental enforcement personnel may be predisposed to perceive regulated entities as socially responsible simply because those entities enjoy favored economic and political status. Inspectors can be prone to assume a priori that large corporations will be competent and cooperative, not only because of those companies' substantial resources and technical staff but because of their political power. One leading critic of regulatory capture theory, who describes tough federal regulations that have been adopted by the US EPA and the US Forest Service, concludes that capture can be avoided only with political leadership and with decision-making processes that self-consciously include the public in meaningful ways. In the end, "Sometimes those conditions hold. Sometimes they do not." Strong, sustained resistance is needed to ensure that polluters are brought into compliance with the law.[11]

The cases presented in chapters 1–3 point to the need for nuance. As such, I have adopted the term "climate of capitulation" to describe the persistent tendency by elected politicians and DEQ staff members and managers to yield to the regulated community's preferences, whether those preferences were explicitly stated or merely anticipated. In a climate of capitulation, powerful business interests are often able to constrain the political agenda and receive favored treatment in the environmental policy arena. Civil servants shrink from taking action that displeases polluting companies, not because those civil servants are unethical but because of longstanding, enforced understandings and patterns of behavior. A climate of capitulation differs from "iron triangle" politics in that iron triangles involve three parties with approximately equal influence: legislative committee members, bureaucrats, and the affected industry. Students of federal policy processes have pointed to evidence that iron triangles in the environmental arena have given way to other, more inclusive forms of policy making.[12]

The kinds of power exerted under a climate of capitulation are not readily apparent to a casual observer, but they can be easily understood within the "faces of power" literature. When companies advance their own interests by keep options off of the table, or when they help shape officials' views and preferences, they are manifesting what political scientists call the "second" and "third" faces of relational power. The second and third faces of power are more subtle but no less effective than the "first" face of power, which involves pushing someone to do that which s/he would not otherwise do via penalties or rewards, such as withholding or providing campaign financing. In many ways, power is "most effective when it is least observable to both participants and observers," as political scientist Steven Lukes has observed. Other studies confirm what chapters 1–3 show, that environmental agency personnel may conciliate or befriend their business counterparts. When that happens, those officials may act out of fear of political retribution or because they want to "stave off outside political criticism and challenges," not because those officials lack integrity.[13]

In a pervasive climate of capitulation, officials may sometimes engage in behavior that resembles outright regulatory capture. Email exchanges among the state's top administrators and environmental officials reinforce the degree to which private interests had special access and influence, especially Dominion in the case of the Wise power plant. In the email exchanges among high-level members of the Kaine administration that have been made publicly available, public health and environmental protection are not the central focus of discussion. Rather, the email messages center around the reactions of the business community or of legislators who favored the Wise facility. The governor's actions and those of his staff call to mind former Virginia Delegate Al Pollard's observation about the extent of Dominion's influence: "Why do you think they call them the 'power' company?"[14]

Origins of Virginia's Climate of Capitulation

Virginia's coal and electric utility interests wield outsize influence in the area of air pollution policy, and their power spills over partisan lines. Democratic and Republican politicians alike opposed the Air Board's actions. Although Republicans have dominated Virginia's House of Delegates since 2000, Democrats controlled the state's senate between 2008 and 2011, when the Board was considering the Wise facility and when the bill that weakened the Air Board's authority was adopted into law. Since 2001 Virginians have elected one Republican and three Democratic governors. These observations fit with multi-state studies have not been able to consistently connect partisanship of the governor or the state legislature with indicators of state-level environmental program strength. To grasp the dynamics of air pollution policy making in Virginia, we must move beyond expectations based on party affiliation.[15]

Virginia's climate of capitulation to regulated interests in the air pollution policy arena has its roots in deeply imbedded structural biases that arise from the state's part-time legislature and the dominance of coal interests and the state's primary electric utility in campaign donations for state elections. Another crucial factor that contributes to those biases is Virginia's political culture, which fosters weak bureaucracies and close ties with business interests. As will be described in detail below, Virginia's traditionalistic political culture reinforces biases against public servants and serving the public interest. In a traditionalistic political culture the status quo is the order of the day. Circles of elites, which include the most powerful businesses, dominate political discourse, and widespread public participation in the making of policy is discouraged.[16]

Virginia's legislature is designed to be a part-time body, with the notion that citizens serving as representatives can remain closely attuned to their constituents' needs and preferences. Political scientists have classified state legislatures along a spectrum from most to least professionalized, based on length of session, pay for legislators, and level of staffing. This ranking scores the most professionalized legislature (California's) as 1 and the least professionalized (New Hampshire's) as 50. In four separate rankings representing the years 1979, 1986, 1996, and 2003, Virginia has consistently scored in the third or fourth quintile, with scores falling between 27 (1996) and 32 (1979 and 2003). Even the most dedicated legislators cannot be independently well informed if they have small staffs, low pay, and short sessions. Legislatures with higher pay are more likely to attract well-qualified representatives. More professionalized bodies, especially those with larger staffs, rely less on the executive branch for policy ideas and measures.[17]

Less professionalized legislatures are handicapped when it comes to analysis of complicated technical issues such as those commonly encountered in the environmental and public health policy arenas. When Virginia's legislators need information they must turn to lobbyists or to the executive branch. Companies take advantage of their ongoing relationships with state civil servants and lawmakers to get deals that favor their interests. Large companies are especially well positioned to push for light-handed regulation, since they can expend considerable resources on attorneys and consultants to fight limits they do not like.[18]

An enduring complication with the making of environmental policy in executive-branch agencies is that regulators often must depend on businesses for technical and process information to establish pollution limits. Elected representatives, at least in Virginia, run into the same problem. Members of Virginia's General Assembly turn to outsiders for legislative language because of short legislative sessions (30 days in odd-numbered years and 60 days in even-numbered years, unless extended for 30 days, at most) and few staff. Each legislator is allocated only one staff member. The General Assembly lacks resources to undertake independent research. Ideas for new legislation often come from the regulated community, and business interests strongly influence whether bills pass or die. General Assembly members cannot undertake more than cursory research themselves. By its very design the body cannot be truly deliberative. Rather, the General Assembly is reactive, converting proposals developed by lobbyists into law.[19]

Although the Joint Legislative and Audit Commission (a research arm of the General Assembly) writes reports on the effectiveness of executive agencies, the Commission does not have experts who can write quick briefing papers on issues before the legislature. This means that power flows to outsiders, and Dominion has an unusual amount of influence. According to former state delegate Albert M. Pollard Jr., Dominion's position on bills determines their fate the vast majority of the time, and the company has vast resources at its disposal to generate convincing factsheets and underwrite campaigns. Mr. Pollard laments, "Any time there's this much power invested in one entity, whether a politician, a railroad, or an electric utility, that is not good for the public interest." W. Tayloe Murphy, Jr., a longtime member of the House of Delegates and Governor Mark Warner's Secretary of Natural Resources, agrees that Dominion's influence has only grown over the years and that Dominion gets what it wants. Jerry McCarthy, who headed the nonprofit Virginia Environmental Endowment for 36 years and who has served almost every Virginia governor elected since 1970, says, "In Virginia's policy-making processes, Dominion usually gets what it wants." Media reports on Dominion's success with its proposals in the General Assembly reinforce these insiders' observations.[20]

The General Assembly's dependence on the regulated community extends to campaign donations, which are unlimited in Virginia's state elections. For another research project, my colleague Vicki Arroyo and I examined campaign donation patterns in nine states between 2000 and 2009. We wanted to know, when a state legislator faces a decision on an issue connected with climate-change policies or energy policies, which of their backers might they feel most compelled to satisfy? We isolated and analyzed donors likely to have a direct interest in policies on climate change or energy—that is, those who fall into categories such as "alternative energy," "transportation," or "energy and natural resources." In Virginia, 61 percent of contributions from donors likely to have an interest in the making of climate-change policy came from energy or natural resources firms, a large category that runs the gamut of major industries such as mining, the electric utilities, steel manufacture, oil and natural gas, and refining. Between 2001 and 2009, 17 percent of energy and natural resources donations came from coal mining companies and donations from Dominion or a handful of the company's top executives constituted 73 percent of those in the electric utilities sub-category. Virginia's pattern of campaign finance resembled those in Texas and Louisiana, where fossil-fuel companies also constituted a sizable percentage of statewide campaign donations.[21]

In a state that allows unlimited donations, those who give generously are likely to find political access. More generally, political science research shows that more money overall flows into campaigns in states (such as Virginia) with no restrictions on campaign donations than in states with campaign finance limits. Candidates in states without campaign donation limits are likely to feel particularly beholden to the largest givers.[22]

The new campaign-financing analyses undertaken for this book examine donations between 2001 and 2015 in order to understand recent long-term trends coincident with the years (2002–2010) during which I was a member of the Air Board. Between 2000 and 2015, Dominion donated more money ($6.2 million) than any other company to candidates in Virginia's state elections, far more than the amount given by the second-most-generous corporate donor, Altria ($2.8 million). Democrats and Republicans alike receive funding from Dominion. In 2015 the Virginian Pilot reported that all forty senators and all but nine of 100 members of the House of Delegates had received campaign funds from Dominion. In that same year Dominion won a freeze for seven years on base rate changes, a law that overrode the State Corporation Commission's usual ability to reduce electricity rates and review earnings.[23]

Concentrated campaign giving in Virginia is not limited to Dominion Power. Coal mining interests give surprisingly large amounts of money to Virginia's politicians relative to amounts donated in other states. During statewide campaigns between 2001 and 2015, Virginia's politicians received $6.8 million from coal mining companies or their executives, the highest amount donated in any state, including states in which much more coal is mined or consumed than in Virginia (e.g., Illinois and Texas). Those $6.8 million in donations accounted for 28 percent of donations to state-level candidates in Virginia from energy and natural resources companies or employees. Only two states in the entire country showed a greater concentration of coal mining interest giving in statewide campaigns. In West Virginia and Kentucky, donations from coal mining interests between 2001 and 2015 for statewide campaigns constituted 45 and 30 percent, respectively, of all donations from energy and natural resources interests.

Coal mining campaign donations in Virginia decreased somewhat in 2015, to equal the amount donated in 2001, but they still constituted 25 percent of funds given by the energy and natural resources sector. The two Democratic governors who were in office during my appointment to the Air Board have relied heavily on the electric utilities, especially Dominion, and on coal companies for campaign financing. Between 2003 and 2010, a period when Tim Kaine was either lieutenant governor, running for governor, or serving as governor, Dominion or its employees and coal company interests gave 45 percent of Mr. Kaine's energy and natural resources support. Giving to Mark Warner between 1999 and 2006, when he was preparing to run for governor, running for governor, or in office as governor, shows similar dominance by Dominion and coal company interests.[24]

Chapter 6 compares Virginia's patterns of campaign donations with those in six leading coal states. But some interstate comparisons are in order here, to put Virginia's campaign finance patterns into perspective. The relatively high level of campaign giving by coal mining interests in Virginia's statewide elections is disproportionate to the relatively low amount of coal produced or used in the state. One might expect heavy concentrations of coal donations in West Virginia and Kentucky because they are among the nation's top coal producers, with 112 million tons and 77 million tons produced in 2014, respectively, out of a national total of 985 million tons. But in 2014 Virginia produced only 15 million tons of coal, approximately half of what the state produced in 2001. In 2014 Virginia's utilities consumed a relatively small amount of coal, 9.5 million tons, which was lower than that in all but a few of the forty states that rely on coal for electricity production. In 2015, only 21 percent of Virginia's electricity came from coal-fired generation, as compared with 35 percent in 2010 and 45 percent in 2005. Virginia's coal mines employed just 3,500 people in 2014. Virginia as a whole is much less dependent than before on coal for electricity or for jobs. Yet donations to state campaigns by the coal mining industry were especially high between 2005 and 2013, when that industry provided between 25 percent and 41 percent of total state-level campaign contributions from the energy and natural resources.[25]

The oddly elevated level of giving by coal interests in Virginia, combined with the state's low economic dependence on coal, leads one to ask about the connection between campaign funds and policy outcomes. There are good reasons to expect that connecting contributions with policy influence might be difficult. Money undoubtedly flows to candidates who are already predisposed to the views their donors favor. Some donors give to members of one political party because of generalized ideological preferences, without an expectation of a quid pro quo.

But what is surprising are findings of weak, if any, links between campaign contributions and legislator behavior at the national level. One much-cited study of contributions and votes in Congress concluded that "legislators' votes depend almost entirely on their own beliefs and the preferences of their party and their votes. Contributions explain a miniscule fraction of voting behavior in the US Congress." Another prominent analysis of policy making in Washington found that "the relationship between money and power is not simple, and the richest side does not always win." These authors observed that "money does not always buy policy outcomes [because] groups work with a diverse collection of allies [and] the mobilization of one side can lead to the counter-mobilization of another."[26]

These latter circumstances do not always occur at the state level. Especially in small or medium sized states, there may be only a handful of groups to counter-mobilize against especially powerful industries. Though fewer studies have analyzed the connection between campaign giving and policy outcomes at the sub-national level, one such study shows that unlimited statewide campaign financing leads to a smaller budget for the poor. That is, as the amount of money flowing into campaigns rises, state-level candidates appear to concentrate their scarce time on wealthy donors. Conversely, receiving fewer funds from wealthy donors bolsters the willingness of state politicians to represent the less fortunate among their constituents.

The political scientist Lynda Powell conducted a comprehensive look at the influence of campaign finance on the behavior of state legislators. Her results, which are based on surveys conducted in 2002, point to connections between legislator pay and donor influence: "my analysis provides the strongest evidence to date that contributions do influence public policy and that viewing contributions as investments explains much of the varied influence of contributions among legislative chambers." Candidates spent more time fundraising as legislator compensation rose, because better-paying positions were considered desirable. More time spent on fundraising meant that donor interests tended to outweigh those of constituents.[27]

But Powell concludes that "these findings should not be taken as simple prescriptions for altering our institutions." Even if legislators seeking positions with higher compensation raise more funds and, therefore, are more likely to turn to their backers for policy counsel, there are strong indications that professionalized legislatures do a better job of representing their constituents. Specifically, state legislators in more professional legislatures "have more contact with their constituents, are more attentive to their concerns, and are more representative of their views than are their counterparts in less-professional legislatures." One way of reconciling these results is to remember that professionalization means more than simply increased compensation. More professionalized state legislatures also have greater staff resources and longer sessions, which means that legislators can collect information, deliberate, and act more independently of government and non-government actors alike in any given policy area.[28]

Virginia's part-time legislature operates against the backdrop of the state's "traditionalistic" political culture, which reinforces cozy relationships between state officials and the regulated community. The very notion of state-based political cultures and their classification comes from Daniel Elazar's enduring work, which was first published in the 1970s. Elazar defined political culture as follows:

Three aspects of political culture stand out as particularly influential in shaping the operations of the state political systems within the context of American federalism. They are (1) the set of perceptions of what politics is and what can be expected from government, held by both the general public and the politicians; (2) the kinds of people who become active in government and politics, as holders of elective offices, members of the bureaucracy, and active political workers; and (3) the actual way in which the art of government is practiced by citizens, politicians, and public officials in the light of their perceptions.[29]

Elazar classified the political culture of every state, and his scheme is in wide use today. By one count, at least 100 studies have relied on Elazar's notions of state-level political culture.[30]

Elazar asserted that states tend to have a dominant predisposition: moralistic, individualistic, or traditionalistic. In moralistic political cultures, "politics ... is considered one of the great activities of humanity in its search for the good society ... . Both the general public and the politicians conceive of politics as a public activity centered on some notion of the public good. Good government, then, is measured by the degree to which it promotes the public good." Individualistic political cultures "emphasize the conception of the democratic order as a marketplace ... . A government need not have any direct concern with questions of the good society ... . Government action is to be restricted to those areas, primarily in the economic realm, that encourage private initiative and widespread access to the market place." Finally, in states with traditionalistic political cultures, we find "an ambivalent attitude toward the marketplace coupled with a paternalistic and elitist conception of the commonwealth." Elazar observed that states don't necessarily fit neatly within one political culture and that subregions within states may exhibit varying cultural tendencies. He classified states along a spectrum according to their dominant political culture and, in some cases, a secondary strong political culture "strain."[31]

In Elazar's scheme Virginia's political culture manifests a "traditionalistic" orientation and he indicated no secondary tendency. Traditionalistic state political cultures "maintain the existing order" and the governing elite exerts tight control. Policy inertia reigns and new programs are initiated only if they serve the interest of elites. Public servants are regarded negatively and there is no deep devotion to serving the public interest. Elazar observed that "where the traditionalistic political culture is dominant ... political leaders play conservative and custodial rather than initiatory roles unless they are pressed strongly from the outside." Civil servants have little power: "Traditionalistic political cultures tend to be instinctively anti-bureaucratic. Bureaucracy by its very nature interferes with the fine web of informal interpersonal relationships that lies at the root of the political system." Of the three cultural predispositions, traditionalistic states show the "most contempt" for bureaucracy and government, "except when they protect entrenched power structures." Political culture persists even when the party in power changes.[32]

When I was a member of the Air Board, DEQ's tendency to capitulate to the business community probably stemmed in part from the longstanding devaluation of the Agency's mission and erosion of personnel and resources by elected politicians. Virginia General Assembly reports from 1996 and 1997 document in some detail staff members' fear of reprisal if they challenged the regulated community and the willingness of management to favor business interests over those of the public and the environment. Those reports also claimed that the DEQ was understaffed.[33]

Studies building on Elazar's pioneering work have framed state political culture as the way in which we define the "proper purpose for government" and how we should undertake to make public policy. In a cross-sectional study of state welfare caseloads, Lawrence Mead observed "three styles of welfare reform" that corresponded well to Elazar's three-category political culture schema. Administrators in moralistic states tried to "use the welfare system to change the lifestyle of the poor" whereas those in traditionalistic states "controlled dependency by keeping people off welfare." In individualistic states officials "were more ambivalent ... relying mainly on sanctions to trim welfare." In another publication Mead reported that states with moralistic political cultures tended to score highest on welfare reform measures relative to states with individualistic or traditional cultures. However, he observed that even moralistic states could run into administrative and political problems, and that one traditionalistic state, Tennessee, undertook welfare reform effectively. Mead described political culture predispositions as tendencies that influence processes and attitudes but do not necessarily determine policy processes or outcomes.[34]

A focus on tendencies, rather than the ironclad outcomes predicted by regulatory capture theories, is precisely what is offered in the notion of a climate of capitulation. In Virginia, the combination of three major factors has created a context in which entrenched business elites can—and do—exercise undue power in the making of air pollution policy, through legislative and administrative processes: (1) campaign donations that, in the energy and natural resources sector, are dominated by one electric utility and coal interests, (2) a reactive part-time legislature that has virtually no independent analytical capacity; and (3) a traditionalistic political culture. Representatives of the regulated community provide technical analysis to information-starved legislators who do not have the resources or time to deliberate over the highly technical matters involved in making environmental policy. Energy and coal mining interests provide a surprising amount of money to state candidates in Virginia, helping the most powerful interests (e.g., Dominion Power) get what they desire in the General Assembly and in administrative regulatory processes.

While I was on the Air Board, the state's environmental civil servants seemed too intimidated to advance strong regulatory proposals. Their basic impulse was to require only what the regulated community would accept by way of emission reductions, and few leaders were willing to push for more. These combined forces explain why the Air Board encountered such fierce resistance to changing the status quo, even if the status quo involved pollution levels that threatened public health or the environment.

The information presented in this and previous chapters leads to the question of which policy or political reforms might be appropriate to counteract the kinds of power imbalances displayed in Virginia. The foregoing analysis highlights important factors that have contributed to Virginia's climate of capitulation. One might logically infer that reforms involving state legislature professionalism and campaign finance could help alleviate the observed biases in Virginia.

But the narratives in chapters 1–3 also highlight the importance of allowing room for effective citizen participation. In Wise and in Alexandria the Air Board adopted emission standards that met the letter of the Clean Air Act and were much lower than those advocated by the Virginia Department of Environmental Quality. Those results would not have been possible without the many citizens, state and local politicians, local and state civil servants, and citizens' groups who presented relevant technical information and who decided to resist the status quo and to stay in the fray, come what may. Financial resources mattered, too. The City of Alexandria spent substantial funds on consultants and legal counsel, and the Sierra Club sponsored a study of airborne particulate matter in Roda. Technical expertise and data were vital, because information is the currency of air pollution policy making.

Legal authority for citizen Boards is important, too. Until 2008, the Air Board could take over permitting processes simply by voting to do so. The Air Board members are term-appointed, unpaid officials, which means they can choose to stay outside of the long-term relationships that entangle paid civil servants and members of the regulated community.

A natural question concerns the generalizability of these observations beyond Virginia. Chapters 5 and 6 investigate whether the patterns of influence observed in Virginia might be found in other coal states, thereby setting the stage for reforms suggested in chapter 7.

5 Shotgun Marriage Federalism

Americans enjoy substantially cleaner air than in the 1970s, both because of, and in spite of, the Clean Air Act's system of collaboration between the US Environmental Protection Agency (EPA) and the states. State-federal partnerships were politically necessary for the birth of many national environmental laws, including the 1970 Clean Air Act and the 1972 Clean Water Act. Members of Congress wanted to know that their constituents and home state agencies would influence how those laws were implemented. The self-proclaimed "new Federalists" in President Richard Nixon's administration believed that state and local government officials should share responsibility for cleaning up pollution, even as the president and his appointees supported centralized authority for cleaning up the nation's air and water. One result of Nixon's advocacy was the EPA, which he formed through executive reorganization by moving programs and statutory mandates from fifteen pre-existing agencies into a single new agency.[1]

The state-federal partnership system adopted in the 1970 Clean Air Act was built on pre-existing foundations. Previously, air pollution regulatory authority had resided at the state and local levels. Even though state and local efforts to control air pollution had been weak and ineffective for the most part, relinquishing that control to an entirely new, untested federal agency would never have been in the cards politically. A practical reason for state-federal cooperation was that the EPA must rely on the states to decide which sources to control and to what extent, since the Agency can never be large enough to undertake that job in all fifty states. Representative Harley Staggers said, when managing the House version of the 1970 Clean Air Act Amendments, "If we left it all to the Federal Government, we would have about everybody on the payroll of the United States. We know this is not practical. Therefore, the Federal Government sets the standards, we tell the States what they must do and what standards they must meet."[2]

Federal-State Collaborations Under the Clean Air Act

"Cooperative federalism" is the phrase widely used to describe such state-federal power sharing arrangements. But "shotgun marriage federalism" might be a better term, since the Clean Air Act threw the states and the EPA into what amounted to a hastily arranged marriage. That partnership can be riven by tension and discord. The states do not always agree with the EPA's assessment of which sources should be controlled and to what extent. Air pollution travels across state lines and is transformed in the atmosphere. As a result, many serious disputes have arisen between upwind and downwind states about who is responsible for which air-quality problems.[3]

Another complication in this supposedly cooperative relationship is that the EPA may not force state air-pollution-control agencies to do anything with respect to the Clean Air Act's statutory directives. Rather, the EPA offers state agencies the opportunity to qualify for delegated authority to implement the act's provisions. When states are offered and then accept that authority for specific Clean Air Act programs, they are eligible to receive Clean Air Act grant funds and they become the primary implementing agency for those programs. If states choose not to request that authority or do not submit acceptable plans for implementing the relevant Clean Air Act sections, the EPA must implement the applicable programs. For programs connected with attaining the National Ambient Air Quality Standards, the EPA may also impose sanctions that could involve freezing new permits for major stationary sources, tightening emission requirements for new major air pollution sources, or withholding air pollution grants or highway construction funds. Some sanctions are nondiscretionary if the EPA determines that a state has either failed to submit an adequate plan or to implement an approved plan. The Clean Air Act permits states to adopt stationary source standards more stringent than those adopted to implement the act's authority.[4]

The character of the EPA's partnerships with the states varies quite a bit. For example, the EPA is the follower in California, whose economy rivals that of Brazil in size and diversity. Federal policies are overshadowed by California's muscular clean-air laws and by the sheer quantity of the state's air-pollution-control resources. California's air pollution regulatory bodies include not only the world-renowned Air Resources Board but also thirty-five air-pollution-control districts, among them agencies in Los Angeles and San Francisco that have long been viewed as among the most progressive in the nation. Federal grant allocations barely dent the budgets of these relatively large agencies. For example, the EPA's funds accounted for only 5 percent of the South Coast Air Quality Management District's overall budget for 2014–2015, and federal grants made up 2 percent of the San Francisco Bay Area Air Quality Management District's 2016 revenues. By contrast, Virginia relies more heavily on delegated federal Clean Air Act authority. In Indiana, 21 percent of the state agency's funding for air-quality programs in 2014–2015 came from the federal government. These differences among the states notwithstanding, a common thread is the impulse for state legislators and governors to want to implement federal laws themselves, rather than cede that authority to the EPA, so they can adjust federal requirements to regional and local circumstances.[5]

Tense relationships between the states and the EPA have played out over both mobile source and stationary source regulations, despite the varying nature of the state-federal partnerships the Clean Air Act sets forth for mobile and stationary source programs. Vehicle inspection and maintenance (I/M) programs are designed to ensure that on-road vehicles do not emit at unacceptably high levels. The states have had primary responsibility for designing I/M programs that would meet federal standards. Disagreements have included whether inspection stations should be centralized or decentralized and which test procedures would achieve the best results at the lowest cost. For the most part, vehicle emission standards per se are the EPA's sole province, with the notable exception of California, the only state empowered to request a waiver from the Clean Air Act's general prohibition on state-established mobile vehicle emission limits. If California is granted a waiver to establish state-specific standards, other states may adopt California's standards.[6]

One important battle over mobile source standard waivers played out between 2005 and 2009. In 2005, under Governor Arnold Schwarzenegger (a Republican), the California Air Resources Board requested from the EPA a waiver so the state could implement standards for greenhouse-gas emissions from vehicles. Those standards were authorized by the state legislature under the 2002 "Pavley rule" (named after Fran Pavley, the California legislator who led the charge for the emissions restrictions). The EPA delayed for two years before denying the waiver request. Under President Obama, the EPA reversed its position, granted the waiver in 2009, and in 2010 adopted national greenhouse-gas-emission standards for vehicles that were harmonized with California's standards.[7]

Emission standards for stationary sources have proved even more divisive. The Clean Air Act envisions that the states will establish standards for existing and new major stationary sources in service of meeting various Clean Air Act goals. Those goals include attaining the National Ambient

Air Quality Standards (NAAQS), which provided the legal basis for the Air Board's actions on the Mirant facility in Alexandria. The EPA sets the NAAQS, which are to be met everywhere in the nation, and the states submit plans specifying the emission reductions from existing sources that are needed to meet the NAAQS. The Clean Air Act also sets forth permitting requirements for new large sources such as power plants. Such facilities may not degrade air quality and they must install the best controls available, goals that framed the Air Board's work in Wise. Another central set of Clean Air Act programs involves "cap and trade" programs for emissions of sulfur dioxide and nitrogen oxides from power plants in which the EPA has set statewide emissions caps and let the states decide how to meet those caps.[8]

Fights have erupted over how the states should meet their obligations under these Clean Air Act programs. States have sued the EPA to force, change, or halt action, and the EPA has required changes to state plans when air-quality goals were not met. A few examples will serve to illustrate the high stakes involved in these disputes. In 1997, eight downwind northeastern states sued the EPA because of interstate pollution transport they alleged was contributing to degradation of air quality in their areas. In response, the EPA demanded that 22 upwind states revise their state air-quality plans to reduce emissions of nitrogen oxides from power plants. When the state of Texas refused in 2011 to implement the EPA's new source permitting program for greenhouse gases, the EPA took over that program until the Texas legislature adopted an enabling state law. In *Massachusetts v. EPA* the US Supreme Court concluded that Massachusetts' coastline had suffered, and would continue to suffer, from sea-level rise linked to the EPA's failure to regulate greenhouse gases. That decision led to the EPA's finding in 2009 that greenhouse gases endanger public health and welfare and therefore must be regulated under the Clean Air Act. Private-sector and public-sector parties have often sued the EPA or the states to change stationary source regulatory decisions. One prominent example is the litigation involving the EPA's initiatives to reduce nitrogen oxides and sulfur dioxide emissions from power plants under the Clean Air Interstate Rule and the Cross-State Air Pollution Rule.[9]

The miracle is that, these many disputes notwithstanding, the Clean Air Act endures and evolves. Not only does the act continue to force improvements to the nation's air quality, the act has morphed into the nation's climate-change law. One legal observer has called the act "surprisingly adaptable, durable and innovative." But the challenge that awaits the EPA and states with respect to regulating carbon dioxide emissions from existing fossil-fuel-fired power plants may prove the act's greatest test to date.[10]

Coal and the Three Faces of Power

Longstanding partnerships between the EPA and the states have been tried as the states have considered their responses to the EPA's Clean Power Plan. The "Clean Power Plan" refers to the EPA's planned use of Section 111(d) of the Clean Air Act, a relatively little-used part of the law, to regulate carbon dioxide emissions from power plants. Under Section 111(d), the EPA established in 2015 a carbon dioxide emission goal in 2030 for each state that corresponds to rates achievable through "the best system of emission reduction that has been adequately demonstrated," considering costs and non-air-quality health and environmental impacts. The EPA also specified interim state-specific performance goals for the period 2022–2029. The Clean Power Plan's broad scope sets it apart from any previous regulations established under Section 111(d), ensuring that there will be many hurdles to full implementation. The attorneys general of 27 states filed lawsuits challenging the Plan. In 2016 the US Supreme Court suspended the Plan to let legal battles play out in court. Donald Trump campaigned against the Plan.[11]

The Clean Power Plan aims to lower carbon dioxide emissions from power plants in 2030 by 32 percent, relative to 2005 levels, which equals 768 million metric tons, and to reduce emissions by 376 million metric tons relative to the projected "business as usual" situation in 2030. The 392 million metric ton difference between these two numbers reflects the decrease in carbon dioxide emissions from power plants that occurred between 2005 and 2014. Market forces have contributed to those reductions. Natural gas prices have fallen as supplies have increased through hydraulic fracturing ("fracking"), and thus natural gas has displaced much coal as a fuel for electricity generation. Further, some energy-intensive and pollution-intensive industries, such as steel manufacturing, have moved outside the United States. State renewable-energy programs and Clean Air Act rules for power plant emissions of toxic air pollutants such as arsenic have also contributed to a decline in electricity generated from coal. The anticipated carbon dioxide reductions from the Clean Power Plan are substantial, important goals that, if realized, would make a palpable dent in national and world greenhouse-gas emissions. For perspective, total carbon dioxide emissions in the nation of Germany in 2014 were approximately 800 million metric tons.[12]

Without full participation from the coal states, carbon dioxide emission reductions from power plants will fall short of the Plan's objectives. "Coal state" here signifies any state in which coal has been, or continues to be, important to electric power generation or in the state's economy or politics.

Efforts to protect coal interests are likely to be strongest in the coal states. Virginia is a longtime coal state, although it is possible that few Virginia residents outside of the state's remote, mountainous southwest corner know much about the state's history as a coal producer or historical reliance on coal for electricity production. Virginia first started producing coal in the 1870s. Production peaked in 1990, when Virginia's coal mines produced 40 million tons.[13]

As measured by coal production or consumption, Virginia does not qualify as a major coal state any longer. By 2014 Virginia's mines were producing 15 million tons, which amounted to only 1.5 percent of total US coal production. Coal consumption in Virginia has decreased steadily since 2000. In 2005 coal provided the fuel for almost half of the state's electricity generation, but by 2015 that proportion had fallen to 21 percent. Coal consumption and production in Virginia pale by comparison with those in many other states. In 2014 Wyoming and West Virginia mined 395 million and 112 million tons of coal, respectively. Kentucky's population is half that of Virginia, yet Kentucky's electric utilities and other industries consumed almost four times as much coal in 2014 as those in Virginia. Still, Virginia remains a coal state because of cultural tradition, which is tied to the now-waning coal mining industry in the state's southwest Appalachian counties, and because coal is still used to generate some electric power. Data presented in chapter 4 and later in this chapter show that coal companies have given heavily to state politicians' campaigns in Virginia, thereby ensuring that the coal industry's concerns are prominent with state legislators.[14]

Chapter 4 argues that political culture, legislative professionalism, and campaign finance donations shape Virginia's climate of capitulation in the making of air pollution policy. These forces reveal themselves in different ways. Political scientists distinguish among "public, hidden, and invisible" kinds of coercion. A public expression of power, sometimes called the "first dimension" of power, involves using overt incentives or punishments, such as campaign donations, to alter someone's preferred behavior. In the first dimension of power, political wins and losses are visible and traceable to particular actors. Those who believe that the first dimension of power is the most important form of power expression claim that everyone who wants to participate in policy making or in politics can do so effectively. Nonparticipation is written down to lack of interest. Joseph Nye encapsulates the first dimension of power as follows: "Someone has the capacity to make others act against their initial preferences and strategies, and both sides feel that power."[15]

Hidden coercion, or the "second" dimension of power, is manifest in control of public policy agendas that constrain policy makers to a cramped set of choices, often termed a "mobilization of bias." Such control might be manifest when part-time legislatures, such as Virginia's, cannot develop their own policy options for especially technical matters but, rather, must rely on information provided by outsiders, such as lobbyists or executive-branch officials. Through the second dimension of power, policy agendas become truncated because of "non-decisions" in which powerful actors prevent specific policy options from being considered in the first place. The voices of the less powerful are simply shut out of the conversation. In this view of power, non-participation is sometimes forced, not voluntary.[16]

The "third" dimension of power involves invisible coercion, in which perceptions are shaped over time without conscious knowledge. Invisible coercion is felt in the effects of Virginia's traditionalistic political culture, which devalues public participation and civil servants, on the one hand, and protects the status quo, on the other hand. Government actors operate in an atmosphere in which elite private interests are of paramount concern to members of both major political parties. Those who might want to oppose those interests feel powerless to do so because of the "shaping of beliefs about the order's legitimacy or immutability." One result in Virginia of this expression of power is the Virginia DEQ's consistent reluctance to require emission reductions that protected public health and the environment. Only strong, sustained leadership can counteract these tendencies. The powerful "prevail simply through the inertia of the situation."[17]

This chapter begins to examine whether the deeply rooted political, economic, and institutional forces that contribute to Virginia's climate of capitulation also characterize six leading coal states: Illinois, Indiana, Ohio, Kentucky, Pennsylvania, and Texas. These coal states merit attention because each is a top consumer of coal, each is a major producer of coal, and each is among the highest emitters in the fifty states of carbon dioxide from the electric utility sector. Together these six states produced 30 percent of the United States' coal in 2014. Together they consumed 37 percent of all coal used to generate electric power in the US in 2014. As percentages of total emissions from the nation's power plants in 2014, the electrical generating units in these six states emitted 35 percent of carbon dioxide, 34 percent of nitrogen oxides, and 48 percent of sulfur dioxide. Their combined power plant carbon dioxide emissions in 2014 (773 million metric tons) exceeded the total carbon dioxide emissions from the burning of fossil fuels (for transportation and other purposes) of every country except China, Russia, India, Japan, and Germany. As a group under the EPA's Clean

Power Plan, these six states would have to reduce their carbon dioxide emissions by 176 million megagrams in 2030 relative to 2012, which constitutes almost half of the overall emission reductions required by the Plan between 2012 and 2030. By every measure, these six states are critical to the success of efforts to reduce US greenhouse gas emissions and to the world's success in combatting climate change.[18]

Yet officials in several of these states have resisted regulation of fossil-fuel-fired power plants. The authors of the 1990 Clean Air Act Amendments explicitly recognized the extra effort needed to win over politicians and electric utilities in the midwestern states, home to the highest-polluting electric utilities. The Act's acid rain program awarded Indiana, Illinois, and Ohio hefty "bonus" sulfur dioxide pollution allowances to ensure that these states' congressional representatives would agree to a scheme whose largest benefits would be felt in the eastern United States. Among the 27 attorneys general who challenged the Clean Power Plan were those from Indiana, Kentucky, Ohio, and Texas.[19]

Partisanship Does Not Explain Action or Inaction of State Policy Makers

It is tempting to posit that the analysis of six coal states could end here by pointing to partisanship and public opinion as the most important factors in shaping policy makers' approaches to regulating greenhouse-gas emissions. After all, in national surveys Democrats and Independents are more likely than Republicans and Tea Partyers to believe that global warming is happening and to be worried about the effects of global warming. Since the 1980s and 1990s Republicans and Democrats in Congress, who previously showed approximately equal tendencies to vote for or against environmental laws, have increasingly lined up against one another on environmentally oriented votes. In 2003 only four Senate Republicans voted for the Climate Stewardship Act, which was co-sponsored by Senator John McCain (a Republican) and Senator Joe Lieberman (a Democrat). In 2009 only eight Republican House members voted for the Waxman-Markey bill, which set forth a comprehensive set of programs on climate change and renewable energy. In November 2015 the US Senate voted along party lines, with only a handful of defections, to disapprove of the EPA's Clean Power Plan, yet another reminder of this continuing partisan divide among national politicians. One comprehensive analysis of voting trends in Congress between 1970 and 2000 linked growing voting gaps between Senate Democrats and Republicans to the defection of Southern Democrats to the Republican Party.[20]

At first glance, the six coal states examined here appear to manifest partisanship patterns that might drive predictably different environmental policies. In the presidential elections of 2000, 2004, 2008, 2012 and 2016, Texas and Kentucky were "red," Illinois was "blue," and Indiana, Pennsylvania, and Ohio were "red" and "blue."[21]

But this parlance oversimplifies and misleads. Few states are all "red" or "blue," in the sense of being made up predominantly of Republicans or Democrats in the electorate or among state-level politicians. In the presidential electoral college system, even if only a few votes separate the leading candidates, as was the case in Florida in 2000, all electoral college votes are granted to the winner, except in Maine and Nebraska. The resulting "red state–blue state" maps imply erroneously that state electorates as a whole can be classified as Republican or Democratic. If we look instead at recent House of Representatives elections, we see that voters in Illinois, Indiana, Kentucky, Ohio, Pennsylvania, Texas, and Virginia, along with those in many other states, have elected a mix of Republican and Democratic House representatives. The fact that popularly used indices of voting records (e.g., the League of Conservation Voters' "scorecards") credit Democratic members of Congress in these seven states with better environmental voting records than most Republicans from those same states does not change the fact that none of these states is thoroughly "blue" or "red."[22]

State-level elections also reflect mixed partisan results. Between 2000 and 2015 all six coal states except Texas had both Democrats and Republicans as governors. Even in Texas, widely considered to be a deeply "red" state, Democrats held the governor's office from 1874 to 1995. Between 2000 and 2015, Virginia had two Republican and three Democratic governors. Republicans controlled the two houses of the Virginia General Assembly for most of that interval, although Democrats controlled the state Senate for three years. A similar pattern is evident in the legislatures of Ohio, Pennsylvania, and Texas. Between 2000 and 2015, state assemblies in Kentucky and Indiana showed mixed partisan control and Democrats were the majority force in Illinois's state legislature. Since residents of all of these states except Texas have chosen Republican and Democratic leaders in relatively recent statewide elections, it would be difficult to attribute to partisanship per se much explanatory power with respect to long-term patterns in state-level environmental policy making.[23]

Partisanship can matter for state-level policy making, but not necessarily in predictable ways. Quantitative analyses of policy "drivers" for state-level renewable-energy laws indicate that partisan control of the state legislature, or what is called "government ideology," can be, but is not always, a significant factor. In those same studies, partisanship of the governor did not correlate significantly with adoption of state-level renewable-energy policies. One comprehensive 2015 study found that the link between partisanship of state governors or legislatures and state environmental program strength varies according to the program measure employed. Such results are consistent with other work, which found that governors of both parties have been active and passive in the areas of climate and renewable energy. Yet another study investigated the correlation between state-level policy activity in a number of areas and results of presidential elections. The results revealed that "red" and "blue" states differed significantly on only 12 of 27 policy indicators.[24]

Perhaps at the root of these surprising findings is that many states resist simple partisan labels. One prominent analysis of voter sentiment and control of state institutions concluded that the American states are neither "red" nor "blue" but, rather, have become increasingly "purple": "At least in terms of distribution of votes and political control of state governments, American states do not sort cleanly into Democratic and Republican camps." While rural areas tend to be more conservative than cities, this difference has shrunk over time, as have "upstate-downstate" differences in Illinois, Indiana, and some other states. We saw in chapter 2 that Democrats and Republicans have represented Virginia's coal mining regions in the Virginia General Assembly simultaneously.[25]

Further, the much-remarked partisan divide in the electorate with respect to climate change, though real, is not the chasm often depicted. One meta-analysis of national polls conducted from 2002 to 2011 points to a consistently higher level of concern about climate change among Democrats than among Republicans. However, these same polls show that "most Americans agree with the overwhelming scientific opinion that climate change is a real problem," that "most Americans express genuine concern about climate change," and that "most Americans want government and industry to take at least some action to address the sources of the problem." A poll conducted before the 2015 UN-sponsored climate talks in Paris yielded similar results: 85 percent of Democrats, 64 percent of Republicans, and 71 percent of Americans overall agreed that reaching an agreement was important.[26]

Republicans' views are not uniform. Republican voters believe by a margin of two to one that the US should decrease its reliance on fossil fuels and invest in renewable energy. In polls conducted from 2012 to 2014, 62 percent of moderate Republicans and 73 percent of liberal Republicans favored strict limits on emissions of carbon dioxide from power plants, while only 40 percent of conservative Republicans and 23 percent of Tea Party Republicans supported such limits. These results indicate why a large majority of Republican voters believe their Republican representatives do not reflect their constituents' views on climate change. One analysis of voting patterns in the US Senate confirms that many Republican senators do not vote in accordance with the concerned views of their constituents when it comes to climate change. A majority of survey respondents supported the Clean Power Plan in many of the states whose officials, many of whom are Republican, challenged the Clean Power Plan. Former EPA Administrator William Ruckelshaus, an Indiana-born Republican, believes national Republican politicians who have repeatedly blocked action on climate change are too eager to appease the party's conservative elements.[27]

Many Republican members of Congress are from the South, an area that was dominated by Democrats from the late 1800s until the late twentieth century. But in the past several decades, conservative Southern Democrats have switched parties. President Lyndon B. Johnson famously predicted after hard-won passage of the 1964 Civil Rights Act that he had "delivered the South to the Republican Party for a long time to come." President Johnson was right to expect widespread defections of Southern Democrats to the Republican Party, not only with respect to members of Congress but for state elective offices, too. In 2015, in the eleven states that constituted the Confederacy, 19 of 22 the US senators were Republicans. Because of partisan realignment and redistricting that has involved concentrating minority voters (who tend to vote Democratic) into fewer districts, Republicans now control at least one house of the state legislature in all eleven former Confederate states. Partisanship, race, and the South are intertwined, a theme that will recur later in this chapter.[28]

Public Opinion and Policy Makers' Decisions Are Not Necessarily Linked

It is reasonable to expect that public opinion should affect how state-level officials undertake air pollution policy making. Such connections have been evident at the national level. In 1970 and in 1989, the Republican presidents Richard Nixon and George H.W. Bush proposed comprehensive changes to the Clean Air Act. Democratic-led Congresses followed suit, enacting strong laws in 1970 and 1990. In both cases strong public demand for action was an important factor.[29]

Climate change has been a highly salient issue with the American public at large for years. National public opinion surveys paint a picture of strong support for reducing greenhouse-gas emissions. In 2008, 2010, and 2012,

70 percent, 74 percent, and 77 percent of Americans, respectively, supported government action to reduce greenhouse-gas emissions. In 2008, 87 percent of Americans said that state governments would boost their economies by requiring greater use of renewable energy. In 2015, 70 percent of Americans approved of strict limits on CO_2 emissions from coal-fired power plants, 67 percent thought global warming was happening, and 53 percent attributed global warming to human actions. Even in 2008 and 2009, during the Great Recession, a survey conducted by Stanford University and the Associated Press found that 14 percent of Americans picked the environment or global warming as the most important problem facing the world in the future, whereas 21 percent chose the economy or unemployment.[30]

Yet poll results tell varying stories about the persistence and the relative levels of Americans' concern over climate change. Gallup data indicate that the percentage of Americans worried about climate change peaked at 72 percent in 2000, and that only 55 percent of Americans showed equivalent levels of concern in 2015. *New York Times* data show that 69 percent of Americans called warming a "very serious" or "somewhat serious" problem in 2015. But European Commission polls indicate that Europeans show a much higher level of concern than Americans. In 2015, 91 percent of Europeans called climate change a serious problem and 47 percent of Europeans considered it one of the world's most serious problems. A 2015 Pew Research poll verifies higher levels of concern over climate change in Europe than in the United States. However, Stanford University researchers have estimated that, on average, US households are willing to pay $134 per year (in 2010 dollars) to reduce greenhouse-gas emissions, for a total national willingness to pay of $15.7 billion.[31]

The available state-level public opinion data indicate that solid public support for reducing greenhouse gases extends to many states, including Virginia and the six coal states included here. An estimated 61 percent of residents in the 27 states whose attorneys general sued the EPA over the Clean Power Plan favor the Plan's carbon dioxide limits. According to a Stanford University analysis of national-level data that were disaggregated to the state level, overwhelming majorities of residents in Virginia and in the six big coal states believe "the government should *require or encourage* [emphasis added] reduction of greenhouse-gas emissions by power plants" (Illinois 82 percent, Indiana 75 percent, Kentucky 78 percent, Ohio 79 percent, Pennsylvania 77 percent, Texas 79 percent, Virginia 81 percent). Unfortunately, these results do not separate respondents who support "requiring" reductions from those who support "encouraging" them, an important distinction to voters and politicians alike.[32]

Other studies seem to confirm that slight to strong majorities of residents in these seven states favor requirements for reducing carbon dioxide emissions. A Yale University modeling analysis combined twelve national surveys on climate change conducted between 2008 and 2013 with state, county, and congressional district demographic data to model opinion at disaggregated levels. The results indicated that the following percentages of statewide residents are likely to support strict regulations for power plant carbon dioxide emissions: Illinois 70 percent, Indiana 56 percent, Kentucky 53 percent, Ohio 63 percent, Pennsylvania 67 percent, Texas 61 percent, and Virginia 66 percent. Perhaps the most striking result of this study's extrapolation is that in these same seven states, in every congressional district except four in Texas, a majority of constituents are expected to favor setting strict limits on existing power plants' emissions of carbon dioxide. As one might expect, the study projects substantial within-state variation. For example, the percentage of Pennsylvania residents expected to support regulating carbon dioxide pollution from power plants varies from 47 percent in Carbon County, in northeastern Pennsylvania's coal mining region, to 76 percent in Philadelphia County. Among Kentucky's counties, projected support varies from 35 percent to 66 percent.[33]

But how intense, how persistent, and how unequivocal must public views be to cause environmental policy action? Politicians of all ideological stripes may resist adopting aggressive greenhouse-gas programs even if those programs appear to be highly salient with the public, because of the large misalignment between those bearing the concentrated costs of controlling pollution and those reaping the climate benefits, which are shared worldwide. Those who experience the costs of greenhouse-gas regulation are likely to lobby much more intensively than those benefitting from the thinly spread benefits. Thus, even though there is evidence of strong public support in Virginia and the other six coal states for reducing greenhouse-gas emissions generally, such support may not necessarily translate into political will to regulate specific sources or industries. Much may depend on whether state officials experience a climate of capitulation like that observed in Virginia. But program configuration can matter, too, when we examine the links between public opinion and programs that reduce greenhouse-gas emissions from power plants. One reason why programs that incentivize investment in wind turbines and other renewable-energy facilities are widely popular is that private investors, farmers, and government authorities reap financial benefits from them.[34]

High public salience is a necessary, but not a sufficient, condition for policy makers' action in issue areas with concentrated costs and diffuse benefits. For example, in Virginia strong public support for action on climate change has not translated into corresponding state-level policies. In public opinion surveys conducted in 2008 and 2010, and in an analysis that combined public opinion results over a decade in the twenty-first century, 72–75 percent of Virginians have signaled their support for government action to reduce emissions of greenhouse gases from private entities. Yet Virginia's politicians have not adopted state-level requirements for renewable energy or for reductions in emissions of greenhouse gases. Similarly, in 2013, 59 percent of Texans supported state government action on global warming, but then-Governor Rick Perry has long proclaimed his skepticism when it comes to human induced climate change. Still, Governor Perry has also pointed proudly to Texas's greenhouse-gas emission reductions, which have stemmed in part from state regulatory incentives to develop wind power.[35]

The apparent gap between voters' inclinations (as expressed in polls) and policy makers' actions extends beyond environmental issues. One comprehensive look at the connection between national public opinion surveys and policy making in Congress finds that "current estimates of the impact of public opinion on policy are probably too high." Part of the problem is methodological: establishing causal, quantitative relationships between inchoate public concern over an overarching issue such as climate change and the enactment of specific policies is an inherently uncertain task. The literature on the effects of public opinion on policy making seems to indicate that the links between public opinion and policy makers' reactions are strongest, and they serve democracy best, when issues are especially salient, when institutional arrangements communicate public opinions effectively, and when citizens are well-informed enough to press for policies that serve the public interest.[36]

Taken as a whole, the evidence shows we must reach beyond partisanship and public opinion polling to anticipate how policy makers in the coal states might react over the long term with respect to reducing carbon dioxide emissions from power plants. Oversimplified "red state"–"blue state" distinctions born of presidential election results do not reflect these states' complicated partisan mixes. Though members of Congress often vote along party lines with respect to environmental proposals, partisan affiliation per se is not an ironclad predictor of public sentiment or of state-level politicians' actions on climate-change policy. While the best estimates indicate that majorities of citizens in the seven states analyzed here support strict carbon dioxide emission reductions from power plants, high public salience does not always translate into political action. Further, each state examined here shows intrastate variations in levels of estimated public support. What other factors might affect how officials in the coal states examined here react to the prospect of reducing power plant carbon dioxide emissions?

6 Six Crucial Coal States and the South

It is not possible to predict what state officials or politicians will or will not do in the air pollution policy arena. Ideas, laws, court decisions, ideology, and public pressure can all affect policy makers' choices, and no model can capture the ways in which these kinds of factors will interact. Chapters 1–3 also show that leadership matters, and one never knows when leaders will emerge. Even in Virginia, policy makers have sometimes resisted the state's persistent climate of capitulation. More generally, environment-related disasters such as hurricanes or drought can shape policy makers' reactions in unexpected ways. But leadership and unanticipated events unfold within state-specific political climates that persist by virtue of institutional capacity, campaign finance patterns, and political culture, the factors examined in this chapter.

The analysis that follows applies the conclusions that emerged in chapter 4 to the coal states of Indiana, Illinois, Kentucky, Ohio, Pennsylvania, and Texas and then to the eleven states that make up the South. We do not have in-depth case-study observations such as those presented in chapters 1–3 for the states examined in this chapter. As such, we cannot say definitively that other states suffer from a climate of capitulation similar to that seen in Virginia, which inclines legislative and executive-branch officials to favor coal and electric utility interests. But we can characterize potential susceptibility to that climate of capitulation, in keeping with the analysis of Virginia undertaken in chapter 4. This chapter documents patterns of coal and electric utility campaign contributions between 2001 and 2015, political culture classification, and legislative professionalism. Virginia is included as a comparative benchmark.

Campaign Finance

The analysis presented in this section asks if there is evidence of especially concentrated giving to state-level candidates' political campaigns by fossil fuel, coal mining or electric utility interests. Dominance by those interests in campaign finance contributions might cause elected politicians to feel pressure to adopt lax air pollution laws or loose regulations for fossil-fuel-fired power plants. The campaign analysis presented in chapter 4 used the interval 2001–2015 to overlap with the years of my service on the Virginia Air Pollution Control Board and to provide a long enough period to dampen short-term fluctuations. That same period is used here.

The fifty states' campaign finance laws represent a laundry list of legal frameworks for mediating the uneasy relationship between money and politics. Only a handful of states, including Virginia, do not regulate campaign contributions or giving in any way, although all states require candidate disclosure of donations and expenditures. Most states restrict the amount that donors may give to specific candidates or committees, with the aim of ensuring that democratically elected officials will not feel they must give preferential access or treatment to the wealthy and well connected. Contribution caps also let campaign donors avoid limitless appeals from candidates and foster more competition from challengers.[1]

One important counterweight to campaign finance limits is US Supreme Court jurisprudence that has supported the right of individuals to donate as much as they like overall, with no restriction on the total amount given to all candidates and campaigns. Some Justices have deemed campaign finance laws as a "crafty plot to silence dissent" that, in the eyes of some, helps counteract self- interested, power-hungry politicians. As a result of the Court's ruling in *Citizens United v. Federal Election Commission*, unions and political action committees may conduct unlimited "parallel" spending opposing or supporting specific candidates. While the Supreme Court's decisions concern federal campaign finance law, several states have decided the Court's decision to ease federal spending restrictions means the states can no longer enforce limits on aggregate contributions by individuals or groups. The wide spectrum of state campaign finance laws illustrates the fact that there is no single obvious solution for balancing these contending, evolving considerations.[2]

One would expect campaign donations by the coal mining industry to be important in states where coal is produced or consumed in significant quantities. Illinois, Indiana, Kentucky, Ohio, Texas and Pennsylvania remain leading coal producers and consumers, despite a notable decline in coal consumption for electricity generation between 2007 and 2015. Figure 6.1 reveals the high concentration of overall national donations in these six states plus Virginia: 74 percent of total national coal mining campaign donations to state-level candidates between 2001 and 2015 went to

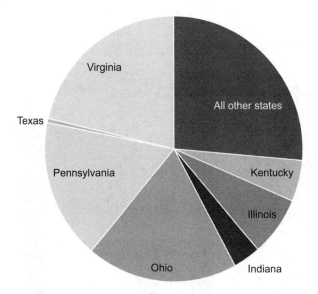

Figure 6.1
Donations to state-level campaigns by the coal mining industry, 2001–2015. Total = $31.9 million.

candidates in these seven states. That percentage barely changes if we look at 2010–2015, so 2001–2015 is not an anomalous period. Total coal mining donations in these seven states from 2001 to 2015 amounted to $23.5 million, as compared with the nationwide total of $31.9 million. One surprise is that since 2001 the coal mining industry has donated very little in Texas, the vast majority of the donations happening in one year (2003). Another surprise is that donations by the coal mining industry in Virginia, the state with the second lowest levels of coal production, are highest in absolute terms at $6.8 million. Pennsylvania and Ohio followed Virginia closely in absolute levels of donations from the coal mining industry.[3]

One might imagine that donations by the coal mining industry should rise and fall with coal production. The bars in figure 6.2 show campaign donations divided by coal production, for 2001 through 2013 (the most recent year for which state-level coal production data were available). Relative amounts of coal production for that same period are indicated in the pie chart. In the states with the lowest coal production, Ohio and Virginia, donations per amount of coal produced were seven to ten times those in Kentucky, the state with the highest coal production. Pennsylvania produced much less coal than Kentucky, but donations per unit

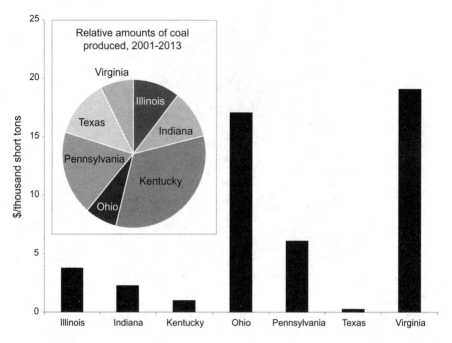

Figure 6.2

The coal mining industry's campaign donations to state candidates per amount of coal produced, 2001–2013 (dollars per thousand short tons).

of coal produced exceeded those in Kentucky by three times. Although Illinois, Indiana, and Texas show coal production levels roughly in the same range, donations per unit of coal production were several times higher in Illinois and Indiana than in Texas. These data indicate that, in these seven states, donations by the coal mining industry to state candidates do not vary predictably with coal production. Coal mining contributions in Ohio, Pennsylvania, and Virginia were high relative to coal produced, while contributions in Texas and Kentucky were low relative to coal produced. This unexpected pattern may reflect the effect of other variables, such as coal companies' financial status, on their donations.[4]

No matter the reasons for these interstate differences, dominant campaign donors within a state are likely to wield power with state politicians. Readily available campaign finance data are grouped by industry categories. The "energy and natural resources" super-category includes a long list of important sectors, ranging from aluminum mining and processing to the electric utilities to the steel industry. If state-level campaign donations from one of these sectors, such as coal mining, constitute a significant fraction of overall donations from the energy and natural resources category, politicians and officials may feel pressure to give special consideration to that sector in pollution policy making that involves coal-fired electric utilities.

Accordingly, the proportion of donations in the energy and natural resources category coming from coal mining interests is taken here as one indicator of the extent to which coal interests generally may be favored in state-level policy decisions. In Kentucky 30 percent of donations between 2001 and 2015 in the energy and natural resources sector came from the coal mining industry. In this measure Virginia rivals Kentucky, where 28 percent of donations in the energy and resources sector came from coal mining in that same period, even though in 2014 Kentucky produced 8 percent of the country's coal while Virginia produced only 1.6 percent. At the opposite extreme is Texas, where only 0.2 percent ($160,000) of energy and natural resources state campaign funds were donated by the coal mining industry, even though Texas produced 4 percent of the nation's coal in 2014. The remaining states fall in between, with the following percentages of energy and natural resource donations coming from coal mining: Ohio 20.9 percent, Pennsylvania 15.9 percent, Indiana 11.4 percent, and Illinois 7.7 percent. The coal industry's CEOs and top executives donate conspicuously to state-level campaigns in Indiana, Virginia, and Ohio, where one, two, or three super-donors, sometimes from the same family, gave combined amounts of $0.4 million, $1.7 million, and $2.2 million, respectively, between 2001 and 2015. In Illinois, one coal company, Foresight Energy, gave $1.2 million to state candidates and campaigns between 2001 and 2015.[5]

Despite the small amounts of money flowing into Texas state election campaign coffers from the coal industry, Texas is an outlier with respect to the state's high campaign donations from oil and natural gas interests. Representatives of these sectors have funded research attempting to debunk the evidence supporting global climate change, and thus their campaign contributions, if significant, are likely to influence state-level decisions involving the regulation of greenhouse gases. In Texas 70.5 percent of campaign donations between 2001 and 2015 ($74 million) in the energy and natural resources category came from oil and natural gas interests, a percentage that far exceeds those in the other six states combined. Five individual oil and natural gas industry contributors gave a combined total of $10.6 million (10 percent of energy and natural resources donations) to state-level campaigns between 2001 and 2015. Lagging far behind Texas with respect to this indicator are Illinois (19.7 percent), Indiana (8.0 percent), Kentucky (28.7 percent), Ohio (16.6 percent), Pennsylvania (25.9 percent), and

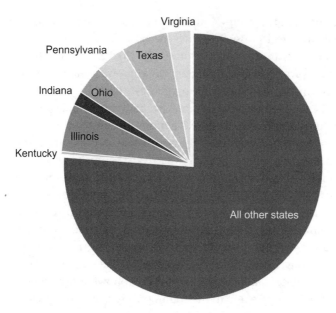

Figure 6.3
Electric utilities' donations to statewide campaigns, 2001–2015. Total = $273,063,867.

Virginia (17.4 percent). In all state-level campaigns nationwide between 2001 and 2015, Texas is outstripped only by California in absolute level of oil and natural gas campaign funds.[6]

While campaign contributions from the coal mining and oil and natural gas industries are distributed in lumpy fashion, electric utility campaign contributions are spread more evenly over all fifty states, as figures 6.3 and 6.4 show. Per capita (state resident) spending by electric utilities varies somewhat among the states examined here, but Kentucky is the only state that stands out, in this case for its relatively low donations per capita. Nationwide electric utility campaign donations to state candidates between 2001 and 2015 exceeded those for the coal mining industry by almost ten times, and donations from the oil and natural gas sectors were $391.2 million, 1.4 times those from the electric utility sector.[7]

Electric utility companies are undoubtedly important, influential political players in any state, including Texas, no matter their levels of campaign contributions. Still, a targeted question that goes to the politics of influence is whether any single electric utility company, or handful of companies, is especially prominent. That is, when a politician thinks of her electric utility backers, do a few or many of them come to mind, and are those dominant

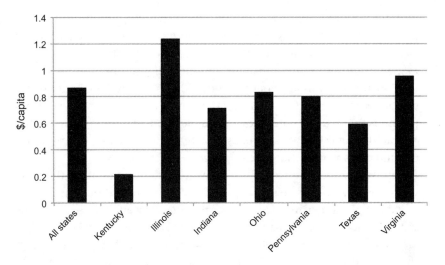

Figure 6.4
Electric utilities' campaign donations to state candidates (dollars per capita), 2001–2015.

donors heavily invested in coal-fired generation? If contributions are spread reasonably evenly among donor utilities, it is likely that no company would spring to mind more often than any other when politicians think of those who have helped their campaigns financially. Studies at the national level suggest the importance of having counterweights, or roughly equal powerful competing entities or groups, to dampen the influence of any single entity or group.[8]

The more dominant a utility in campaign finance, the more state politicians are likely to feel pressure to cater to that entity in air pollution policy making, as has happened in Virginia. Between 2001 and 2015 Dominion donated $5.3 million, or 67 percent of all electric utility funds provided to state-level candidates in Virginia. The donor that provided the second-highest percentage of overall electric utility funds, at 33 percent ($3.2 million) of total electric utility contributions, was FirstEnergy Corp. in Ohio. The highest absolute amount given by any electric utility outside of Virginia was $4.3 million, by Ameren (27 percent of all electric utility contributions), in Illinois. In Illinois, Indiana, Kentucky, and Pennsylvania, individual utility companies provided between 16 and 28 percent of total electric utility campaign contributions. All of the top utility donors in these six states operated coal-fired power plants as of mid 2016. In Texas, which by one official count has the largest number of electric utility companies of the seven states examined here, no single company gave more than 11 percent of total donations from electric utilities. In fact, between 2001 and 2015, T. Boone Pickens, an oil and wind power investor, donated more money to Texas politicians than any electric utility company.[9]

It's natural to wonder about the connection between these patterns and the presence or absence of campaign finance limits for state-level campaigns. None of these states provides public financing for state candidates. We can distinguish three categories of state limits on private contributions to candidates per election cycle: category 1, few or no limits (Virginia, Pennsylvania, Texas); category 2, some contributions limited (Indiana, Ohio, Kentucky), and category 3, all contributions limited (Illinois).[10]

Table 6.1 summarizes the results of the foregoing analysis, ordering the states by category of campaign finance limits and assigning relative industry dominance ratings in columns three through five that are summed in the far right column. Columns three and five assign scores according to the percentages of energy and natural resources donations that were given by coal, oil, and natural gas interests and the percentage of overall electric utility donations that came from the top utility donor. The scores attached to the percentages given in columns 3 and 5 are assigned as follows: 4 for 75–100 percent, 3 for 50–74 percent, 2 for 25–49 percent, and 1 for 0–24 percent. In column 4, Yes and No responses receive scores of 1 and 0,

Table 6.1
Relative campaign finance dominance ratings (dominance ratings for columns 3 and 5: 0 to 25 percent, 1; 26 percent to 50 percent, 2; 51 to 75 percent, 3; 76 percent to 100 percent, 4. See text for explanation.)

	Campaign finance limits category	Fossil % of energy and Natural resources donations (dominance rating)	Coal giving high relative to coal production (dominance rating)	Percent of all electric utility donations from top utility donor (dominance rating)	Overall industry dominance rating (sum of ratings, 2 to 9)
Pennsylvania	1	42 (2)	Yes (1)	21 (1)	4
Texas	1	71 (3)	No (0)	11 (1)	4
Virginia	1	46 (2)	Yes (1)	67 (3)	6
Indiana	2	19 (1)	No (0)	16 (1)	2
Kentucky	2	59 (3)	No (0)	28 (2)	5
Ohio	2	38 (2)	Yes (1)	33 (2)	5
Illinois	3	27 (1)	No (0)	27 (2)	3

respectively. The scores presented in table 6.1 indicate that state campaign finance limits do not prevent particular companies or industries from giving a high proportion of overall funding. Ohio and Kentucky, with some campaign finance limits, show overall dominance ratings higher than those in Texas and Pennsylvania, states with few or no campaign finance limits.

Patterns of campaign financing between 2001 and 2015 in the six big coal states and in Virginia thus reveal a spectrum in the amount of pressure state legislators and administrators might experience from industries with interests in the regulation of air pollution from fossil-fuel-fired power plants. However, every state examined here manifests at least some evidence of concentrated giving by oil and natural gas, coal mining, or electric utility interests. This kind of influence corresponds most closely to the first dimension of power, as discussed in chapters 4 and 5, when one party has the ability to coerce another into acting against her initial preferences and both parties understand that power has been expressed.

Of course, in some cases contributors may simply give to those whose preferences align with theirs. But as former Virginia Delegate Albert Pollard put it, even if a legislator votes against Dominion's position, campaign gifts might alter how strongly that legislator argues for views that might be regarded unfavorably by donors. Although the presence of dominant donors does not guarantee that politicians' views will change, there is much potential for donations to cause subtle or marked shifts in behaviors. Former US Senator Bob Kerrey, a Democrat, corroborated former Mr. Pollard's observation concerning the "bending of perspectives":

There's a big difference between corrupt and corruption … . Corruption implies a state, a constant state in which everyone is groveling and everyone is behaving in almost a bestial fashion. Whereas corrupt is, I make a decision to say something I don't really believe … . I persuade myself I've always been against raising the minimum wage and people are contributing to me because I've always been against raising the minimum wage. But the fact is I've closed my mind off to any thought of raising the minimum wage because I know it's going to cut off a significant amount of financial support if I do.[11]

Political Culture

According to Daniel Elazar, political culture is an "orientation to political action in which each political system is embedded." Political culture is durable because it is "rooted in the cumulative historical experiences of particular groups of people." The very idea that distinguishable political cultures exist and shape political processes, institutions, and outcomes is controversial. Some researchers have appeared to link "good" political culture with US democratic institutions, leading to criticisms that political culture analysis amounts to little more than smug parochialism. But leading scholars have built strong arguments about the existence and power of political cultures to shape differing, enduring political attitudes and institutions. Robert Putnam's much-cited book *Making Democracy Work* argues that political institutions and civic engagement in Italy differ regionally as a function of attitudes that originated in the Middle Ages. His claim that democratic capacity rises and falls with civic engagement rests on the identification of deep-seated political cultures.[12]

Elazar's comprehensive classification of state political cultures is a mainstay in the political science literature, even though he introduced his scheme in 1966 and the last revision was published in 1984. According to Elazar, migration patterns to and within the United States caused deeply rooted, persistent differences in political outlook. Whereas the Puritans aimed to imbue all aspects of political life with religious principles, thereby establishing a "moralistic" political culture, many settlers in Pennsylvania and other mid-Atlantic states sought to maximize individual opportunity outside of religious practice. Those immigrants favored "private pursuits from the first," and their individualistic political culture accommodated that inclination. In the South, racism and slavery fostered an elitist, aristocratic political culture that "reached its apogee in Virginia and South Carolina." Those traditionalistic tendencies were ameliorated in North Carolina and Georgia, where "a measure of equalitarianism was introduced by the arrival of significant numbers of Scotch-Irish immigrants whose traditional culture was strongly tempered by moralistic components."[13]

Elazar identified three basic state-level political culture orientations: traditionalistic (T), individualistic (I), and moralistic (M). He then classified each state and its sub-regions as, for example, as T or IT or IM, the first initial indicating the stronger strain. In a traditionalistic political culture, the status quo is the order of the day. Circles of elites, which include the wealthy and well connected, dominate political discourse, and widespread public participation in policy making is discouraged. Citizens do not feel welcome in policy-making arenas, and civil servants are viewed negatively. Policy makers in traditionalistic states will initiate new programs "if the program serves the interest of the governing elite." Leaders play "conservative and custodial" roles "unless they are strongly pressed from the outside." In individualistically oriented states, officials focus on helping maintain a healthy marketplace and will not start new programs "unless demanded by public opinion." Personal relationships and a "system of mutual obligation" animate politics in individualistic political cultures, where politics is viewed as a "dirty business" left to professionals. Some corruption "is expected in the normal course of things." Bureaucracies are viewed "ambivalently." In moralistic states, widespread participation in politics is standard. Officials in moralistic states will initiate new programs if they are deemed in the public interest, and bureaucrats are viewed positively.[14]

Elazar was careful to avoid favoritism toward any particular political culture. Thus he emphasized the strengths and weaknesses of each type, indicating that moralistic political cultures embody both "the continuing American quest for the good society" and "inflexibility and narrow-mindedness." In the individualistic political culture we find the most tolerance "of out and out political corruption" but also the "framework for the integration of diverse groups into the mainstream of American life." Moralists advocate social orderings that individualists deem violations of private freedoms, putting these two cultures somewhat in tension with one another. With the traditionalistic political culture we see both "the search for continuity in a society whose major characteristic is change" and a political economy built first on slavery and later on violation of civil rights. Traditionalistic political cultures have produced great leaders, said Elazar, but "without a first-rate elite to draw upon, traditionalistic culture political systems degenerate into oligarchies of the lowest level."[15]

Elazar recognized that political culture is "dynamic" and that every state contains elements of each political culture. For example, he described shifts in traditionalistic political cultures in the South as follows:

The traditionalistic political culture has tended to adopt individualistic elements as its traditional social bases have been eroded. With its older elites no longer in positions of power, many of its old traditionalistic attitudes transformed into bigotries designed to maintain the old racial caste system, or became unchallenged efforts, by men seeking personal profit from the changes, to maintain the political status quo. On the other side of the coin, traditionalistic modes of operation have been adapted by the economic leadership in major southern cities to create organized business dominated oligarchies committed to civic progress as a means of economic betterment. The Dallas Citizens' Council is one of the best known of these organizations, but they are to be found in most major southern cities.[16]

More than a hundred studies have used Elazar's classification scheme. Despite criticism that Elazar's scheme was not based on empirical work and that state populations have changed over time, many researchers have found strong empirical support for his basic typology. One early skeptic, Ira Sharkansky, quantified Elazar's typology on a scale of 1 to 9 and scored the states accordingly. Then Sharkansky investigated the quantitative relationship between state political culture and 23 measures of political participation, size and perquisites of the bureaucracy, and scope and character of government programs. Fifteen of the 23 variables varied with political culture in statistically significant fashion, and all varied in accordance with Elazar's typology, even when controlling for region, income and degree of urbanism. Researchers have found convincing connections between Elazar's political culture classification scheme, on the one hand, and restrictiveness of voter registration laws, voter turnout, and state government expenditures, on the other hand. In studies published just since 2002, Elazar's typology has helped explain interstate differences in the 2008 presidential primary outcomes, attitudes toward the bureaucracy, social welfare reforms, and funding for higher education.[17]

No one claims that state-level political culture determines policy outcomes. Rather, the differences Elazar identified constitute distinctive, lasting contextual circumstances that help explain variations in state-level political processes and institutions that, in turn, affect policy choices. The fact that Elazar based his scheme on immigration patterns that occurred in the seventeenth, eighteenth, and nineteenth centuries could be regarded as a strength, not a weakness, since state-level political institutions were shaped and established in those eras. Still, we must also recognize that, in the decades since Elazar crafted his typology, the US's immigration patterns have changed and racist laws that biased patterns of political participation have been overturned.

So while Elazar's scheme continues to help explain state-level differences in policies and programs, we must stay open to the possibility of cultural shifts that might modify the patterns he identified. For example, Joel Lieske supports the use of cultural strains (e.g., "global," "pluralistic," "blackbelt," and "Latino") that he derives from current US census data. Lieske does not tie these classifications to generalizations about political attitudes and the functioning of political institutions, and he uses the term "state culture" rather than "state political culture." Lieske's system provides a useful point of comparison. However, Elazar's scheme is appropriate for the purposes of this analysis, which asks questions about attitudes and norms that affect policy making.[18]

Elazar classified each state's political culture, either as a dominant strain or as a dominant plus a secondary strain. States with moralistic (M) or individualistic (I) dominant strains occur almost everywhere in the country, but the traditionalistic (T) states are found almost exclusively in the South and Southwest. Ohio and Illinois are IM, Texas and Kentucky are TI, Indiana and Pennsylvania are I, and Virginia is T. Elazar also identified subcultures

Table 6.2

Political culture classification scores. (See text and note 19 for an explanation of how these scores were derived.)

	Elazar	Thomson (based on Sharkansky)
Ohio	Individualistic-Moralistic	4.5
Illinois	Individualistic-Moralistic	4.7
Pennsylvania	Individualistic	4.9
Indiana	Individualistic	5.5
Texas	Traditionalistic-Individualistic	6.8
Kentucky	Traditionalistic-Individualistic	7.6
Virginia	Traditionalistic	8.0

within each state. So, for example, Virginia and Illinois have pockets of TM and TI subcultures, respectively. Table 6.2 shows Elazar's overall classification for Virginia and the six coal states analyzed in this chapter, as well as a numeric value derived from Elazar's assignment of state subcultures. A value of 1 indicates a purely moralistic culture, 5 corresponds to a purely individualistic culture, and 9 indicates a purely traditionalistic culture. This scoring system was derived using Sharkansky's method.[19]

Elazar identifies moralistic tendencies in Ohio and Illinois, but the scores presented in table 6.2 show those states to be more individualistic than moralistic, a conclusion that squares with Lieske's 2012 analysis. So in Illinois, Indiana, Ohio, and Pennsylvania, Elazar's scheme predicts the following political culture attitudes, which bear on who participates and how power is distributed in the making of environmental policy: ambivalent attitudes toward civil servants and bureaucracies, but a recognition that they are necessary to "enhance efficiency"; a willingness by politicians to adopt new programs if demanded by public opinion; government action to "keep the marketplace in working order"; and a sense that politics should be left to the professionals, who are expected to indulge in corrupt behavior at times. In Texas and Kentucky we would expect to find a some of these same individualistic political culture traits mixed with those found in Virginia's squarely traditionalistic culture: negative attitudes toward civil servants and bureaucrats, strong control of bureaucracies by the elite, no new programs unless supported by the elite, government viewed as a means of maintaining the existing order, and an expectation that only the elite will participate in government policy making.[20]

In political cultures with individualistic elements we would expect bureaucrats to feel somewhat empowered and to find politicians receptive to public preferences, especially if environmental programs mesh with economic goals. In traditionalistic political cultures, even strong public opinion on an issue such as climate change may not translate into public action, because of the background expectation that political elites control decision making tightly and that they will not adopt new programs unless they gain from them. Civil servants in traditionalistic states will be unlikely to challenge the status quo with information or ideas that contradict those in positions of political and economic power.

Shifts in state populations stimulated by immigration in the late twentieth century and the early twenty-first century could change longstanding institutional frameworks and policy practices. With respect to the states analyzed here, Latinos are increasingly important in Texas, and we see the growth in Illinois of what Lieske calls the "Global" subculture, a "diverse polyglot of ethnic groups," around major urban areas. An interesting thread appearing in both Elazar's and Lieske's typologies is the distinctiveness of the South, which in Elazar's scheme is dominated by traditionalistic political cultures and in Lieske's typology by "blackbelt" culture. In his classic 1949 study of Southern politics, V. O. Key placed the "black belt," regions with relatively high concentrations of African Americans, at the heart of racialized Southern politics. To this day, demographic maps show that African Americans live in high concentrations in a belt that bends to the east and the northeast from Houston to Washington. Key concluded that regional support among white Southerners for discriminatory policies was correlated with the African American population.[21]

State Legislative Professionalism

In 1948 the National Council of State Governments issued a plea for state legislatures to strengthen and professionalize. The report's authors quoted Woodrow Wilson as having said "It is the proper duty of a representative body to look into every affair of government and talk much about what it sees. It is meant to be the eyes and the voice, and to embody the wisdom and will of its constituents." Wilson wanted legislators to analyze and deliberate in deciding how to represent the public good. Around the middle of the twentieth century, some state legislatures embraced enthusiastically reforms along the lines of the National Council's recommendations, but many did not. Some state traditions applaud the idea of a citizen legislature that meets for brief sessions, has virtually no expert staff, and is poorly paid, precisely so the legislators do not become "professional politicians" who might become distant from their constituents.[22]

There are special challenges to deliberative capacity when part-time lawmakers are faced with the highly technical and politically charged issues that are part and parcel of regulating air pollution emissions from power plants. The ability to obtain and interpret specialized information is necessary to achieve independent action in the arena of air pollution policy. The more professionalized the state legislature, the more likely that body can exercise independent judgment in the environmental policy arena and the less likely that outsiders will control legislative agendas.

Peverill Squire and Gary Moncrief have indexed state legislatures on a professionalism scale that incorporates salaries of lawmakers, numbers of staff members, and length of legislative sessions. These relative rankings have remained stable with repeated computations, although Squire and Moncrief caution against making fine distinctions between states that have similar scores. In the states examined here, four legislatures (Illinois, Ohio, Pennsylvania, and Texas) are among the 15 most professionalized. By contrast, Indiana, Kentucky, and Virginia rank in the middle.[23]

Highly professionalized legislatures are more likely to possess capabilities for information gathering that reduce dependence on outsiders, whether lobbyists or executive-branch agencies, and to spend time deliberating over that information. Low staff numbers and short sessions increase vulnerability to hasty, poorly informed lawmaking. Less professionalized legislatures in Indiana, Kentucky, and Virginia have relatively small staffs (numbering 239, 406, and 391, respectively), as compared with 980 in Illinois, 2,918 in Pennsylvania, and 2,090 in Texas. However, the relatively professionalized Ohio state legislature, which meets throughout the year, has a staff of only 465. The legislatures in Illinois, Ohio, and Pennsylvania do not limit the length of their sessions, whereas those in Indiana, Kentucky, Texas, and Virginia meet for specified numbers of days. In Texas the legislature meets only every other year, for a maximum session length of 140 days; the legislatures in Kentucky and Virginia meet for one or two months every year.[24]

All the state legislatures examined here employ staffers who write reports. But the nature and scope of those reports varies, with the more professionalized legislative bodies showing a greater propensity to commission in-depth analytical studies. The Pennsylvania legislature has employed a nonpartisan Joint State Government Commission that has served as a research and policy investigation arm and has undertaken detailed analytical studies of issues such as tire recycling. The Pennsylvania legislature has also formed advisory committees of experts who have provided input to the

Commission's reports. Committees in the Texas legislature have gathered information through public hearings and have written brief reports, for example, on the potential impacts of the Clean Power Plan on electricity supply and reliability. Committees in the Illinois General Assembly have researched and written their own reports on pressing issues such as the care of elderly prison inmates, and the Illinois General Assembly has ordered executive agencies to report on issues such as the shutdown of nuclear power facilities. In Ohio, the Legislative Services Agency has written reports called "member briefs" that have provided information on complicated issues such as land conveyance. The Kentucky Legislative Review Commission has apparently spent most of its research effort on executive agency management reports, but has written occasional research reports on topics such as the equine industry and the effects of cap-and-trade policies for controlling air pollution. Legislative commissions in Indiana and Virginia appear to have focused their efforts on management evaluations of state agency performance, rather than on independently conducted research and analysis.[25]

Salary bears on legislator independence, or lack thereof. In 2015, the annual salaries of legislators in Illinois, Ohio, and Pennsylvania were, respectively, $75,884, $60,584, and $95,237, with per diem allowances (except in Ohio) while the legislatures were in session. In Indiana, Texas, and Virginia, legislators' annual salaries were, respectively, $31,238, $17,700, and $24,840, (The last figure is for Virginia state senators; House of Delegates members received $24,100.) Per diem and mileage allowances can increase compensation, as can use of campaign funds for reimbursement of travel expenses. For example, legislators in Kentucky received total compensation in 2013 that ranged from $40,327 to $90,161, but their salaries alone ranged from $13,175 to $41,975. Low paid legislators are often forced to devote considerable time to other salaried activities, despite the fact that, even in 2004, one study reported that three fourths of state legislators felt their legislative job demanded at least half of their professional time. "Citizen" legislatures have become representative bodies that demand, but do not remunerate appropriately, a professional commitment from their members. When the gap between salary and job demands is large, many talented individuals may not be attracted to elective office and state legislators may work for the industries they are supposed to regulate. Alternatively, legislators might try to set themselves up for high-ranking executive agency jobs to compensate for years of low remuneration.[26]

In the environmental policy arena, power flows to those who can collect and interpret complicated scientific, legal, and economic information. The question is, who will provide legislators with that information and how will we know who those sources are? State legislators who do not develop independent analytical capacity must depend on informal interactions, either with lobbyists or executive agency staff, or on executive agency reports. Such dependence transfers power away from the legislatures, makes their operations less transparent, and increases their susceptibility to action based on ad hoc, biased information. The second face of power anticipates that policy makers will exclude less powerful participants and points of view from consideration because of dependence on powerful entities for the very information needed to set policy agendas. Regulated entities in states with citizen legislatures can become trusted "go to" sources for analysis and information. "When you compensate a legislator well and give them a staff," Squire has concluded, "they're able to put more time into their work and actually develop some knowledge around different policies."[27]

Established rankings and this look at staff resources and current legislator pay point to the Pennsylvania legislature as having the most capacity for deliberation and independent analytical capacity. Illinois and Ohio rank next; then comes Texas, with high staff numbers but low pay and short sessions. Indiana, Kentucky, and Virginia are the weakest in terms of deliberative and analytical capacity, because of short sessions, low legislator salaries, and low staff numbers. The professionalism scores used here are derived from the inverse of Squire and Moncrief's scores and extend from 0 (high professionalism) to 10 (low professionalism). As the scores ascend, they indicate increasing level of legislator dependence on outsiders.[28]

Table 6.3 displays and adds the summary scores assigned in each subsection to show how these states rank relative to one another with respect to susceptibility to the climate of capitulation described for Virginia in chapter 4. Since the summary scores are based on simple ranking systems, they are best used to gauge relative susceptibilities. For perspective, states that do not use or produce coal to any great extent and that have relatively professionalized legislatures and strong strains of moralistic political culture, California, Massachusetts, New York, and Washington earn scores of 12.3, 13.6, 11.0, and 13.8 on this susceptibility scale. As such, we might consider that a score between 10.0 and 16.0 indicates lowest susceptibility of capitulation to electric utility and coal interests, a score between 16.1 and 22.0 indicates medium susceptibility, and a score between 22.1 and 28.0 indicates highest susceptibility.

Using this scale, of the states displayed in table 6.3, Illinois and Pennsylvania show relatively low susceptibility to a climate of capitulation, Ohio and Indiana show low to medium susceptibility, Texas and Kentucky fall

Table 6.3

Relative susceptibility to a climate of capitulation with respect to coal-related air pollution. (As explained in note 28, the most professionalized state legislature in Squire and Moncrief's analysis receives a score of 3.7 on this transformed scale. Thus, the empirical lower bound for the state legislative professionalism scale is 3.7, although the theoretical lower bound is 0. See text for description of the susceptibility score range. See text for explanation of the summed susceptibility range.)

	Campaign finance (2 to 9)	Political culture (1 to 9)	Legislative professionalism (0 to 10)	Susceptibility
Pennsylvania	4	4.9	5.2	14.1
Illinois	3	4.7	7.2	14.9
Ohio	5	4.5	6.2	15.7
Indiana	2	5.5	8.3	15.8
Texas	4	6.8	7.9	18.7
Kentucky	5	7.6	8.6	21.2
Virginia	6	8.0	8.6	22.6

into the medium susceptibility range, and Virginia shows relatively high susceptibility to a climate of capitulation. The coal states Minnesota and Maryland provide a point of comparison to these scores. Both states rely on coal for electrical power generation, but little (Maryland) or no (Minnesota) coal is mined in those two states. Their susceptibility scores using the methods outlined above are 13.3 (Minnesota) and 16.6 (Maryland).

The South stands out in table 6.3. The three states with the highest scores are Kentucky, Texas, and Virginia. The US Census includes Kentucky in the "South," but many political analysts exclude Kentucky from the South because Kentucky was not a member of the Confederacy. In Kentucky there is a spirited debate over the state's regional affinities. One online commenter remarked, "As someone who has lived in Kentucky his whole life, I can say we're a very confused state." So perhaps it's safest to say that parts of Kentucky have Southern affinities.[29]

The fact that Kentucky, Texas, and Virginia show the highest susceptibility to a climate of capitulation leads to this question: Might other Southern states prove similarly vulnerable with respect to the regulation of air pollution from fossil-fuel-fired power plants?[30]

The South

The Southern states are as vital to Clean Air Act programs concerning coal-fired power plants as are the coal states examined earlier in this chapter.

Coal is an important fuel in the eleven states of the South, taken here to mean the eleven states that formed the Confederacy during the Civil War: Alabama, Arkansas, Florida, Georgia, Louisiana, Mississippi, North Carolina, South Carolina, Tennessee, Texas, and Virginia. In 2014 the power plants in these states consumed 32 percent of coal used for electric power in the United States. Collectively the power plants in these states discharged 37 percent of carbon dioxide, 33 percent of sulfur dioxide, and 28 percent of nitrogen oxides emitted from US electrical power plants in 2014.[31]

But most of the South differs from the coal states examined earlier in this chapter because of lower coal production. In 2014, Florida, Georgia, North Carolina, and South Carolina produced no coal, and production levels in Arkansas, Louisiana, Mississippi, and Tennessee were relatively low. The South's main coal-producing states are Alabama, Texas, and Virginia, whose combined production in 2014 was about equal to that in Kentucky.[32]

For the most part, the South's low coal production is accompanied by low coal company campaign giving. In the eight Southern states outside of Alabama, Virginia, and Texas, total coal industry giving to state candidates or committees between 2001 and 2015 totaled only $593,000. We have already seen that coal interests gave relatively low amounts ($160,000) between 2001 and 2015 to support state campaigns in Texas, despite that state's relatively high coal production levels. By contrast, in Virginia coal interests provided high amounts ($6.8 million), disproportionate to the relatively small amount of coal mined in Virginia. Even though Alabama's coal mines produced about three fourths of the amount produced by Virginia's coal mines between 2001 and 2013, in that same period coal interests donated to Alabama state candidates only $1.6 million, about 20 percent of the amount given to state candidates in Virginia. Even more puzzling, campaign finance laws in both Alabama and Virginia are equally liberal: both states allow unlimited contributions by any individual or group to any candidate or committee. With respect to campaign financing by the coal industry, Virginia is an outlier as compared with its sister states in the South.[33]

Electric utility contributions to state campaigns in the South are low overall relative to the region's share of national population. Between 2001 and 2015 electric utilities provided $64.3 million to state-level candidates and committees in the South, or 22 percent of electric utility state campaign financing for the nation as a whole. The population of the South in 2014 (106 million) was 33 percent of the US total.

Table 6.4 displays the results of an analysis of dominance in campaign finance rating whose methods are identical to those used in table 6.1.

Table 6.4

Relative campaign finance dominance ratings. (Dominance ratings for columns 2 and 4: 0 to 25 percent, 1; 26 percent to 50 percent, 2; 51 to 75 percent, 3; 76 percent to 100 percent, 4. See text for explanation.)

	Fossil % of energy and Natural resources donations (dominance rating)	Coal giving high relative to coal production (dominance rating)	Percent of all electric utility donations from top utility company donor (dominance rating)	Overall industry dominance rating (sum of ratings, 2 to 9)
Alabama	35 (2)	No (0)	70 (3)	5
Arkansas	55 (3)	No (0)	42 (2)	5
Florida	10 (1)	No (0)	56 (3)	4
Georgia	43 (2)	No (0)	20 (1)	3
Louisiana	67 (3)	No (0)	44 (2)	5
Mississippi	48 (2)	No (0)	24 (1)	3
N. Carolina	28 (2)	No (0)	34 (2)	4
S. Carolina	20 (1)	No (0)	23 (1)	2
Tennessee	59 (3)	No (0)	4 (1)	4
Texas	71 (3)	No (0)	11 (1)	4
Virginia	46 (2)	Yes (1)	67 (3)	6

This analysis cannot capture the political influence of the Tennessee Valley Authority, a "corporate agency of the United States," which operates coal-fired power plants in Alabama, Kentucky, and Tennessee but gives no money to political campaigns. Considering oil and natural gas interests contributions in the South as a whole, Texas candidates were the major recipients, receiving 67 percent of funds given in state elections in the South between 2001 and 2015.[34]

When it comes to political culture, Elazar's classification scheme and numeric calculations based on his map of state subcultures put all eleven Southern states into the traditionalistic category, with many also showing individualistic elements and a few showing traditionalistic-moralistic pockets. Table 6.5 displays political culture rankings for the South derived from Elazar's classification scheme. North Carolina is almost unique in Elazar's classification scheme, sharing an overall traditionalistic-moralistic classification with only one other state, Arizona. In Lieske's 2010 typology of state cultures, which is derived from extensive analyses of census and religious

Table 6.5
Relative susceptibility to a climate of capitulation with respect to coal-related air pollution. (As explained in note 28, the most professionalized state legislature in Squire and Moncrief's analysis receives a score of 3.7 on this transformed scale. Thus, the empirical lower bound for the state legislative professionalism scale is 3.7, although the theoretical lower bound is 0. See text for description of the susceptibility score range. See text for explanation of the summed susceptibility range.)

	Campaign Finance (2 to 9)	Political Culture (1 to 9)	Legislative Professionalism (0 to 10)	Susceptibility
Texas	4	6.8	7.9	18.7
S. Carolina	2	8.8	8.4	19.2
Florida	4	7.5	7.9	19.4
Georgia	3	8.3	8.8	20.1
N. Carolina	4	8.4	8.2	20.6
Mississippi	3	9.0	8.9	20.9
Tennessee	4	8.5	8.8	21.3
Louisiana	5	7.9	8.4	21.3
Virginia	6	8.0	8.6	22.6
Arkansas	5	8.8	8.9	22.7
Alabama	5	8.6	9.2	22.8

survey data, two cultures predominate in the South: "blackbelt" and "border." Lieske identifies in these subcultures similar political-economic-social markers, to wit, low "social capital," high income inequality between races, higher voting rates for George W. Bush, and higher rates of electing African American officials. Social capital means "social networks and the associated norms of reciprocity and trustworthiness." Robert Putnam quantified social capital for all fifty states, and the eleven states that formed the Confederacy rate low on that scale.[35]

Elazar's typology and Lieske's analysis together imply a tendency in the South toward political inertia, aversion to new programs, exclusive decision making dominated by elites, weak and poorly regarded bureaucracies, persistent racial disparities, and a low sense of shared community. But strong individualistic elements allow for the possibility of government decisions supporting private initiative. Distinctive to the South as a whole is the overlap among strongly traditionalistic political cultures, deeply imbedded race-based rifts borne of slavery and Jim Crow-era discrimination and civil rights violations, and low levels of social engagement. The historian Dan Carter has layered onto this portrait a patina of "white Southern-ness," which means a "defensive conservatism" and a "need to protect a besieged social order" that has persisted even as the region's economics and culture have shifted.[36]

Table 6.5 displays susceptibility scores for the South, combining analysis for campaign finance, political culture, and legislative professionalism in a fashion similar to that for the coal states. Many state legislatures in the South fall on the lower end of the legislative professionalism scale. Legislators in those less professionalized assemblies will tend to be more dependent on outsiders for analysis and information than their legislative counterparts in states with more professionalized lawmaking bodies. The scores displayed in the last column of table 6.5 show that the Southern states show a higher susceptibility to a climate of capitulation to coal and electric utility interests than the coal-producing states of Illinois, Indiana, Ohio, and Pennsylvania.

One must exercise caution when generalizing about the politics and culture of the South as a whole. Despite the shared proclivities described here, each state's policies are distinctive and unpredictable. North Carolina and Texas have become leading producers of electricity generated by solar and wind, respectively, because of state renewable energy laws and, in North Carolina, generous tax credits for investment in renewables. In North Carolina, where Democrats and Republicans have won state offices, legislators adopted in 2002 the Clean Smokestacks Act, which required steep reductions in sulfur dioxide, nitrogen oxides, and mercury emissions from existing coal-fired power plants. Some observers are concerned that early retirement of those facilities to meet the Clean Air Act's requirements for reducing greenhouse gases might "strand" the considerable costs imposed by the Clean Smokestacks Act. In Texas, Republican politicians continue to expand the state's wind resources even while resisting climate-change policy making per se. Texans support the pursuit of energy security and a mixed energy base, inclinations shared by many US Republicans generally, who favor by a wide margin moving away from fossil fuels and toward renewables. In 2008, Florida's politicians, led by then-Republican Charlie Crist, adopted the South's only statewide law aimed at reducing greenhouse gases. Four highly populated counties in South Florida have formed a climate-change compact.[37]

Then there are the reversals and the skeptics. North Carolina lawmakers decided in 2015 not to renew generous renewables tax credits. Residents of North Carolina's Outer Banks have resisted long-term forecasts of sea-level rise because of fears over the effects of those predictions on property values. Florida's greenhouse-gas legislation was "gutted" under Governor Rick Scott (a Republican). As of 2015 Florida's state civil servants reportedly were under pressure to avoid using the term "climate change."[38]

Even if we can't predict the specific shifts and changes that typify state-level policy making, we can identify structural tendencies. This overview of political culture, campaign financing patterns, and legislative professionalism suggests the strong possibility of high susceptibility in the South generally to the climate of capitulation described for Virginia. The Southern states do not produce much coal. But they rely heavily on coal for electricity generation, even after a multi-year decline in the use of coal and a concomitant increase in the use of natural gas.[39]

Most Southern states have citizen legislators who are likely to rely on the business community for technical analysis in issue areas like energy and air pollution policy making. In two states with somewhat more professionalized legislatures, Florida and Texas, we find either a dominant electric utility (Florida) or overwhelming strength of oil and natural gas interests (Texas). The South's political cultures and long history of racial rifts reinforce political inertia, exclusivity in decision making, a regionally defensive posture, and a relatively lower inclination to engage with community concerns. These deeply imbedded tendencies, which stand outside of partisanship or public opinion and are likely to foster resistance to reducing air pollution from electrical generating facilities, complicate the Clean Air Act's shotgun marriage between the EPA and the Southern states with respect to their shared responsibilities for reducing power plant air pollution.

7 "Thus Always to Tyrants": Lessons and Reforms

The Commonwealth of Virginia's official seal, which depicts Virtue triumphant over Tyranny, features the motto "Sic semper tyrannis" ("Thus always to tyrants"). When the seal was originally designed, in 1779, the colonies were rebelling against the British for unjust exercises of power. A different kind of tyranny challenges Virginians now: the power imbalances detailed in chapters 1–3 that, in the air pollution arena, have favored electric utilities and coal interests.[1]

Power imbalances in public administration have a long history in American politics. During Franklin Delano Roosevelt's second term as president, a team of researchers led by Louis Brownlow, a noted expert on public administration, investigated whether the White House needed reorganization. A central question was how to empower the president with appropriate administrative management tools. An unstated but understood objective of the report was to help the president become a more effective executive in the face of a strong Congress and a Supreme Court that had steamrollered much of the president's New Deal legislation.[2]

In perhaps its most famous pronouncement, the Brownlow report declared, "The president needs help." Roosevelt suffered from an information deficit that diminished his capacity to govern, particularly the effectiveness of his administrative management. It was impossible for the president to locate information in the vast wilderness that was the US government. At the time, the executive branch consisted of perhaps a hundred separate agencies not gathered under department umbrellas, forming an impenetrable thicket. But the report's authors did not recommend a large executive office apparatus with a crowd of special assistants. The Brownlow Commission recommended that six executive aides help the president "obtain and interpret without delay all pertinent information possessed so as to guide him in making his responsible decisions." The entire Executive Office of the President was to consist of perhaps ten staff, "a number permitting the president to give personal direction to his staff and to have regular meetings of the whole group."[3]

The vision of a small, tightly knit, carefully selected group of aides seems quaint in an age when the Executive Office of the President commands a budget of $694 million and the White House staff alone number 450. The Brownlow Commission's purpose was to "help" strengthen the president's administrative capacity, not create a huge new bureaucracy. Still, the point remains: information is power, and presidents who do not have information at their fingertips are at a handicap.[4]

Franklin Roosevelt and his successors would certainly anticipate the tendency of legislators to micro-manage policy decisions in executive agencies and to introduce their own analyses into policy debates. Congress regularly uses its oversight and budget authority to direct or block agencies' activities. Legislatures and courts invariably weigh in on administrative decisions that might appear at first glance to lie within the purview of the executive branch. In Virginia the state legislature has often inserted itself into what some might regard as the province of executive agencies, by changing regulators' authority and mandating policy choices. Legislative oversight of, and interference with, executive agencies is common and inevitable.

Information is a critical weapon in such struggles. Presidents, heads of executive agencies, and legislators arm themselves with assistants who can obtain information and negotiate successfully to manipulate its use in policy debates. But key questions are: Who provides the information that is the basis for action by policy makers? Who "calls the fiddler's tune"? Where are the loci of decision-making power?

In the realm of air pollution policy, some state policy makers need help, much as Roosevelt did, to mitigate policy biases that result in information distortions. Virginia's climate of capitulation, described at length in chapter 4, has resulted in information biases, entrenched reluctance by civil servants and politicians to challenge regulated entities, and the propensity to adopt weak permits and regulatory limits. Important forces contributing to Virginia's climate of capitulation are the predominance of the coal industry and one electric utility in state-level campaign finance, a citizen legislature that depends on outsiders for information and analysis, and a traditionalistic political culture that fosters inertia and elite control.

But Virginia is not alone in experiencing these vulnerabilities. Chapter 6 asked if similar political, institutional, and economic forces are found in other states. That analysis indicated that all Southern states are strongly susceptible to a climate of capitulation described in chapter 4 for Virginia.

The coal states of Illinois, Indiana, Ohio, and Pennsylvania show low or low to medium evidence of susceptibility to a climate of capitulation.

This chapter sets forth a summary of the policy-making strengths and weaknesses that emerge from the three Virginia State Air Pollution Control Air Board decisions described in chapters 1–4. Those points necessarily repeat some information previously presented, to set the foundation for reforms discussed later in the chapter. Next come conclusions about the generalizability of the climate of capitulation observed in Virginia. That section draws on information, ideas, and analysis presented in chapters 5 and 6.

The final part of this chapter suggests national and state-specific reforms. Their goal is to ensure that implementation and enforcement of Clean Air Act standards, including those for greenhouse gases, can happen effectively and well even in states with constraints born of deeply imbedded political and economic predilections. The reforms also emphasize the importance of decentralized power generation in achieving the nation's goals for reducing greenhouse gases and the need to address longstanding inequalities in Appalachian communities and in low-income communities of color. Reform suggestions are linked to the faces of power literature, which helps connect biases in the exercise of political power with appropriate solutions.

Strengths in How the Virginia Cases Unfolded

Permit writing is a vitally important form of environmental policy making. Air-quality standards or regulations for large pollution sources become reality only when source-specific permit limits are written. The stakes are high, and the associated technical-legal-scientific issues involve specialized terminologies that can easily exclude the uninitiated. These challenges notwithstanding, the Virginia State Air Pollution Control Board adopted air pollution permits for the Mirant and Dominion coal-fired power plants with legally viable, technically achievable limits that were far stricter than those advocated by the staff and the management of Virginia's Department of Environmental Quality.

The Board's independent legal powers were a necessary condition for these results, and the Board members chose to exercise their authority. But the Board also depended on a large extended network of citizens and public officials. The Mirant facility's permit limits resulted from the combined efforts of citizens, the Board's majority, the City of Alexandria's staff and outside legal counsel, local and state politicians, and the Assistant Attorney General, who defended the Board's actions in court. Before the Board became involved, the City of Alexandria had established a formal community group that monitored the situation at Mirant, disseminated information to interested citizens, and provided feedback to the city council. The monitoring group constituted a bridge between the public at large and the elected politicians.

Of particular note in Alexandria were ordinary citizens who rose to the occasion. Those individuals contracted for expert analysis that cost thousands of dollars. They kept showing up, meeting after meeting, year after year, even as government officials expressed skepticism over their questions and hampered their efforts to collect information. At one point, staff members of Virginia's DEQ responded to citizens' inquiries about Mirant's production by ushering Elizabeth Chimento and Poul Hertel into "a room with 10,000 boxes" and telling them they were allowed to read documents but not to copy them.[5]

The Board also obtained large amounts of useful information from the City of Alexandria's staff and from the city's consultants. The City's outside legal counsel on Mirant, John Britton, coordinated and oversaw technical and legal analyses that illuminated the consequences of the Board's choices. The City was willing to spend a lot of money, estimated at a million dollars, on those efforts.

The Board's deliberations on Mirant, Wise, and Roda happened in the public spotlight. For all three cases, much valuable information came from the Board members' independent research and from the public comment process. The Southern Environmental Law Center repeatedly questioned the emission limits proposed by the DEQ and, through court action after the Board's issuance of the Wise County permit, ensured that Dominion would adhere to the permit's strict mercury limits. Citizens' groups brought attention to the fugitive dust problem in Roda. The Sierra Club contracted with Professor Viney Aneja, who collected air-quality data that revealed disturbingly high levels of particulate matter near people's homes.

The federal Clean Air Act was the relevant statutory authority, providing a strong framework for the Board's deliberations and decisions in Wise and in Alexandria. In Alexandria the Board relied on the Clean Air Act's prohibition against violations of the National Ambient Air Quality Standards. In Wise, a complicated set of Clean Air Act technology-based permitting requirements came into play. Determining "best" and "maximum" available technology involved research that Board members undertook personally after becoming convinced that DEQ staffers would write lax limits acceptable to Dominion Power.

Weaknesses in How the Virginia Cases Unfolded

The regulated community's incentives are to minimize costs and to pressure decision makers in the legislature and in the executive branch to write lenient standards. In 2005 DEQ Director Robert Burnley wrote a stern letter to Mirant in which he demanded strict compliance with state and federal law. Secretary of Natural Resources W. Tayloe Murphy Jr. and Governor Mark Warner supported Burnley's efforts. But after Mr. Burnley retired from government service in early 2006, and after Governor Warner and Secretary Murphy were no longer in office, DEQ staffers and managers evinced a consistent reluctance to press companies to achieve the lowest emissions possible within the constraints of the law, technological availability, and reasonable cost. Governor Kaine and his advisors supported the DEQ's inclinations and questioned the Board's decisions.

Virginia's Air Board members are unsalaried and they have no staff. Consequently, many Board members may be disinclined to undertake their own research and to make proposals independent of those suggested by the DEQ. To avoid being ciphers, Board members must be able to collect and interpret technical-legal information. State law prescribes procedures that add a thick layer of complicated administrative mandates. But because it is so difficult to master this wide variety of regulatory requirements, many Air Board members tend to defer to the DEQ's substantive and procedural suggestions.

When the Board decided, in response to public pleas, to exercise its independent legal authority for Mirant's permit, the Virginia General Assembly, the DEQ's leadership, and Governor Kaine's administration rushed to diminish the Board's powers, well before the Board had proposed any permit limits. The General Assembly's audit and reporting arm, the Joint Legislative Audit and Review Committee, did not investigate the situation or inquire into the basis for the Board's actions. Individual Virginia General Assembly members could not rely on staff members for policy analysis because their aides serve as personal assistants, not as policy experts. No matter how well intentioned a state legislator may be, Virginia's legislature meets for only a few weeks every year, making it virtually impossible to deliberate thoughtfully over complicated technical matters. In the end, two judges upheld the Air Board's permit decisions, demonstrating that the Board was an expert citizen body fully capable of understanding and implementing air pollution law.

A willingness to defend with little scrutiny the interests of coal-fired electric utilities could be related to the flow of money from companies to candidates in state elections. In Virginia, donations by the coal mining industry are unusually high relative to the state's coal production, and, as a proportion of overall energy and natural resources campaign financing, are almost unrivaled in the coal states examined in chapter 6. Of the states examined in chapters 5 and 6, only in Kentucky, one of the nation's primary coal producers, have coal mining interests given more than they do in Virginia, as a fraction of overall energy and natural resources giving. In Virginia the state's primary electricity provider, Dominion, gave 67 percent of funds provided to state candidates by the electric utilities between 2001 and 2015. Dominion sprinkles its giving far and wide and, as a result, the company has special influence with state politicians and officials of all ideological stripes, whether in the executive branch or in the legislature. In 2016 a public radio station revealed that in 2013 the DEQ's longtime director, David Paylor, had accepted from Dominion a trip to a golf tournament worth an estimated $2,370 and that during the trip he attended an expensive dinner paid for by Dominion.[6]

In the cases examined here, ordinary citizens and the City of Alexandria's local government officials showed a willingness to become involved and to undertake appropriate analyses that would illuminate policy makers' decision paths. Those actions mattered a great deal. But even in flush times not all local governments can afford the analyses needed to support such efforts. Not all citizens can act as forcefully and over as many years as did Alexandria's citizens, nor can all rural communities expect NGOs to sponsor monitoring studies, as the Sierra Club did in Roda.

Chapters 1–3 reveal an atmosphere in which state civil servants and legislators alike, from both major political parties, deferred to the regulated community on the highly technical decisions flowing from the federal Clean Air Act. The resulting imbalance of power, which favors private interests, is not a function of partisanship but, rather, of deeply imbedded attitudes and institutional structures. State-level administrative and legislative deference to coal and electric utility in the making of air pollution policy will affect the EPA's ability to coax from Virginia strong Clean Air Act plans for any air pollutant, including greenhouse gases.[7]

Public opinion has not proved to be a predictably strong driver of state-level action on climate change. As discussed in chapter 4, surveys in Virginia since 2008 have shown strong support for government action to reduce greenhouse gases. Yet the state's leadership, Republican and Democratic alike, have failed to translate that will into policies.

Implications for Other States

Coal dependence by itself does not determine a state's vulnerability to biased air pollution policy making. Of the fifty states, Illinois was the fifth-highest producer and the second-highest consumer of coal in 2014. Yet Illinois has a relatively professionalized legislature, which should enhance that body's analytical independence, and a mixed individualistic-moralistic political culture that is likely to be more receptive to action on behalf of the public good relative to traditionalistic states. Chapter 6's analysis concludes that Illinois shows low susceptibility to the climate of capitulation documented in Virginia.[8]

Some coal states have adopted policies to reduce emissions of greenhouse gases from fossil-fuel-fired power plants. Maryland's electric utilities consumed 7.4 million tons of coal in 2014, as compared with 9.5 million tons in its neighbor to the south, Virginia. By contrast with the passivity of Virginia's politicians, Maryland's legislature adopted a renewable energy act in 2004 and a plan for reducing greenhouse gases in 2009; the latter aims to reduce greenhouse-gas emissions by 25 percent in 2020 relative to 2006 levels. Maryland officials have cited the potential harm of sea-level rise in a state with a 3,190-mile coastline and 3.8 million residents who live on the coast. Virginia's coastline length and coastal population exceed those of Maryland. In America's heartland, Iowa has shown a striking dedication to wind farms, even though 53 percent of the state's electricity was fueled by coal in 2015. In that same year, wind power accounted for 31 percent of electricity generated in Iowa. Coal-dependent Minnesota has launched aggressive energy efficiency and renewable energy programs.[9]

Still, the analysis presented in chapter 6 points to coal states that are vulnerable to the climate of capitulation observed in Virginia. Particularly in the eleven states constituting the South, we find a high susceptibility to a climate of capitulation, because of part-time legislatures lacking independent analytical capability, a generalized resistance to regulation born of traditionalistic political cultures, and campaign finance donations dominated by coal, other fossil fuel, or electric utility interests. More professionalized legislatures in Pennsylvania and Ohio seem to have the institutional resources to resist manipulation by coal and utility interests, but campaign finance donations in these states have tilted toward coal interests. A handful of coal industry super-donors in Illinois, Indiana, Ohio, and Virginia are undoubtedly influential with state officials. Constrained contexts such as these can make it difficult for state legislators to keep policy agendas broad or for state civil servants to imagine taking action that displeases the business community.

Fortunately, these are susceptibilities, not inevitabilities. With appropriate state and national reforms, the potential for power biases in state-level air pollution policy making can be reduced. Reforms that address those susceptibilities should establish more democratic and inclusive processes, allow for independent development of regulatory options, and make politicians less dependent on private entities for analysis and campaign financing.

The Clean Air Act as the Nation's Climate-Change Law

At this writing, the Clean Air Act is the United States' national climate-change law. It's safe to say that no one envisioned this result in 1970, when the Clean Air Act introduced for the first time a strong federal regulatory role in cleaning up the nation's air pollution. The US Supreme Court's *Massachusetts v. EPA* ruling in 2007 paved the way for the EPA's decision to recognize greenhouse gases as pollutants and regulate their emissions from mobile and stationary sources under the Clean Air Act. Prominent environmental law scholars have asserted that, once the EPA declared greenhouse gases to be air pollutants under the Clean Air Act, regulation of existing power plant carbon dioxide emissions was legally unavoidable. Disputes in the courts have revolved around issues such as the extent of the EPA's power to reach "beyond the fence line" of electrical generating plants to include renewable sources of electricity as a possible control measure for reducing carbon dioxide emissions.[10]

The many calls for a new law that revolves around a national carbon tax or a cap-and-trade system are well intentioned. The Clean Air Act's cap-and-trade systems for sulfur dioxide and nitrogen oxides limit overall emissions and allow trading of pollution allowances among affected companies, thereby helping to foster cost-effective, innovative solutions. Pollution allowances become assets that are used only when necessary, encouraging polluters to lower their emissions below required levels and save allowances for future use or sale. Clean Air Act cap-and-trade systems for sulfur dioxide and nitrogen oxides emissions from power plants have accomplished substantial reductions whose estimated social benefits far outweigh their social costs. To take but one example, the Cross State Air Pollution Rule, which limits power plant nitrogen oxides and/or sulfur dioxide emissions in 25 states, is estimated to yield between $120 billion and $280 billion in annual health benefits, as compared with $0.81 billion in annual costs.[11]

Yet market-based systems do not necessarily hit the right environmental mark or price emission allowances correctly. The 1990 Clean Air Act's national emissions goal for sulfur dioxide emitted from power plants, 8.9 million tons in 2010, was too high, allowing too much sulfur dioxide to be pumped into the nation's air. With pollutants whose effects are felt regionally or locally, pollution "hot spots" can accompany emissions trading schemes, because regional or national pollution caps do not guarantee adequate protection in localized areas. Considerable health and environmental costs have been avoided because the EPA has used other Clean Air Act provisions to lower power plants' sulfur dioxide emissions, which stood at 3.16 million tons in 2014. One prominent economist offered this observation: "If the nation's fate with respect to sulfur dioxide emissions were left to Congress, tens of billions of dollars in additional public health and environmental costs would have been incurred. ... Fortunately, the inability of Congress to act was backstopped by the regulatory ratchet of the Clean Air Act that triggers a procession of regulatory initiatives based on scientific findings."[12]

Experts continue to argue over how to appropriately price emissions of pollutants that contribute to global warming. Debates tend to center on the virtues and flaws of cap-and-trade systems vs. carbon taxes. Trading systems require thorny decisions about the level of the emissions cap, which determines how many emissions allowances to distribute, who should receive allowances and in what quantities, and whether polluters should pay for allowances. Carbon taxes could be the source of significant revenues, in the hundreds of billions of dollars a year just in the United States, that could be used to mitigate the regressive effects of higher prices on low-income individuals or, alternatively, to lower other taxes. But setting a tax rate involves heroic assumptions about the damages and social costs imposed by greenhouse gases and the effects of those taxes on greenhouse-gas emissions. Some of the best efforts to determine the "right" carbon tax have produced estimates that vary by a factor of 5. Further, taxes tend to change behaviors—and, therefore, emissions—only over time and in unpredictable fashion.[13]

Cap-and-trade systems can generate substantial revenues, too, if polluters purchase emission allowances rather than having them allocated for free. While the European Union's carbon trading system has experienced difficulties with allowance over-allocation, low trading prices, and recalcitrant Member States, in the US regional carbon trading systems in the northeastern states and in California have already yielded valuable lessons in how to design those systems for optimal impacts. Cap-and-trade systems produce certainty about emission levels while letting the market prices of those allowances vary. Close analysis of the relative advantages and disadvantages of taxes vs. cap-and-trade systems for greenhouse gases points to the latter as providing more certainty with respect to lowering emissions predictably and timely.[14]

These debates notwithstanding, the notion of a new nationwide carbon tax or trading system enacted by Congress remains, politically, simply a theoretical idea. Although the House of Representatives passed comprehensive climate and energy legislation in the 2009 Waxman-Markey bill, Congress has not adopted a climate-change law, nor has any president, Democrat or Republican, advanced climate-change legislative proposals. Of course, carbon is already taxed in various ways, at the national and state levels, through gasoline taxes and similar policies. But when it comes to national legal frameworks, the shotgun marriage between the states and the EPA that was created in the 1970 Clean Air Act has evolved for the time being into a partnership that will set the nation's course in reducing emissions of greenhouse gases from power plants. The success or failure of that partnership will help determine whether the United States can fulfill its climate-change obligations to the world community.

Virtually all of the Clean Air Act's programs depend on strong political will and robust institutional capacity at the state level. Susceptibility to a climate of capitulation in some coal and Southern states could translate into regulatory favoritism toward big donors, information biases when policy makers depend overly on the regulated community, exclusionary participation in policy making, regulatory blind spots with respect to the effects of pollution on vulnerable communities, and reluctance by civil servants to displease regulated entities. Any of these biases could weaken the plans for controlling air pollution that the states submit to the EPA.

One does not have to look far to identify such soft spots. For example, some major utilities, including Dominion in Virginia, have advocated a "rate-based" system, rather than the alternative "mass-based" system, to control carbon dioxide emissions. Under a rate-based system, utilities in a given state must meet an average emissions rate, expressed as tons of carbon dioxide allowed per unit of electrical generation. With rate-based systems, if electrical generation increases, emissions will increase too. In a mass-based system, a state's overall greenhouse-gas emissions would be capped, pushing utilities toward greater energy efficiency and greater use of solar and wind power and other renewable power sources. Reports have indicated that, like Dominion, other utilities in the southeastern US may press for rate-based state plans. US Department of Energy forecasts have predicted increases in carbon dioxide emissions if many states adopt rate-based standards for controlling emissions from electric utilities. With mass-based systems, states' carbon dioxide emissions for power plants cannot increase, even if demand for electricity grows.[15]

The Clean Power Plan also suffers from a truncated time horizon. No provisions exist for further emission reductions after 2030. The consensus is that deep, sustained reductions in the emission of greenhouse gases (on the order of 2 percent per year), starting in 2011, from the United States and other industrialized nations will be needed to avoid catastrophic global damage from a warming atmosphere.[16]

A relatively unused part of the Clean Air Act, Section 115, offers possible statutory authority for the EPA to require increasingly stringent reductions that could stretch past 2030 and cover a wide variety of greenhouse-gas emitting sources from all US states. Section 115 says that, when the EPA Administrator "has reason to believe that any air pollutant or pollutants emitted in the United States cause or contribute to air pollution which may reasonably be anticipated to endanger public health or welfare in a foreign country," the Administrator shall require revised plans from the polluting states. A reciprocity determination is necessary to demonstrate that the nation adversely affected by the United States' emissions will provide, with respect to pollution emitted within its borders, "essentially the same rights with respect to prevention or control" to the United States. Careful legal analysis indicates that the reciprocity test could be met, given the many substantive commitments to reducing greenhouse gases that other nations have provided, and that by invoking Section 115 the US does not appear to risk undue interference by other nations in the making of domestic air pollution policy. Section 115's authority could provide the framework needed to set state caps for greenhouse gases that continue to decrease over time, much as has been the case for sulfur dioxide emissions from power plants, while allowing states the chance to decide how to implement those limits.[17]

New Opportunities for Meaningful Citizen Engagement

Provide Grants for Citizen Analysis

In the early years of my work on the Virginia State Air Pollution Control Board, one fellow member seemed incredulous at the notion that the Board would adopt policy options stricter than those advocated by regulated entities. As I recall this brief exchange, which happened long ago but made a strong impression, the other Board member said, why should we consider options that the regulated community doesn't support? Aren't they our constituency? A well-placed manager at the DEQ was fond of saying that there were no air-quality problems in the Commonwealth of Virginia. These sentiments reflect the characteristics of traditionalistic political cultures in which elite interests matter most, new programs are viewed with skepticism, and inertia reigns. States with traditionalistic political cultures, such as those in the South, are especially likely to manifest worldviews that resist change or that, in the words of one historian, "defend a besieged social order."[18]

The acceptance of an order in which polluting sources are viewed as the ultimate authority on how they should be regulated implies a deeply imbedded shaping of perceptions that happens through the third face of power. In the third face of power, wants and beliefs are shaped over time through relationships between agents and subjects of power. The powerful come to assume their views will prevail and that their ideas will be regarded as the most legitimate. Traditionalistic political cultures involve hierarchies and exclusiveness that come about via the third face of power. Those in inferior positions, such as civil servants, defer to those in power and allow themselves to be coerced because they assume that is the natural, immutable order. Government authorities have legitimacy, but their role is "limited to securing maintenance of the existing social order." Agency representatives are expected to know their place.[19]

Traditionalistic political cultures found in many Southern states are inseparable from the region's long history of racial oppression and slaveholding. Slavery and Jim Crow laws involved overt expressions of power and institutionalized racism. But since the civil rights era, and as political processes and participation have become more open to African Americans and other minorities, subtler kinds of framings have helped maintain embedded systems of power. In the place of overt race-based oppression, we see in the South a yearning by some to protect old forms of order, a "defensive conservatism."[20]

In environmental policy making, such value systems privilege the views of the regulated community, foster a low regard for civil servants, make it difficult for members of the general public to participate meaningfully, and overlook the full spectrum of needs in economically and politically vulnerable communities such as those in southwest Virginia. Chapters 1–3 illustrate the many ways in which DEQ staffers and managers, despite good intentions, deferred to corporate interests. Institutionally enforced timidity likely played a role in DEQ staffers' behaviors and attitudes. When I joined the Air Board in 2002, it had only been a few years since the General Assembly's Joint Legislative Audit and Review Commission had reported that, "nearly half of DEQ's employees fear for their jobs if they make a decision consistent with law or regulation that upsets a member of the regulated community."[21]

Some of Virginia's elected politicians have been staunch defenders of the economic and political status quo. The General Assembly and two Democratic governors decided summarily that a new coal-fired power plant in southwest Virginia would be in the public interest. Members of the General Assembly asserted that Dominion would be a responsible corporate actor and control its pollution to the extent necessary to comply with the law. In challenging the regulated community's views, the Air Board was by definition "rogue" and suspect, even though the Boards' permit limits for the Wise and Mirant facilities, which were far stronger than those proposed by the DEQ and the regulated companies, held up in court.

Favoritism toward the regulated community manifests itself in other ways. The Virginia DEQ's "stakeholder" group on the state's Clean Power Plan had fourteen members, nine of whom represented electric utilities, a coal company, the state's manufacturing association, or a power plant management firm. Biases favoring regulated entities can take the form of small budgets for regulatory agencies, to weaken those organizations. An agency's size is not always correlated with its strength. When agencies are kept small, however, staff members imagine their authority as circumscribed.[22]

Independent analysis and outside oversight can help when agencies are either resource lean or susceptible to bias toward regulated entities. In Virginia, citizen research and input helped point the way to appropriately stringent standards. Federal or state funds should be available for citizens to undertake independent assessments of air pollution problems. Under Sections 103(a) and (b) of the Clean Air Act, the EPA may "make grants to air pollution control agencies, to other public or non profit private agencies, institutions, and organizations, and to individuals" for studies "relating to the causes, effects (including health and welfare effects), extent, prevention, and control of air pollution." These provisions include the possibility of citizen grants used to study local air pollution problems.[23]

The EPA already provides grant support for such endeavors in specialized areas. State air pollution agencies and Indian tribes are the main awardees. In 2015, Section 103 grants amounted to $37 million. Most of that funding underwrote monitoring of ambient fine particulate matter, and some of it was devoted to monitoring for air toxics and nitrogen dioxide. With an enlarged Section 103 grant program, citizens or local government authorities could hire experts and undertake studies, with the purpose of illuminating state and federal legal requirements, interpreting permit precedents,

developing regulatory options, and collecting relevant economic, demographic, public health, and environmental data. Even a modest amount
of funding, perhaps $10 million a year for projects around the country,
would reinforce greatly the ability of citizens and citizen regulatory authorities to undertake independent analyses. Some states have resources that
might be used for similar purposes, such as Virginia's Emergency Response
Fund, which is fed by fines and penalties. That fund's resources can be used
for "development and implementation of corrective actions for pollution
incidents." At the end of 2015, that Fund had a balance of $14.2 million,
although the Virginia DEQ plans to use those resources over the next ten
years to remediate contaminated sites.[24]

Form Regional Citizen Oversight Bodies

The case studies described in chapters 1–3 underscored the importance of
the Air Board's expertise, its independent decision-making authority, and
its members' choice to exercise that authority in service of Clean Air Act
goals. A reform deriving from this observation would institute new air pollution citizen oversight committees for each of the EPA's ten geographic
regions. The EPA's regional offices, located in San Francisco, Philadelphia,
and other major cities, provide the agency's interface with state pollution-control agencies. Citizen oversight committees would help the EPA's
regional office staff evaluate Clean Air Act plans submitted by the states,
to include, but not be limited to, anticipated regulation of carbon dioxide
from power plants.

These committees would not have legal decision-making power, following the general model of national government advisory committees formed
under the Federal Advisory Committee Act of 1972. Rather, they would
be advisory. The EPA has appointed many such committees. As is the case
for many federal advisory committee members, air pollution planning
oversight committee appointees would be compensated for their time and
travel expenses.[25]

To counterbalance conversations about policy making that are too often
biased toward the regulated community, each planning oversight committee should be made up of citizens who bring relevant background with air
pollution issues but who do not work for private entities directly regulated
under state plans. To ensure that the committee members speak independently and not on behalf of any organization, they should not employed
by an environmental or public health advocacy group. In each EPA region,
a committee of five to seven individuals would be appointed for fixed terms
of several years, to help evaluate the adequacy of state Clean Air Act plans.

The committees' charge would be to advise the EPA's Regional Administrators, the top officials in the EPA's regional offices, on technical, policy, and legal aspects of the state plans submitted in that particular region. Each state in the region would have at least one committee member responsible for being knowledgeable on air pollution issues in that particular state. A part-time staff member for each regional committee would organize meetings and help perform research. Committees could share information across regions.

The oversight committees would advise the EPA on whether to approve or disapprove state plans, and they would provide input for the federal backup plans that the EPA must adopt for states submitting unacceptable plans. The committees could commission independent analyses, using Clean Air Act or state funding sources such as those described in the section immediately above. Their deliberations would be open to public comment and they would vote in public on their recommendations. Meetings would be held several times a year in locations scattered across each EPA region— some in economically vulnerable and minority communities, whose input should be actively sought and whose exposures to air pollution should receive special attention from the oversight committees.

Independent citizen oversight advisory committees can help the EPA make difficult judgment calls on state-proposed air pollution plans, on a case-by-case basis. In theory, state-level agencies can foster more widespread participation in state-level air pollution policy decisions than can the EPA's regional offices. But policy makers in states susceptible to a climate of capitulation may not have the institutional capacity or the political will to implement the Clean Air Act in unbiased fashion. The ongoing efforts to provide clean air for all Americans and the nation's climate-change commitments to the world community are at risk in states characterized by a climate of capitulation. Disapproving state plans, or parts thereof, is a non-trivial decision, and the EPA must then find the resources to implement the particular Clean Air Act provisions that would have been delegated to the state, had they not failed to meet federal standards. The oversight committees could help mitigate the corrosive effects of state-level favoritism toward the regulated community and provide an extra set of helping hands for the formidable task of evaluating state plans submitted under the Clean Air Act.[26]

The oversight committees' perceived legitimacy and power would hinge on their members' expertise, lack of obligation or ties to the regulated community or to advocacy groups, and independence. In the recent past, such committees have suffered from a reputation for providing business representatives yet another avenue for molding government policies to their liking. In the early 2000s, the EPA's Science Advisory Board came under fire for violating conflict-of-interest procedures and failing to ensure that members brought independent views to the table. Because of perceptions that government advisory committees had been "stacked" with business-sector lobbyists, the Obama administration banned registered lobbyists from such committees. In the 1970s, representatives of the private sector dominated some state-level citizen environmental boards. With the citizen oversight committees proposed here, it would be crucial to ensure careful appointments. Attracting leaders for these committees is possible only if they have their own staff member and if members are compensated fairly for their time, in keeping with practices used for other federal advisory committees.

EPA policy makers must take these committees seriously, to avoid having them become "nothingburgers," the term former EPA Administrator Anne Gorsuch famously gave to one such federal advisory body for which President Reagan had nominated her. The committees must have clear, regular access to high-level officials in the EPA's regional and headquarters offices. They must actively seek input from members of the public who might be intimidated to speak up and the committees must deliberate in public. They must set their own agendas and have independent analytical capability. With strong appointees not affiliated with the regulated community and genuine access to the EPA's decision makers, these oversight committees can help counteract state-level climates of capitulation that threaten to slow the nation's progress in improving air quality and meeting global responsibilities to reduce greenhouse-gas emissions. [27]

"You've Got to Dance with Them What Brung You": Campaign Finance Reform

It's hard to resist the conclusion that, in Virginia and some other states, state-level politicians accept funds in exchange for company access and influence. Texas journalist and satirist Molly Ivins adopted the adage, "You've got to dance with them what brung you," as the title for one of her books. In a C-SPAN interview she explained: "This is one of the oldest expressions in politics and what it means is, when you get to public office, you vote with the folks who put you there. That used to mean your constituents, the people who voted for you. But more and more what it means is, you vote with the special interests who put up the money to get you to public office." Some politicians accept campaign finance funds from companies whose positions match theirs. But in other cases, campaign donors win the opportunity to present their side and to remind candidates of their financial clout. Candidates and politicians can undoubtedly name their most important backers and the state's dominant campaign finance donors, too.[28]

The figures and analyses presented in chapters 4–6 bear repeating, for they underscore the varying degrees to which companies and industries dominate giving in state-level campaigns. Unless otherwise specified, all figures given here refer to donations between 2001 and 2015 to candidates for state-level political office. Virginia's dominant electric utility, Dominion, donated far more money to state political candidates than any other company. In election year 2015, most candidates for state-level office accepted funds from Dominion. In Virginia, coal companies gave 28 percent of all funds donated by energy and natural resources interests to state candidates, an unusually high proportion relative to all the other coal states examined. In Kentucky, with much higher coal production and consumption than Virginia, the coal industry provided 30 of campaign donations from the energy and natural resources sector as a whole. A handful of coal industry super-donors in Illinois, Indiana, Ohio, and Virginia donated between $400,000 and $2.2 million to state candidates. In Texas 70 percent of funds contributed by energy and natural resources interests came from the oil and natural gas sectors, and five super-donors gave together individually $10.6 million, or 10 percent of all funds from the energy and natural resources sector. Individual electric utility companies are dominant donors in campaign contributions for some of the Southern and coal states examined in chapter 6.

State campaign contribution limits do not prevent a company or industry from becoming a predominant force. Ohio, Kentucky and Illinois limit contributions in some fashion, but individual electric utility companies or the coal industry generally have been powerful donors in each of those states. Contribution limits that cap the amount an entity can give to a particular candidate or political committee do not keep that entity from spreading contributions far and wide, thereby become a powerful funding force overall.

The solution to this problem seems obvious: state reforms that limit overall giving by any individual donor might help remedy a system in which donors are likely to feel compelled to "pay to play" and in which candidates feel pressure to listen closely to their most generous backers. But the US Supreme Court has struck down restrictions on the total amount donors may give in national-level political campaigns, with the view that aggregate limits unconstitutionally burden donors' participation ("speech") in the electoral process. Wealthy individuals can donate to as many candidates for national elective office or political action committees as they like, up to the contribution caps for each candidate or committee. The expected effect is that corporate political action committees will receive even more money than before from rich individuals. Those committees will then be able to contribute up to the applicable limit for even more candidates than before. As a result of the Supreme Court's decisions, six states have already decided not to enforce their aggregate donation limits. The National Conference on State Legislatures predicts that any remaining state-level aggregate finance limits will disappear.[29]

Critics point out that allowing the rich to donate even more money to campaigns will magnify existing policy biases toward wealthy individuals and corporations. Former Senator Alan Simpson, a Republican, practically breathed fire when he wrote in December 2015: "Money's dominance over politics isn't merely one of the problems our country faces. It is *the* problem ... . Either we are a country that makes decisions based on the common good, or one where the size of your wallet determines the validity of your ideas. Either we uphold the values of a representative democracy, or we allow greed and wealth to destroy the world's greatest experiment in self-governance."[30]

With respect to adopting restrictions for greenhouse-gas pollution, former Senator Bob Kerrey, a Democrat, spoke about parallel campaigns by advocacy groups and their ability to make him "afraid to do what I think is right": "You're sitting there saying, 'Is Americans for Prosperity going to advertise against me in a primary, yes or no?'" The very prospect of a negative parallel campaign is enough to make politicians change their votes and attitudes. These are classic expressions of the first and second dimensions of power: sometimes, powerful interests donate funds to make politicians indebted to them. Sometimes implied threats of a negative campaign suffice to make politicians change their positions and votes.[31]

In late December 2015, Virginia Governor Terry McAuliffe (a Democrat) announced a circumscribed set of recommendations from his climate-change commission. By the governor's side was Thomas Farrell II, the CEO of Dominion. Farrell is one of Virginia's wealthiest donors and gave $267,996 to state campaigns between 2001 and 2015. Dominion has been Governor McAuliffe's top Virginia campaign donor in the energy and natural resources sector, even though, during his campaign for governor in 2009, McAuliffe claimed he would take no money from Dominion. In the wake of the scandal surrounding former Virginia Governor Robert McDonnell's corrupt practices while in office, observers of Virginia politics say it's time to implement ethics reforms that include campaign finance reforms. McDonnell was convicted of accepting money and favors from a businessman in exchange for promoting the business. The US Supreme Court subsequently overturned McDonnell's conviction because of questions about whether the quid pro quo in question involved an official act.[32]

In light of these considerations, the best readily available reform may be for states to provide public financing to candidates who refuse private financing of any kind. Such "clean election" systems exist in Arizona, Connecticut, and Maine. In Arizona a candidate who raises $5 from each of at least 200 individuals receives public funds. Of course, these systems are not fail-safe. Candidates may still choose to raise private funds rather than receive public financing, and privately financed candidates may well raise funds exceeding those available to publicly funded candidates.[33]

Public financing systems do not prevent the financing of parallel campaigns by political action committees. But with public financing, voters know which candidates have accepted funds from wealthy interests and which candidates have opted out. Small contributors become important because they help candidates become eligible for public financing. Candidates who win with public financing are not directly beholden to superdonors or corporate interests. Many state legislature candidates might be relieved to accept public funds, especially those who need only a few thousand dollars to run their campaigns. Candidates might relish the prospect of never feeling obligated, of being free to make decisions without fear of alienating financial backers.[34]

Such reforms would take time and considerable public pressure to come into being, no matter the state. In the short term, interested citizens might undertake a "sunshine in government" campaign. It would be a reasonably straightforward matter to post on a website the amounts politicians accept from energy interests, accompanied by a list of those politicians' policy decisions, non-decisions, or legislative votes related to air pollution.

Increase State Legislators' Independence

In the making of environmental policy we must keep the policy agenda open to a wide variety of options and players. Achieving that seemingly simple goal requires a great deal of vigilance. Scholars who have studied the exercise of the "second face of power" have shown that powerful actors can easily restrict the range of ideas considered. When the second face of power comes into play, "Power is exercised when A devotes his energies to creating or reinforcing social and political values and institutional practices that limit the scope of the political process to public consideration of only those issues which are comparatively innocuous to A."[35]

In his study of how the second face of power manifests itself, the political scientist Matthew Crenson described US Steel's ability to keep air pollution regulation off of the local government agenda in Gary, Indiana, during the 1950s. US Steel wielded power not through any overt action but simply by being the biggest gun in town: "The reputation for power may have been more important than its exercise. It could have enabled US Steel to prevent political action without taking action itself, and may have been responsible for the political retardation of Gary's air pollution issue."[36]

Another example of the exercise of the second face of power involved the Virginia General Assembly's decision in 2006 to preclude the Air Board from considering a particular regulatory option for mercury air pollution from power plants. In that incident, related in detail in chapter 2, the General Assembly prevented the Board from even taking comment on a rule that many other states had already adopted. Instead, the General Assembly enacted, without analysis or consultation with Board members, a law that ordered the Board to adopt the EPA's cap-and-trade program, which was widely regarded as illegal. Dominion and the state's other electric utilities were never forced to speak publicly for or against the choices offered by the Board. The EPA's cap-and-trade approach was eventually struck down in federal court as a violation of the Clean Air Act. The General Assembly's willingness to constrain the Board's agenda to the legally questionable option favored by the electric utilities is a classic example of how the powerful can manipulate policy agendas.[37]

Part-time citizen legislatures do not have sufficient tools at their disposal to keep interest groups from suppressing legitimate environmental policy alternatives. By contrast, members of professionalized legislatures are more likely to accumulate knowledge comparable to that of other political actors, and, consequently, they are less likely to be at a disadvantage with respect to the executive branch or lobbyists. For example, in the professionalized California legislature, Assemblywoman Fran Pavley was able to lead legislative efforts to regulate greenhouse gases. Despite the institutional limits of their positions, some Virginia legislators develop environmental expertise and are recognized for proactive leadership. Former Secretary of Natural Resources and longtime state delegate W. Tayloe Murphy Jr. personifies such an exception, but he has bemoaned Virginians' "tradition of passing the buck" with respect to environmental protection.[38]

Nine of the legislatures in the sixteen coal or Southern states examined in chapter 5 rank middling to low with respect to indices of professionalization.

When state legislators in less professionalized assemblies are faced with highly technical problems such as those confronted in the air pollution arena, they are likely to lack independent sources of information to inform their debates and decisions. Especially when legislatures meet for only a few weeks a year, members do not have sufficient time to collect and absorb background information needed to develop a list of policy options, discuss those options among themselves, and decide based on a deliberative, informed process. States with citizen legislatures generally lack staff attorneys and analytical experts.[39]

The political traditions of many states with citizen legislatures rest on the idea that legislators should keep their regular jobs and conduct short legislative sessions to avoid becoming professionalized. But there are compelling arguments for citizen legislatures to consider professionalizing themselves. Scholars who have studied all fifty legislatures conclude that professionalized legislatures perform better on a variety of important measures:

Lawmakers in more professional legislatures have more contact with their constituents, are more attentive to their concerns, and are more representative of their views than are their counterparts in less-professional legislatures. Member voting is affected, with lawmakers in more professionalized legislatures asserting greater independence from their parties. Legislative efficiency—the percentage of bills passed and the number of bills enacted per legislative day—goes up with professionalization level … . More professionalized legislatures are better able to counter gubernatorial influence in the budget process, to resist a governor's policy agenda … . Bureaucrats are more effectively constrained and have less influence on legislative outcomes in more professionalized legislatures … . Higher levels of professionalization are associated with … stronger environmental and renewable energy programs … . More generally, professionalized legislatures are also better able to mediate policy disputes, thereby reducing the motivation for interest groups to turn to citizen initiatives in the states that allow them.[40]

In fact, many legislatures are part-time in name only. Legislators in citizen assemblies complain they are overworked and undercompensated, and academic observers agree. Further, low levels of compensation make these bodies unrepresentative of the state population at large. One Republican representative in North Dakota's House put it this way: "I think when we make it a policy to underpay ourselves so we look good to the public, we limit this chamber to people of a certain amount of means. I don't think that's right." State legislators fear that "We're missing young people because they cannot afford to be here." These are not just intuitions. A comparison of the average ages of all state legislators in 2015 with Squire's index of legislative professionalism shows that, with some scatter and a few exceptions, average age of state legislators tends to decline as professionalization increases.[41]

There are many degrees of professionalization, and there is plenty of room for citizen legislatures to pick the path that makes the most sense without surrendering dearly held identities. But the evidence indicates that expert staffs, longer sessions, and higher pay make state legislatures more responsive to their constituents' views, more knowledgeable on the matters that come before them, and better able to stand their ground when faced with interest groups. The combination of more resources and higher pay seems to motivate state legislators to listen carefully to public opinion. More professionalized legislatures are younger, which encourages an infusion of new ideas. Professionalized legislatures are better able to change public perceptions that state legislatures are places where representatives debate frivolous matters, such as how to style the possessive form of "Arkansas," or that they are susceptible to incompetence and corruption.[42]

Term limits weaken state legislatures relative to the executive branch. At the same time, term-limited legislators seem to be more inclined to think about the interests of the state as a whole than about just those of their constituents. Unfortunately, it does not follow that term-limited legislators would free themselves of manipulation by corporate interests, in light of evidence that some state legislators use their political positions as stepping stones to more lucrative positions in the private sector.[43]

Among the tools available for increasing professionalization are lengthening sessions and hiring bipartisan research staffers who can provide independent analysis. Even a small cadre of staffers with the appropriate technical-legal backgrounds would improve legislators' ability to exercise thoughtful, independent judgment. A few examples illustrate this point. Through Pennsylvania's bipartisan Joint State Government Commission, legislators form task forces, inform themselves through advisory committees of experts, and sponsor lengthy staff-written reports. For one example, in 2015 the Commission authored a 117-page study on truancy, with extensive analysis and associated policy recommendations. The Commission also conducts short-term staff studies. In North Carolina a research division in the legislature employs attorneys and analysts who analyze proposed legislation. The North Carolina legislature undertakes studies with the help of staffers in a Research Division.[44]

At the same time, there is evidence that increased pay for state legislators goes hand in hand with higher dependence on campaign donors, before and after elections. It would be counterproductive to increase legislators' pay, with the goal of enhancing their capacity to govern well and to represent constituents in environmental policy, without establishing protections against dependence on campaign funding by special interests. As was elaborated above, providing public funding for campaigns may help relieve pressure on legislators to favor powerful members of the business community.

In most endeavors, when we want competent help, we hire professionals. This expectation should apply to state assemblies, too—especially those in the coal states and the South, whose strength and capacity in the environmental arena should be bolstered by thoughtfully professionalizing them in order to counteract manipulation by interests opposed to regulatory standards that meet the letter of the Clean Air Act.

Encourage Decentralized Power Generation and Address Longstanding Inequalities

Public financing for state-level candidates, professionalization of state legislatures, and oversight of states' air-pollution-control efforts by citizens' committees should help diminish the political power that fossil-fuel interests and electric utility interests wield in the making of air pollution policy. But those reforms will not change the concentrated economic power of the electric utilities and those who supply them with fuel. Fortunately, technological and policy shifts that help diffuse control over electricity generation can also serve to decrease our reliance on fossil fuels.

Americans have become voracious consumers of electricity. In 1960 the per capita generation of electricity in the United States was approximately 4,000 kilowatt-hours. By 2015 it had increased to about 13,000 kilowatt-hours. The US Energy Information Administration predicts that growth in electricity use and growth in gross domestic product will continue to be linked, but that electricity consumption will grow more slowly than the overall economy for the foreseeable future. Slower rates of growth in electricity consumption could happen because of greater efficiency brought about by government standards, the trend in the US economy toward less energy-intensive industries, and a slowing of population growth. Predictions of slow growth in electricity consumption present a problem for the industries that supply electricity and for those that sell fuels to electricity generators.[45]

The electric utilities may not have to worry about stimulating demand for their product. Americans depend heavily on electronic devices for communication, shopping, and research, among other activities. For that reason, power outages are not merely inconvenient; in addition, they decrease productivity and are debilitating and isolating. Electric utilities use our addiction to our electrically powered devices to justify the construction of more huge generating stations, warning that, without new capacity, outages will become more frequent. Even more than before, such prospects threaten to interfere with productivity and our everyday lives. State utility regulators can be hard pressed to argue for increasing energy efficiency or for programs whose goal is to manage electricity demand.

Fortunately, the twenty-first century promises modes of renewable and decentralized electricity generation that can save energy and put more control in the hands of individual residences and businesses. If government entities continue to subsidize and incentivize these possibilities, we can reduce the economic clout of electric utilities and fossil-fuel interests and reduce power plant air pollution simultaneously. We can also eliminate a part of the huge energy losses that occur during electricity generation, transmission, and distribution. At present, 65 percent of the primary energy that goes into making electricity is simply lost.[46]

In some states, these possibilities are already being realized through distributed generation (i.e., the use of small generators close to the point of use) and through systems that rent land from individuals for solar energy harvesting or for wind towers. In Hawaii the combination of high energy prices, tax credits, and plentiful sunshine has led many homeowners to install solar photovoltaic systems. Tax incentives in sunny Arizona fostered a similar rush to install rooftop solar systems. States have stimulated solar installation by crediting individuals for self-generated electricity that flows back into transmission lines ("net metering"), through strong policies for connecting individual generators to the grid ("interconnection"), by requirements that electric utilities invest in renewable sources of generation, and through "creative financing."[47]

Distributed generation and demand-side management hold great promise for releasing us from our dependence on centralized utilities and on producers of fossil fuels. However, the policies that support these systems can be unpredictable because government authorities sometimes change them or abandon them in midstream. Distributed generation is not problem-free. When customers reduce their demand for conventionally generated electricity, the cost of maintaining infrastructure like transmission lines must be spread across fewer customers. If rates then rise to compensate for lower demand, even more customers will have incentives to reduce their use of centrally provided electricity by investing in energy efficiency measures or in distributed generation systems. Analysts warn utility investors of a disruption comparable to that when the telephone industry, previously a regulated monopoly, transformed utterly because of changes in government regulation and technological development. Wind farms built by the electric utilities do not pose the same threats to the industry's profits and economic strength, although investment in wind power has the potential to reduce the economic power of the fossil-fuel industries.[48]

State policies for promoting wind power have worked in part because of their equitable impacts, which come about when such programs benefit households and small businesses. Iowa and Texas are leaders in wind power generation despite being coal states. Iowa has attracted many businesses because of the state's dedication to wind power and the state's ample wind resources. One report indicates that in Iowa "Farmers kind of see wind as a second cash crop" because of property tax incentives and lease arrangements. In 2014, wind farms in Texas produced 20 percent of the wind-generated electricity in the United States—a result attributable to the state's renewable portfolio standard and various subsidies, including state support for transmission lines. In Texas and Iowa these policies have been embraced by Republicans.

In both states a vital factor in promoting wind farms has been economic stimulus to rural or economically depressed areas. Such programs have succeeded because of their financial benefits to a broad segment of the population and because they help people of ordinary means. Many states will undoubtedly incorporate wind power when reducing carbon dioxide emissions from power plants in ways that will fuel economic development where it is most needed.[49]

Revenues from state and regional cap-and-trade programs to reduce carbon dioxide emissions from power plants can also help address important equity concerns. Carbon trading systems can involve the sale of emissions allowances. To give but one example of the possible scale of revenues generated from cap-and-trade programs, revenues from carbon allowances sales in Ohio could exceed $500 million per year. Some of those revenues could be directed to communities traditionally dependent on coal mining that have satisfied our electricity appetites for decades.[50]

Coal mining regions deserve a helping hand in the form of sustained economic development and waste cleanup. Such support could take the form of renewable energy development and remediating the damaged lands and ecosystems coal mining companies have left in their wake. Addressing those inequities is only fair, given the extensive social, health, and environmental costs coal communities have borne on behalf of the rest of the nation. Land restoration in Appalachia would also help revive some of the nation's richest temperate ecosystems.[51]

No matter how future decisions shape future state-federal partnerships to reduce power plant emissions, the federal and state governments can follow the example of Germany and continue to foster emission reductions through energy policy. Even though Germany has no national climate law, and despite the fact that Germany mines and burns a great deal of coal, national energy laws there have fostered widespread investment in energy efficiency and in solar and wind energy. A host of related national regulations have aimed to reduce energy consumption, boost investment in renewable sources of energy (wind, solar, and biomass), increase energy efficiency, lower greenhouse-gas emissions, and increase energy independence. Germany's feed-in tariff system, which guarantees to investors in renewable electricity payment over the long term for electricity returned to the grid, has let communities take charge of their own electrical generation. One result of this system is that individuals, not utilities, hold almost half of Germany's renewable energy capacity. Between 2003 and 2014 renewable generating capacity in Germany tripled, increasing to 28 percent of electricity generated in 2014. By equating renewable energy investment with personal profit that can be realized by individual households, low-carbon solutions have become widely popular. Still, Germany's system has been criticized for regressive effects on consumers of modest means, pointing to the need to design systems in the United States that spread program costs equitably.[52]

"Intervening on Behalf of National Values"

Equity and democracy are at the core of this book's observations and recommendations about the politics of influence at the state level. Ideally, many groups and voices should have power in policy making. Government authorities should not listen preferentially to certain groups over others. Citizens generally should control their government

It would be nice to believe this balance establishes itself naturally in the US political system. However, the political scientist E. E. Schattschneider observed that the problem with those who believe in the "pluralist heaven" is that "the heavenly chorus sings with a strong upper-class accent." The Clean Air Act's shotgun marriage between the states and the EPA has worked unevenly and, especially in coal states, is susceptible to a climate of capitulation that rests on deeply embedded constraints born of political culture, institutional design, and patterns of campaign finance. In a climate of capitulation, coal and energy interests thwart state-level efforts to protect public health and welfare in accordance with the Clean

Air Act's mandates. Unless powerful elites are checked, they tend to muscle others out of the environmental policy arena. As the Pulitzer Prize–winning author Marilynne Robinson has pointed out, sometimes the national government must intervene to protect national values when subnational governments oppress, rather than protect, the public good.[53]

Much ink has been spilled over whether, and to what extent, private interests have captured government regulators and lawmakers. Based on my thirty years of experience as a policy maker and as professor of environmental policy, I do not subscribe to public choice theory generally, which holds that companies manipulate and control elected and appointed public servants to a great and catastrophic extent. Resistance is possible. Strong leaders can and do emerge. But when fossil-fuel interests, biased institutions, and entrenched elites stymie realization of the public good, change must come.

Appendix

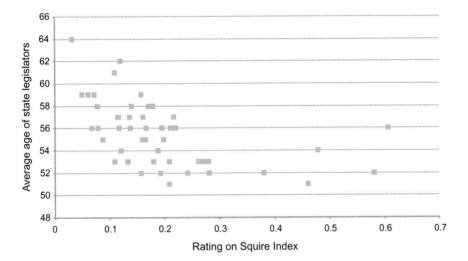

Ratings on Squire Index of legislative professionalization vs. average age of state legislators.

Notes

Introduction

1. United Nations Framework Convention on Climate Change, "Intended Nationally Determined Contributions: United States," 1. The International Energy Agency reports that global energy-related carbon dioxide emissions in 2014 were 32.3 billion Mg CO_2 eq (megagrams of carbon dioxide equivalent, the widely used measure that normalizes in one metric the atmospheric impact of all greenhouse gases). See International Energy Agency, "Global Energy-Related Emissions of Carbon Dioxide Stalled in 2014," 13 March 2015, http://www.iea.org/newsroomandevents/news/2015/march/global-energy-related-emissions-of-carbon-dioxide-stalled-in-2014.html. Total 2005 greenhouse-gas emissions in the United States were 7.38 billion Mg CO_2 eq. In 2005 net national emissions, which deduct absorption of carbon dioxide by plants, were 6.68 billion Mg CO_2 eq. The US submission to the United Nations Framework Convention on Climate Change appears to use the latter figure as its 2005 baseline. A 28 percent reduction from 2005 levels therefore amounts to 1.87 billion Mg. US Environmental Protection Agency, *Inventory of US Greenhouse Gas Emissions and Sinks: 1990–2014 (April 2016)*, ES-7; Baumert, Herzog, and Pershing, *Navigating the Numbers*, 32.

2. US Environmental Protection Agency, *Inventory of US Greenhouse Gas Emissions and Sinks: 1990–2014 (April 2016)*, ES-7; European Environment Agency, *Annual European Union Greenhouse Gas Inventory 1990–2013 and Inventory Report 2015*, 87. Data cited are for 2013, the most recent available for the European Union as a whole.

3. The US EPA projects that the states' plans will achieve 750 to 782 million Mg in carbon dioxide emission reductions in 2025 relative to 2005. US Environmental Protection Agency, *Regulatory Impact Analysis for the Clean Power Plan Final Rule*, 3-20, 8-3, 8-4; US Environmental Protection Agency, "Carbon Pollution Emission Guidelines for Existing Stationary Sources: Electrical Utility Generation Units; Final Rule," *Federal Register* 80, no. 205 (23 October 2015): 64661–65120, at 64664; US Environmental Protection Agency, *Inventory of US Greenhouse Gas Emissions and*

Sinks: 1990–2014 (April 2016): Executive Summary, ES-5, ES7. Carbon dioxide emissions figures are for 2014, the most recent available.

4. US Environmental Protection Agency, "Sulfur Dioxide," https://www3.epa.gov/airquality/sulfurdioxide/; US Environmental Protection Agency, *Regulatory Impact Analysis for the Clean Power Plan Final Rule*, see generally chapter 4; US Environmental Protection Agency, "Environmental Justice State Guidance," see 13–4 for statistics on disproportionate effects felt in minority communities.

5. For a typical "demise of coal" article, see Danielle Pacquette and Steven Rich, "The (Possible) Slow Death of Coal," *Washington Post*, 24 July 2014, https://www.washingtonpost.com/news/storyline/wp/2014/07/24/the-death-of-coal/; US Energy Information Administration, "Power Sector Coal Demand Has Fallen in Nearly Every State Since 2007," http://www.eia.gov/todayinenergy/detail.cfm?id=26012; US Environmental Protection Agency, *Inventory of US Greenhouse Gas Emissions: Executive Summary*, ES-5, and chapter 3, *Energy*, 3–5; US Environmental Protection Agency, *Regulatory Impact Analysis for the Clean Power Plan Final Rule*, 3–27; US Energy Information Administration, "Effects of the Clean Power Plan," figure IF1–3, http://www.eia.gov/forecasts/aeo/section_issues.cfm#cpp; US Energy Information Administration, "What Is US Electricity Generation by Energy Source?" https://www.eia.gov/tools/faqs/faq.cfm?id=427&t=3; US Environmental Protection Agency, "Sulfur Dioxide," https://www3.epa.gov/airquality/sulfurdioxide/.

6. Adam Liptak and Coral Davenport, "Supreme Court Deals Blow to Obama's Efforts to Regulate Coal Emissions," 9 February 2016, http://www.nytimes.com/2016/02/10/us/politics/supreme-court-blocks-obama-epa-coal-emissions-regulations.html.

7. Those sixteen states are Alabama, Arkansas, Florida, Georgia, Illinois, Indiana, Kentucky, Louisiana, Mississippi, North Carolina, Ohio, Pennsylvania, South Carolina, Virginia, Tennessee, and Texas, which together emitted a total of 1.33 billion metric tons of carbon dioxide in 2014, as compared with 2.04 billion tons from all US power plants. Germany, Umweltbundesamt, *Submission Under the United Nations Framework Convention on Climate Change*, 67; US Environmental Protection Agency, *Inventory of US Greenhouse Gas Emissions and Sinks: 1990–2014 (April 2016)*, E-5; US Environmental Protection Agency, "Air Markets Program Data," https://ampd.epa.gov/ampd/.

8. Megan Holohan, "Probing Question: What Gives the Sunrise and Sunset Its Orange Glow?" *Penn State News*, 5 March 2007, http://news.psu.edu/story/141337/2007/03/05/research/probing-question-what-gives-sunrise-and-sunset-its-orange-glow; "M.S.L.J.," "Sunsets and Scientists," *The Economist*, 8 April 2014, http://www.economist.com/blogs/babbage/2014/04/air-pollution.

9. Reitze, *Stationary Source Air Pollution Law* 8–9; Hurley, *Environmental Inequalities*, 183–184; *The Guardian*, "60 Years Since the Great Smog of London, in Pictures,"

https://www.theguardian.com/environment/gallery/2012/dec/05/60-years-great
-smog-london-in-pictures; Dewey, *Don't Breathe the Air*, 19; US Environmental Protection Agency, *Costs and Benefits of Reducing Lead in Gasoline: Final Regulatory Impact
Analysis* (US EPA, 1985); Jane E. Brody, "Despite Reductions in Exposure, Lead
Remains Danger to Children," *New York Times*, 21 March 1995, http://www.nytimes
.com/1995/03/21/science/despite-reductions-in-exposure-lead-remains-danger-to
-children.html; Woodin, "Environmental Effects of Air Pollution in Britain," 753.

10. Cook et al., "Selective Bird Predation on the Peppered Moth," 609–612.

11. US Environmental Protection Agency, "Benefits and Costs of the Clean Air
Act 1990–2020, the Second Prospective Study," https://www.epa.gov/clean-air-act
-overview/benefits-and-costs-clean-air-act-1990-2020-second-prospective-study;
Pope et al., "Fine Particulate Air Pollution and Life Expectancies in the United
States," 129; US Environmental Protection Agency, "EPA Takes Final Step in Phase-
out of Leaded Gasoline," 29 January 1996, https://www.epa.gov/aboutepa/epa-takes
-final-step-phaseout-leaded-gasoline. The statistics given are for total sulfur deposition (US Environmental Protection Agency, *2012 Progress Report*, 6).

12. US Environmental Protection Agency, "Summary Nonattainment Area Population Exposure Report" (as of 17 June 2016), https://www3.epa.gov/airquality/
greenbook/popexp.html; Darryl Fears, "Pollution Will Kill 5 Million People," *Washington Post*, 13 February 2016, http://www.philly.com/philly/news/nation_world/
20160213_Pollution_will_kill_five_million_people.html; Richard Read, "Estimated
35,200 US Traffic Deaths Reported in 2013," *The Christian Science Monitor*, 15 February 2014, http://www.csmonitor.com/Business/In-Gear/2014/0215/Estimated-35
-200-US-traffic-deaths-reported-in-2013; US Environmental Protection Agency, 2012
Progress Report, 18–21; Morello-Frosch et al., "Environmental Justice and Southern
California's 'Riskscape,'" 570–572; Aneja et al., "Characterization of Particulate
Matter (PM10) Related to Surface Coal Mining Operations in Appalachia," 500.

13. Rabe, "Contested Federalism," 518–519; Kaswan, "Decentralizing Cap-and-
Trade," 340, 400–401. On the history of federal efforts to regulate grandfathered
electric utilities, see Revesz and Lienke, *Struggling for Air*; Adam Liptak and Coral
Davenport, "Supreme Court Deals Blow to Obama's Effort to Regulate Coal Emissions," *New York Times*, 9 February 2016, http://www.nytimes.com/2016/02/10/us/
politics/supreme-court-blocks-obama-epa-coal-emissions-regulations.html.

14. Dwyer, "The Practice of Federalism Under the Clean Air Act," 1193–1195; US
Environmental Protection Agency, "Ozone Protection Under Title VI of the Clean
Air Act," https://www.epa.gov/ozone-layer-protection/ozone-protection-under-title
-vi-clean-air-act.

15. Bolton et al., "Organizational Capacity," 26–27.

16. See generally R. Douglas Arnold, *The Logic of Congressional Action*.

17. For these competing schools of thought, see generally Waterman and Meier, "Principal-Agent Models: An Expansion?"; Croley, *Regulation and Public Interests*; Carpenter and Moss, *Preventing Regulatory Capture*; Derthick, *Agency Under Stress*; Derthick and Quirk, *The Politics of Deregulation*; and, Quirk, "In Defense of the Politics of Ideas."

18. Chapter 4 provides more background on relevant scholarship concerning state environmental politics, law, policies, and policy processes, including the work of Pete Andrews, Vicki Arroyo, Michael Berry, Bill Buzbee, Elizabeth Haskell, Alexander Heckman, Alice Kaswan, David Konisky, Michelle Pautz, Sarah Rinfret, Barry Rabe, and Neal Woods.

19. For example, "good government" measures rely on highly generalized indicators, such as the presence or absence of long-term budgeting and the nature of contracting procedures, that have no obvious relationship to the processes of making policies related to air pollution. Pew Trusts published summary grades for state government performance in "Grading the States 2005: A Look Inside," http://www .pewtrusts.org/~/media/legacy/uploadedfiles/pcs_assets/2004-2006/gppreport 2005pdf.pdf.

20. Gelpe, "Citizen Boards," 453–462.

21. Haskell and Price, *State Environmental Management*, 64.

22. California Air Resources Board, "Board Member List, Photos, and Bios," http:// www.arb.ca.gov/board/members.htm, "Organization of the California Air Resources Board," http://www.arb.ca.gov/html/org/org.htm; State of California, "Governor's Budget, 2016–17: Air Resources Board," http://www.ebudget.ca.gov/2016-17/ StateAgencyBudgets/3890/3900/department.html; Tollefson,"America's Top Climate Cop," 268; Arbuckle, "The Role and Implications of Citizen Environmental Boards in State-Level Policymaking: Does Agency Structure Matter?," 42.

23. State of Alabama, "The Environmental Management Commission," http:// adem.alabama.gov/commission/default.cnt; South Carolina Code of Laws, "Title 44—Health, Department of Health and Environmental Control," http://www .scstatehouse.gov/code/t44c001.php; Illinois Pollution Control Board, "About the Board," http://www.ipcb.state.il.us/, and "Staff Directory," http://www.ipcb .state.il.us/AboutTheBoard/StaffDirectory.asp; Illinois General Assembly, Legislative Research Unit, "Boards and Commissions Salaries or Other Compensation, August 2015," 8, http://www.ilga.gov/commission/lru/salaries.pdf; Haskell and Price, *State Environmental Management: Case Studies of Nine States*, 37; Texas Commission on Environmental Quality, "History of TCEQ and Its Predecessor Agencies," https:// www.tceq.texas.gov/about/tceqhistory.html, and "TCEQ Organization Chart," https://www.tceq.texas.gov/about/organization/orgchart.html.

24. § 9 Virginia Administrative Code 5, "State Air Pollution Control Board: Agency Summary," http://law.lis.virginia.gov/admincode/title9/agency5/preface/, § 10.1–

1302, "Qualifications of Members of Board," http://law.lis.virginia.gov/vacode/title10.1/chapter13/section10.1-1302/, and § 10.1–1306, and "Air Pollution Control Board," http://law.lis.virginia.gov/vacode/title10.1/chapter13/.

25. Karl Blankenship, "Murphy Selected as VA Secretary of Natural Resources," *Bay Journal*, 1 March 2002, http://www.bayjournal.com/article/murphy_selected_as_va_secretary_of_natural_resources; Karl Blankenship, "Tayloe Murphy Receives Flanigan Award," *Bay Journal*, 1 September 2006, http://www.bayjournal.com/article/tayloe_murphy_receives_flanigan_award; Rusty Dennen, "Tayloe Murphy Guards Resources in Tight Budget Times," Fredericksburg.com, 18 January 2003, http://www.fredericksburg.com/coming_sunday/tayloe-murphy-guards-resources-in-tight-budget-times/article_96375f5a-e845-559d-8e61-38e16e0c52a2.html.

26. W. Tayloe Murphy Jr., personal interview, 3 September 2015.

27. Hansell, "The Electricity Fairy"; Glenn Hurowitz, "Virginia Gov, Possible Veep, Afraid of Big Coal," *Grist*, 18 June 2008, http://grist.org/article/calamity-kaine/.

28. Aneja et al., "Characterization of Particulate (PM10)," 496–501.

29. Robert G. Burnley, email message to the author, 22 July 2015; *TimesNews*, "Judge Rejects Dominion Power Plant Air Permit," 11 August 2009, http://www.timesnews.net/article/9015939/judge-rejects-dominion-power-plant-air-permit.

30. Debra McCown, "Appeals Court Upholds Hybrid Energy Center's Air Permit," *Bristol Herald Courier*, 24 December 2012, http://www.tricities.com/news/article_9e44ceb4-8589-55a3-b345-e58d24995a40.html?mode=jqm; Kirstin Downey, "Compromise Preserves Board's Permitting Clout," 20 March 2008, *Washington Post*, http://www.washingtonpost.com/wp-dyn/content/article/2008/03/18/AR2008031803909_pf.html.

31. EasyBeingGreener, "Update on Wise County Virginia Coal Plant," http://easygreener.blogspot.com/2009/09/update-on-wise-county-va-coal-plant.html; Dominion, "Virginia City Hybrid Energy Center Joins the Fleet," https://www.youtube.com/watch?v=iF4vA6C-Hqs, at 3:32; Environment News Service, "Polluting Potomac River Generating Station to Close," 30 August 2011, available at ens-newswire.com/2011/08/30/polluting-potomac-river-generating-station-to-close.

32. League of Conservation Voters, "National Environmental Scorecard," http://scorecard.lcv.org/#.

33. Brigid Schulte and Chris L. Jenkins, "So Close and Yet So Far Apart," *Washington Post*, 16 November 2006, quoting Robert Lang, demographer and director of the Metropolitan Institute at Virginia Polytechnic Institute and State University, http://www.washingtonpost.com/wp-dyn/content/article/2006/11/15/AR2006111501395.html.

34. Union of Concerned Scientists, "Burning Coal, Burning Cash: Ranking the States That Import the Most Coal—2014 Update," http://www.ucsusa.org/clean _energy/smart-energy-solutions/decrease-coal/burning-coal-burning-cash-2014 -update-state-coal-imports.html; US Energy Information Administration, "US Energy Mapping System: Coal," http://www.eia.gov/state/maps.cfm; US Energy Information Administration, "What Is the Role of Coal in the United States?," http://www .eia.gov/energy_in_brief/article/role_coal_us.cfm.

35. See generally Arnold, *The Logic of Congressional Action*.

36. Thomson, *Sophisticated Interdependence in Climate Policy*, see generally chapters 1 and 2.

37. Crenson, *The Unpolitics of Air Pollution*, 77–80; Nye, *The Future of Power*, 14.

38. Nye, *The Future of Power*; Arnold, *The Logic of Congressional Action*; Rabe, "Contested Federalism"; Yeager, *The Limits of Law*; Bosso, *Pesticides and Politics*; Croley, *Regulation and Public Interests*; Bachrach and Baratz, "Two Faces of Power"; Kearns and Lukes, "In Conversation with Steven Lukes"; Crenson, *The Unpolitics of Air Pollution*; Derthick, *Agency Under Stress*; Derthick, "Compensatory Federalism"; Gaventa, *Power and Powerlessness*; Krosnick, "Public Opinion on Climate Change"; Elazar, *American Federalism*; Squire and Moncrief, *State Legislatures Today*.

39. Dan Carter, "More Than Race," 149.

Chapter 1

1. US Department of Energy, *Special Environmental Analysis*, 85.

2. National Park Service, "Shenandoah National Park: Traveler Information Coordination Survey," September 2011, vi, http://ntl.bts.gov/lib/42000/42800/42885/ Shenandoah_TIS_Final_Report_09-11_final.pdf; Shenandoah National Park, "Visibility and Haze," https://www.nps.gov/shen/naturescience/visibility_and_haze.htm; Tennesen, "On a Clear Day," 28; see generally Eshleman et al., "Surface Water Quality Is Improving."

3. US Environmental Protection Agency, "Nitrogen Dioxide," https://www.epa.gov/ air/nitrogenoxides/; US Environmental Protection Agency, "Air Emission Sources: Nitrogen Oxides," https://www.epa.gov/cgi-bin/broker?_service=data&_debug=0& _program=dataprog.national_1.sas&polchoice=NOX; US Environmental Protection Agency, "National Emissions Inventory (NEI) Air Pollutant Emissions Trends Data and Estimation Procedures"; US Environmental Protection Agency, "Milestones in Mobile Source Air Pollution Control and Regulations," https://www3.epa.gov/otaq/ consumer/milestones.htm; US Environmental Protection Agency, "Cars and Light-Duty Trucks—Tier 2," https://www.dieselnet.com/standards/us/ld_t2.php.

Comparison of NOx emission rates in 1970 and in 2014 is based on "VMT," or "vehicle miles traveled."

4. US Department of the Interior, National Park Service, letter from Marie Rust, Regional Director, to Donald S. Welsh, Regional Administrator, US Environmental Protection Agency, 19 February 2004, http://www2.nature.nps.gov/air/hot/archive/200404/docs/Shenandoah.pdf; US Environmental Protection Agency, Proposed Rule, "Approval and Promulgation of Air Quality Implementation Plans; Virginia; Redesignation of the Shenandoah National Park Ozone Nonattainment Area To Attainment and Approval of the Area's Maintenance Plan," US Federal Register Vol. 70, No. 213, 67109–20, 4 November 2005, https://federalregister.gov/articles/2005/11/04/05-22031/approval-and-promulgation-of-air-quality-implementation-plans-virginia-redesignation-of-the.

5. US Environmental Protection Agency, "National Ambient Air Quality Standards (NAAQS)," https://www.epa.gov/air/criteria.html. In some cases, the EPA has set multiple standards for the same pollutant that are tied to different averaging times. The idea is to ensure protection of public health from high short-term exposures as well as unsafe chronic exposures. So, for example, the 24-hour standard for fine particular matter is 35 micrograms per cubic meter while the annual standard is 12 micrograms per cubic meter. When discussing quantitative estimates for air pollution levels and their relative levels of safety, it is vital to specify the averaging time represented by the measures in question. A level of 25 micrograms of fine particulate matter per cubic meter would be alarming if it represented an annual average, but that same measurement would be considered in compliance with the 24-hour NAAQS for fine particulate matter. In Shenandoah National Park violations of the eight-hour ozone standard threw the area into nonattainment.

6. US Environmental Protection Agency, "Nonattainment NSR Basic Information," https://www.epa.gov/nsr/nonattainment-nsr-basic-information.

7. Blue Ridge Environmental Defense League, letter to Laura Justin, Department of Environmental Quality, 8 March 2004, http://www.bredl.org/pdf/CPVWarren_comments030804.pdf.

8. Virginia State Air Pollution Control Board, Meeting Minutes for 29 June 2004, http://townhall.virginia.gov/L/GetFile.cfm?File=C:\TownHall\docroot\Meeting\1\4246\minutes_deq_4246_v3.pdf; Rex Springston, "Panel Oks Power Plant Near Shenandoah National Park," *Richmond Times-Dispatch*, 30 June 2004; Virginia Department of Environmental Quality, "Ozone and $PM_{2.5}$ Regional Planning Activities," http://www.deq.virginia.gov/Programs/Air/AirQualityPlans/OzoneandPM25RegionalPlanningActivities.aspx; US Environmental Protection Agency, Direct Final Rule, "Approval and Promulgation of Air Quality Implementation Plans; Virginia; Fredericksburg and Shenandoah National Park 8-Hour Ozone Areas Movement from the Nonattainment Area List to the Maintenance Area List," *Federal Register* 73, No. 9, 2210–1, 14 January 2008, https://federalregister.gov/articles/2008/01/14/E8-290/

approval-and-promulgation-of-air-quality-implementation-plans-virginia
-fredericksburg-and-shenandoah; Thomas Strickland, Acting Assistant Secretary for
Fish and Wildlife and Parks, memorandum to Anita Riggleman, Virginia Department of Environmental Quality, 22 November 2010, 3, http://www.deq.virginia
.gov/Portals/0/DEQ/Air/Permitting/PowerPlants/DominionWarren/Thomas
_Strickland.pdf.

9. US Department of Energy, *Special Environmental Analysis*, appendix A, 2; Jerome
Brooks, Virginia Department of Environmental Quality, "Mirant Potomac River
Generating Station," Clean Air Act Enforcement Lessons Learned Work Shop, 19
June 2009, http://www.marama.org/calendar/events/presentations/2009_06Lessons
Learned/2009_06LL_MirantPRGS.pdf; US Department of Justice, "Clean Air Act Set-
tlement to Eliminate Almost 29,000 Tons of Harmful Emissions in Virginia and
Maryland," 8 May 2006, https://www.justice.gov/archive/opa/pr/2006/May/06
_enrd_278.html.

10. Memorandum from Kelly Lease, Air Compliance Inspector, and Charles D.
Forbes, Air Compliance Manager, to Jeff Steers, Director, Northern Virginia Regional
Office, Department of Environmental Quality, 10 August 2003, included as appendix F in Chimento and Hertel, "Mirant Power Plant Emissions"; Chris L. Jenkins,
"Digging Up Dirt On Mystery Ash in Alexandria," *Washington Post*, 20 November
2003, https://www.washingtonpost.com/archive/local/2003/11/20/digging-up-dirt
-on-mystery-ash-in-alexandria/0e43aea8-73e4-42b4-9ecf-eb2d239fbda0/.

11. The term "anticipatory politics" is borrowed from Yeager, *The Limits of Law*, 39.

12. Virginia General Assembly, Joint Legislative and Audit Review Commission,
Interim Report, IV; Virginia General Assembly, Joint Legislative and Audit Review
Commission, *Review of the Department of Environmental Quality*, 30–31, 111.

13. W. Tayloe Murphy Jr., personal interview, 3 September 2015.

14. Chimento and Hertel, "Mirant Power Plant Emissions," 6; letter from Elizabeth
Chimento and Poul Hertel, 12 September 2005, to Joseph T. Kelliher, Chairman,
Federal Energy Regulatory Commission, http://energy.gov/sites/prod/files/oeprod/
DocumentsandMedia/mirant_111805_a.pdf.

15. Sullivan Environmental Consulting, "Screening-Level Modeling Analysis of the
Potomac River Power Plant Located in Alexandria, Virginia," 29 March 2004, https://
www.alexandriava.gov/uploadedFiles/tes/info/Sullivan%20Modeling.pdf; Elizabeth
Chimento, letter to David Sullivan, 7 April 2005, author's copy.

16. John Britton, former counsel to the City of Alexandria, personal interview, 11
June 2012; Elizabeth Chimento, personal communication, 7 July 2015.

17. Commonwealth of Virginia, State Air Pollution Control Board, "Consent
Order," 3 September 2004, https://www.alexandriava.gov/uploadedFiles/tes/info/
2004-09-23%20-%20Consent%20Order%20-%20Downwash%20Modeling.pdf; Aero

Engineering Services, "Ambient Air Quality Analysis: Potomac River Generating Station, Alexandria, Virginia (August 2005)," 1, author's copy.

18. Letter from Robert G. Burnley, Director, Virginia Department of Environmental Quality, to Lisa D. Johnson, President, Mirant Potomac Power, LLC, 19 August 2005, author's copy; Elizabeth Chimento, personal communication, 5 July 2015; Robert G. Burnley, personal communication, 14 July 2015; email message from W. Tayloe Murphy Jr. to Robert Burnley, 24 August 2005, available through the Library of Virginia's Digital Collections, http://digitool1.lva.lib.va.us:8881/.

19. Letter from Governor Mark R. Warner to Ms. Lisa Johnson, President, Mirant Potomac River, LLC, 21 September 2005, author's copy; *The Connection*, "Pressure on Mirant Builds: PEPCO Says Mirant Can Cease in 18 to 24 Months," http://www.connectionnewspapers.com/news/2005/sep/28/pressure-on-mirant-builds/.

20. The 2005 order and subsequent DOE orders are described in Department of Energy, Order No. 202–07–2, 13 January 2007 http://energy.gov/sites/prod/files/oeprod/DocumentsandMedia/EO-05-01.pdf; Southern Environmental Law Center letter described and cited in Moeller, "Clean Air v. Electric Reliability," 51, note 148; letter from Ira T. Kasdan and Steven L. Humphreys, Counsel to the Virginia Department of Environmental Quality, to Kevin Kolevar, US Department of Energy, 23 November 2005, http://energy.gov/sites/prod/files/oeprod/DocumentsandMedia/mirant_112305.pdf; Robert G. Burnley (former Director, Virginia Department of Environmental Quality), in discussion with author, 9 July 2015; email message from Robert G. Burnley, Director, Virginia Department of Environmental Quality, to Virginia Secretary of Resources W. Tayloe Murphy Jr., 21 October 2005, available through the Library of Virginia's Digital Collections http://digitool1.lva.lib.va.us:8881/; letter from Robert G. Burnley, Virginia Department of Environmental Quality to Samuel Bodman, Department of Energy, 5 January 2006, 3, 4 http://energy.gov/sites/prod/files/oeprod/DocumentsandMedia/mirant_010506_b.pdf.

21. Department of Energy, *Special Environmental Analysis*, S-4; US Environmental Protection Agency, "Administrative Compliance Order by Consent," 1 June 2006, included as appendix B to Department of Energy, *Special Environmental Analysis*; John Britton (attorney, Schnader, Segal & Lewis LLP, former outside counsel, City of Alexandria), personal interview, 11 June 2012.

22. Elizabeth Chimento, "August 8th [2006] Mirant Plant Incident and Subsequent Conversations with NVDEQ Director Jeff Steers," 3, author's copy.

23. *The Connection*, "Air Pollution Control Board to Monitor Mirant," 26 September 2006, http://www.connectionnewspapers.com/news/2006/sep/26/air-pollution-control-board-to-monitor-mirant/; Virginia State Air Pollution Control Board, Meeting Minutes, 25 September 2006, http://townhall.virginia.gov/L/GetFile.cfm?File=C:\TownHall\docroot\Meeting\1\7739\minutes_deq_7739_v2.pdf.

24. Department of Energy, *Special Environmental Analysis*, 85; Schnader Attorneys at Law, counsel to the City of Alexandria, "Letter to Air Pollution Control Board members, 22 March 2007," 2, author's copy; V. Thomson, comments at 26 March 2007 meeting of the Virginia State Air Pollution Control Board, author's notes. The health effects included in this analysis were mortality, nonfatal heart attacks, and bronchitis.

25. Staffing levels from Valerie Thomson, Department of Environmental Quality Director of Administration, personal communication, 23 July 2015; Burnley, "How Will Virginia Regulate Uranium Mining?" 43.

26. Robert G. Burnley, email message to author, 24 July 2015; Joint Legislative Audit and Review Commission of the Virginia General Assembly, *Interim Report: Review of the Department of Environmental Quality*, 17.

27. Email message from Vivian Thomson to Bruce Buckheit, 17 March 2007; email message from Vivian Thomson to Cindy Berndt, Regulatory Affairs Director, Virginia Department of Environmental Quality, 29 March 2007.

28. Virginia State Air Pollution Control Board Meeting Minutes, 10 April 2007, http://townhall.virginia.gov/L/GetFile.cfm?File=C:\TownHall\docroot\Meeting\ 1\9134\minutes_deq_9134_v1.pdf.

29. Hunton & Williams, 16 May 2007 letter to the Honorable Timothy M. Kaine, author's copy; Pepco Holdings Co., letter from Dennis R. Wrasse to the Honorable Tim Kaine, 16 May 2007, author's copy.

30. Virginia State Air Pollution Control Board, Meeting Minutes, 23 May 2007, 3–4, http://townhall.virginia.gov/L/GetFile.cfm?File=C:\TownHall\docroot\Meeting\ 1\9226\Minutes_DEQ_9226_v2.pdf; Maria Hegstad, "Mirant Sues State's Board Over Tightened Emission Restrictions," *The Washington Examiner*, 2 and 3 June 2007, 4; *Mirant Potomac River LLC v. State Air Pollution Control Board*, 13 June 2007, 10-2, author's copy; *Mirant Potomac River LLC v. State Air Pollution Control Board*, transcript of 16 August 2007 hearing in the Circuit Court of the City of Richmond before the Honorable Melvin R. Hughes, 13, 67, 77, 90, author's copy.

31. Britton, interview; Ignacio Pessoa, former City Attorney, City of Alexandria, email correspondence with author, 11 February 2016.

32. Carl Josephson, "Answer of Respondents, *Mirant Potomac Power LLC v. State Air Pollution Control Board, Virginia*," 9 July 2007, author's copy; *Mirant Potomac Power LLC v. State Air Pollution Control Board*, transcript of 16 August 2007 hearing in the Circuit Court of the City of Richmond before the Honorable Melvin R. Hughes, 13, 67, 77, 90, author's copy.

33. Memorandum from David Paylor, Virginia Department of Environmental Quality, to Preston Bryant, Secretary of Natural Resources, 19 June 2007, available

through the Library of Virginia's Digital Collections, http://digitool1.lva.lib.va
.us:8881/.

34. Letter from Malay Jindal, Maureen Barrett, and William Skrabak, City of Alexandria Department of Transportation and Environmental Services, to State Air Pollution Control Board, 12 September 2007, author's copy; State Air Pollution Control
Board, Meeting Minutes, 13 September 2007, 1–2, http://townhall.virginia.gov/L/
GetFile.cfm?File=C:\TownHall\docroot\Meeting\1\9822\Minutes_DEQ_9822_v3
.pdf.

35. Letter from Ignacio Pessoa, Alexandria City Attorney, and John B. Britton,
Schnader Harrison Segal and Lewis LLP, to David K. Paylor, DEQ Director, and members of the State Air Pollution Control Board, 29 November 2007, author's copy.

36. Virginia State Air Pollution Control Board Meeting Minutes, 10 October 2007, 3,
http://townhall.virginia.gov/L/GetFile.cfm?File=C:\TownHall\docroot\Meeting\
1\9825\Minutes_DEQ_9825_v2.pdf.

37. Memorandum from Mark Rubin to David Paylor and Preston Bryant, 3 October
2007, available through the Library of Virginia's Digital Collections, http://digitool1
.lva.lib.va.us:8881/; Memorandum from Kate Paris, Confidential Assistant to Governor Kaine's Chief of Staff, to Wayne Turnage, Chief of Staff to Governor Kaine,
"Major Cabinet Issues," 9 October 2007, available through the Library of Virginia's
Digital Collections, http://digitool1.lva.lib.va.us:8881/.

38. *Mirant Potomac L.L.C. v. State Air Pollution Control Board et al.*, 75 Va. Cir. 117
(Circuit Court of Richmond 2008).

39. Virginia State Air Pollution Control Board, Meeting Minutes, 20 March
2008, 1–18, http://townhall.virginia.gov/L/GetFile.cfm?File=C:\TownHall\docroot\
Meeting\1\10733\Minutes_DEQ_10733_v4.pdf. http://townhall.virginia.gov/L/Get
File.cfm?File=C:\TownHall\docroot\Meeting\1\10733\Minutes_DEQ_10733_v4
.pdf; City of Alexandria, "Alexandria City Council Approves Settlement with Mirant
on Its Potomac River Generating Station," 1 July 2008, https://www.alexandriava
.gov/news_display.aspx?id=14346; Virginia State Air Pollution Control Board Meeting Minutes, 30 July 2008, http://townhall.virginia.gov/L/GetFile.cfm?File=C:\
TownHall\docroot\Meeting\1\11413\Minutes_DEQ_11413_v2.pdf.

40. Patricia Sullivan, "GenOn Power Plant in Alexandria Is Set to Close," *Washington Post*, 29 September 2012, https://www.washingtonpost.com/local/genon-power
-plant-in-alexandria-is-set-to-close/2012/09/29/daa355ea-08d7-11e2-858a
-5311df86ab04_story.html; Stephen Miller, "Breaking: Alexandria Coal Power Plant
to Close Next Year," **Greater** Greater Washington, 30 September 2011, http://
greatergreaterwashington.org/post/11870/breaking-alexandria-coal-power-plant-to
-close-next-year/; Environment News Service, "Polluting Potomac River Generating
Station to Close," August 30, 2011, available at ens-newswire.com/2011/08/
30/polluting-potomac-river-generating-station-to-close; Virginia Department of

Environmental Quality, "Mirant Potomac River Generation Station Selected Emissions Periods," 2007 (exact date not indicated), author's copy; US Environmental Protection Agency, "The 2011 National Emissions Inventory," https://www3.epa.gov/ttnchie1/net/2011inventory.html, indicates that in 2011 electric utilities' sulfur dioxide emissions in Virginia were 67,979 tons.

41. Email message from Mark Rubin, Senior Advisor to the Governor, to Brian Shepard, Larry Roberts, and Bill Murray, 30 October 2006, available through the Library of Virginia's Digital Collections, http://digitool1.lva.lib.va.us:8881/; email message from Preston Bryant, Virginia Secretary of Natural Resources, to Mark Rubin, 29 December 2006, available through the Library of Virginia's Digital Collections, http://digitool1.lva.lib.va.us:8881/.

42. Email message from Secretary of Natural Resources Preston Bryant to Governor Tim Kaine, 29 January 2007, available through the Library of Virginia's Digital Collections, http://digitool1.lva.lib.va.us:8881/.

43. Kirstin Downey, "Compromise Preserves Board's Permitting Clout," *Washington Post*, 20 March 2008, http://www.washingtonpost.com/wp-dyn/content/article/2008/03/18/AR2008031803909_pf.html; Virginia Department of Environmental Quality, "Citizen Board Legislation: House Bill 3113/Senate Bill 1403, A Progress Report on the Efforts of the HB 3113/SB 1403 Stakeholder Group," November 2007, 1, file:///Users/VET4Y/Desktop/Coal%20Nation/DEQ%20Board%20Bill%20HB_3113_Report_Final_111607.pdf; email message from Shelton Miles, Chair, State Water Pollution Control Board, to Secretary of Natural Resources Preston Bryant, 29 January 2007, available through the Library of Virginia's Digital Collections, http://digitool1.lva.lib.va.us:8881/.

44. Letter from W. Tayloe Murphy Jr. to Delegate Kirk Cox, 1 February 2007, as appended to an email message from Hullie Moore, Member, State Air Pollution Control Board, to Mark Rubin, Counselor to Governor Tim Kaine, 2 February 2007, available through the Library of Virginia's Digital Collections, http://digitool1.lva.lib.va.us:8881/.

45. Robert G. Burnley, "Let's Not Gut Our Citizen Boards: Busting the Citizen Environmental Boards Myths," *Virginian-Pilot*, 3 February 2008.

46. "Kaine Silence Mystifies Local Leaders," *Alexandria Connection*, 6 February 2007, http://www.connectionnewspapers.com/news/2007/feb/06/kaine-silence-mystifies-local-leaders/; Cale Jaffe, Environmental Law Center, letter to Governor Tim Kaine, 24 January 2007, available through the Library of Virginia's Digital Collections http://digitool1.lva.lib.va.us:8881/).

47. Virginia General Assembly, Acts of Assembly 2008: S 423, http://lis.virginia.gov/cgi-bin/legp604.exe?081+ful+CHAP0276Kirsten Downey, "Compromise Preserves Board's Permitting Clout," *Washington Post*, 20 March 2008, http://www

.washingtonpost.com/wp-dyn/content/article/2008/03/18/AR2008031803909_pf
.html; Burnley, "How Will Virginia Regulate Uranium Mining?" 42.

48. Tim Craig, "Kaine Says Coal-Burning Power Plant Is Necessary," *Washington Post*, 30 March 2008, http://www.washingtonpost.com/wp-dyn/content/article/2008/03/29/AR2008032901844.html.

Chapter 2

1. Smithsonian Institution, "The Roots and Branches of Virginia Music: The Past Is the Present," http://www.folkways.si.edu/roots-branches-virginia-past-present/bluegrass/music/article/smithsonian; Wise County History, http://www.wisecounty.org/wise_history.html.

2. Film interview with Kathy Selvage, Southern Appalachian Mountain Stewards video, 2007, https://www.youtube.com/watch?v=GZoQ5Gw0r7Q; Staff report, "Coal Waste Piles Across Southwest Virginia Feeding Wise Power Plant," *TimesNews*, http://www.timesnews.net/article/9076166/coal-waste-piles-across-sw-virginia-feeding-wise-power-plant; Dominion Virginia Power, response to question of Bruce Buckheit, 14 April 2008, http://www.deq.virginia.gov/Portals/0/DEQ/Air/Permitting/PowerPlants/VCHEC/Dominion/Buckheit/Buckheit_5.pdf.

3. Film interviews with Dr. Ron Heller, University of Kentucky, and Kathy Selvage, *The Electricity Fairy*; Gaventa, *Power and Powerlessness*, 35; Lewis, *Black Coal Miners*, 191–193.

4. Hank Hayes, "Report Indicates Manufacturing Could Replace Lost SW Virginia Coal Jobs," *Times News*, 10 February 2015, http://www.timesnews.net/article/9084962/report-indicates-manufacturing-could-replace-lost-coal-jobs-in-sw-va; US Bureau of Labor Statistics, "State Employment Seasonally Adjusted: Virginia," http://www.bls.gov/web/laus/tabled1.pdf; Katie Dunn, "Economic Future Must Address Decline of Coal," *Coalfield Progress*, 24 July 2015, reposted on Wise County's website, http://www.wisecounty.org/planupdate/Economic_Future_072514.pdf.

5. US Department of Agriculture, Economic Research Service, "County-Level Data Sets: Percent of Total Population in Poverty, 2014, http://www.ers.usda.gov/data-products/county-level-data-sets/poverty.aspx; US Department of Agriculture, "Small Area Income and Poverty Estimates," http://www.census.gov/did/www/saipe/data/interactive/saipe.html?s_appName=saipe&map_yearSelector=2014&map_geoSelector=mhi_s&s_measures=mhi_snc; Megan Brantley, WCYB, "Southwest Virginia Tops the Charts in Drug Abuse," 23 April 2013, http://www.wcyb.com/news/watercooler/Southwest-Virginia-tops-the-charts-in-drug-abuse/19863944; Nick Miroff, "Dark Addiction," *Washington Post*, 13 January 2008 http://www.washingtonpost.com/wp-dyn/content/article/2008/01/12/AR2008011201181.html; Ezzati et al., "The Reversal of Fortunes," specific county figures in Data Set S-2.

6. Virginia General Assembly, SB651, 2004, https://leg1.state.va.us/cgi-bin/legp504 .exe?ses=041&typ=bil&val=SB651; Tim Craig and Sandhya Somashekhar, "Dominion Gets Initial Approval for Coal Plant," *Washington Post*, 31 March 2008, B2; Virginia State Corporation Commission, "Petition of Virginia Electric and Power Company, Case No. PU-2006-0075," 16 October 2006, 40, http://www.scc.virginia .gov/docketsearch/DOCS/2%24xg01!.PDF; Scott Harper, "Power Plant is Ground Zero in Battle of Energy vs. the Environment," *The Virginian-Pilot*, 22 June 2008, http://hamptonroads.com/2008/06/power-plant-ground-zero-battle-energy-vs -environment; Abt Associates, Assessing the Economic Impact, E-2.

7. Commonwealth of Virginia, State Corporation Commission, "Case No. PUE-2006-0075: Petition of Virginia Electric and Power Company," 17 October 2006, 40, http://www.scc.virginia.gov/docketsearch/DOCS/2%24xg01!.PDF; Tim Craig, "Kaine Says Coal-Burning Power Plant Is Necessary," *Washington Post*, 30 March 2008, http://www.washingtonpost.com/wp-dyn/content/article/2008/03/29/AR20080 32901844.html; Stephen Igo, "Wise Administrator Believes Power Plant Will Get State OK," *Times News*, 9 January 2008, http://www.timesnews.net/article/9004595/ wise-administrator-believes-power-plant-will-get-state-ok; Hansell, *The Electricity Fairy*, interviews with Robert Adkins and Robby Robbins, Wise County Board of Supervisors, 2008, specific dates not given.

8. Mike Tidwell, Chesapeake Climate Action Network, *Washington Post* editorial, 27 January 2008; Film interview with Cale Jaffe, undated, *The Electricity Fairy*.

9. Staff report, "Utility Reaches Deal on Plant," *Richmond Times-Dispatch*, 6 March 2008, http://www.richmond.com/news/article_41763293-ef4e-5ce0-94f4 -7c3f48b24e61.html; Tim Craig and Sandhya Somashekhar, "Dominion Gets Initial Approval for Coal Plant," *Washington Post*, 31 March 2008; Tim Craig, "Kaine Irks Environmentalists By Supporting Coal-Burning Plant," *Washington Post*, 30 March 2008, C1; Kathy Still, "Wise County Supervisors Hear More from Power Plant Opposition," 15 February 2008, *Bristol Herald-Courier*, http://www.tricities.com/news/ article_9940c095-6bed-5b3e-bfc7-0daa41c8bc94.html?TNNoMobile.

10. Email message from Preston Bryant to Tim Kaine, 22 May 2008, available through the Library of Virginia's Digital Collections, http://digitool1.lva.lib.va .us:8881/.

11. Dominion Virginia Power, PSD Preconstruction Permit Application: Dominion Southwest Power Project, Virginia City, Virginia, July 2006, author's copy; testimony of Catharine Gilliam, National Parks and Conservation Association, State Air Pollution Control Board meeting, 10 October 2007, author's copy; Virginia State Air Pollution Control Board, Meeting Minutes, 25 January 2008, http://townhall .virginia.gov/L/GetFile.cfm?File=C:\TownHall\docroot\Meeting\1\10453\Minutes _DEQ_10453_v2.pdf.

12. US Environmental Protection Agency, "Prevention of Significant Deterioration: Basic Information," https://www.epa.gov/nsr/prevention-significant-deterioration-basic-information.

13. US Environmental Protection Agency, "National Emission Standards for Hazardous Air Pollutants," 6 April 1973, 38 Federal Register 8824, http://www.epa.gov/ttnatw01/asbes/fr/38fr8820.pdf; US Environmental Protection Agency, "Mercury: How People Are Exposed to Mercury," http://www.epa.gov/mercury/exposure.htm; Virginia Department of Health, "Fish Consumption Advisories for Tennessee and Big Sandy River Basin," http://www.vdh.state.va.us/epidemiology/dee/publichealthtoxicology/advisories/TennesseeBigSandy.htm; US Environmental Protection Agency, "Mercury and Air Toxics Standard: Cleaner Power Plants," http://www.epa.gov/mats/powerplants.html; Jastremsky, "Comment: Cracking Down on Coal," 435.

14. US Environmental Protection Agency, "Clean Air Mercury Rule," http://www.epa.gov/camr/; Jastremsky, "Cracking Down on Coal," 443.

15. National Association of Clean Air Agencies, "State Mercury Programs for Utilities, December 4, 2007," http://www.4cleanair.org/Documents/StateTable.pdf; State Air Pollution Control Board, Meeting Minutes, 27 January 2006; National Public Radio Interview with Dr. Charles Driscoll, 19 January 2007, http://www.npr.org/templates/story/story.php?storyId=6921983; Virginia General Assembly, "HB 1471, Mercury Emission Controls."

16. Rex Springston, "First Step Toward Cleaner Skies: State Pollution Board Weighs Rules Cutting Mercury Emissions," *Richmond Times-Dispatch*, 14 January 2007, B-7; See generally Meltz and McCarthy, "The D.C. Circuit Rejects EPA's Mercury Rules"; *New Jersey v. EPA*, 517 F.3d 574 (D.C. Cir. 2008). In 2011 the EPA adopted a MACT rule to require reductions of mercury and other "air toxics" from coal- and oil-fired power plants. In 2016 an estimated 77 percent of the coal-fired power plants in the United States were preparing to install, or already had installed, controls to meet those standards. Reid Frazier, "Coal-Fired Power Plants Clean Up Their Act," *Inside Energy*, 6 January 2016, http://insideenergy.org/2016/01/06/coal-fired-power-plants-clean-up-their-act/.

17. Dominion Virginia Power, "PSD Permit Application for the Proposed Virginia City Hybrid Energy Center in Southwest Virginia," June 2006, updated 10 August 2007, 3-13, 5-24, author's copy; Virginia City Hybrid Energy Facility, Response to Data Request from Vivian Thomson, undated, http://www.deq.virginia.gov/Portals/0/DEQ/Air/Permitting/PowerPlants/VCHEC/Thomson/Thomson_22.pdf; Chesapeake Climate Action Network, "Mile Long Petition," http://www.youtube.com/watch?v=h-BEczrvzM0, 21 May 2008; Hansell, "The Electricity Fairy."

18. Virginia Department of Environmental Quality, Draft PSD Permit for Virginia Power and Electric, Virginia City, Virginia, January 2008, 8–9, author's copy;

Virginia Department of Environmental Quality, Draft Engineering Analysis for the Case-by-Case MACT Permit to Construct and Operate the Virginia City Hybrid Energy Center, 4 March 2008, author's copy; Southern Environmental Law Center et al., "Comments Regarding the Draft PSD Permit for the Virginia City Hybrid Energy Center," 12 March 2008, author's copy.

19. Vivian Thomson, Memorandum to Cindy Berndt, 30 June 2008, 1, author's copy.

20. Virginia General Assembly, Joint Legislative Audit and Review Commission, *Review of the Department of Environmental Quality*, v.

21. Virginia State Air Pollution Control Board, Meeting Minutes, 20 March 2008, 20–25, http://townhall.virginia.gov/L/GetFile.cfm?File=C:\TownHall\docroot\ Meeting\1\10733\Minutes_DEQ_10733_v4.pdf.

22. Air Board Meeting Minutes, 20 March 2008, 25.

23. Air Board Meeting Minutes, 20 March 2008, 26–27.

24. Air Board Meeting Minutes, 20 March 2008, 27-28.

25. National Park Service, "Comments on Virginia City Hybrid Energy Center PSD Permit Application," 12 March 2008, author's copy; Air Board Meeting Minutes, 20 March 2008, 26–28, 34.

26. Email messages between Secretary of Natural Resources Preston Bryant and Governor Tim Kaine, 22 January 2008, available through the Library of Virginia's Digital Collections, http://digitool1.lva.lib.va.us:8881/; email messages between Governor Tim Kaine and Tim Dunn, 19 March 2008, available through the Library of Virginia's Digital Collections, http://digitool1.lva.lib.va.us:8881/.

27. Andrea Hopkins, "Our Position on Power Plant Has Evolved with Evidence," *Bristol Herald-Courier*, 20 January 2008, http://www.heraldcourier.com/news/our -position-on-power-plant-has-evolved-with-the-evidence/article_15e46227-d931 -5d18-a2c7-11c65a63d2db.html; email messages among Governor Tim Kaine, Secretary of Natural Resources Preston Bryant, Steven Waltz, Director of the Department of Mines, Minerals and Energy, and various executive office staff members, 18 through 21 February 2008, available through the Library of Virginia's Digital Collections, http://digitool1.lva.lib.va.us:8881/.

28. Email messages among Mark Rubin, Senior Advisor to Governor Kaine, Secretary of Natural Resources Preston Bryant, Brian Shepard, and Carol Denson, 14 March 2008, available through the Library of Virginia's Digital Collections; email messages among Wayne Turnage, Preston Bryant, Mark Rubin, and Larry Roberts, 18 March 2008, available through the Library of Virginia's Digital Collections, http://digitool1 .lva.lib.va.us:8881/; email messages between Brian Shepard, Director of Policy for Governor Kaine, and Cathy Ghidotti, Director of Scheduling, 19 March 2008,

available through the Library of Virginia's Digital Collections, http://digitool1.lva .lib.va.us:8881/; email messages among Wayne Turnage, Chief of Staff to Governor Tim Kaine, Mark Rubin, Senior Advisor to Governor Kaine, and Preston Bryant, Secretary of Natural Resources, 14 March 2008, available through the Library of Virginia's Digital Collections, http://digitool1.lva.lib.va.us:8881/; email message from Preston Bryant, Secretary of Natural Resources, to Wayne Turnage, Chief of Staff to Governor Kaine, Larry Roberts, Mark Rubin, and Brian Shepard, 17 March 2008, available through the Library of Virginia's Digital Collections, http://digitool1.lva .lib.va.us:8881/; email message from Bruce Buckheit, former Air Board member, to Vivian Thomson, 10 September 2016.

29. Email message from Mark Rubin, Senior Advisor to the Governor, to Governor Tim Kaine, 24 March 2008, available through the Library of Virginia's Digital Collections, http://digitool1.lva.lib.va.us:8881/.

30. Email messages among David Paylor, Director, Department of Environmental Quality, Preston Bryant, Secretary of Natural Resources, and Mark Rubin, senior aide to Governor Kaine, 26 March 2008, available through the Library of Virginia's Digital Collections, http://digitool1.lva.lib.va.us:8881/; email messages among Governor Tim Kaine, Senior Advisor to the Governor Mark Rubin, Secretary of Natural Resources Preston Bryant, and DEQ Director David Paylor, 18 April 2008, available through the Library of Virginia's Digital Collections, http://digitool1.lva.lib.va .us:8881/.

31. Email message from David Paylor, Director, Department of Environmental Quality, to Preston Bryant, Secretary of Natural Resources, and Mark Rubin, Senior Advisor to Governor Kaine, 5 February 2008, available through the Library of Virginia's Digital Collections, http://digitool1.lva.lib.va.us:8881/.

32. Chesapeake Climate Action Network, "Mile-Long Petition," http:// chesapeakeclimate.org/blog/mile-long-petition/.

33. Bruce Buckheit, Memo to David Paylor, Richard Langford, John Hanson, Hullie Moore, and Vivian Thomson, 14 April 2008, "Further Data Gathering Activities In Support of VAPCB Consideration of Permit Applications Respecting the Virginia City Hybrid Energy Center," author's copy.

34. US Environmental Protection Agency, "Prevention of Significant Deterioration Basic Information," http://www.epa.gov/nsr/psd.html#best.

35. Vivian Thomson, Memorandum to David Paylor, Department of Environmental Quality, 14 April 2008, author's copy.

36. Hullihen Williams Moore, memorandum to David Paylor, " Information re Wise County Permits," Department of Environmental Quality, 9 April 2008, revised 13 April 2008, author's copy.

37. US Energy Information Administration, "State Energy-Related Carbon Dioxide Emissions by Year, 2000–2011."

38. *Massachusetts et al. v. US Environmental Protection Agency*, 549 US 497 (2007), 3, 4; Daniel Shean, memorandum to Vivian Thomson, 20 April 2008, 2–3.

39. Bloomberg, "Virginia Regulator Rejects Electric Coal Gasification Plant," 14 April 2008, http://www.bloomberg.com/apps/news?pid=conewsstory&refer=conews&tkr=AEP:US&sid=asojU7dOVsOk.

40. Email message from Preston Bryant, Secretary of Natural Resources, to Larry Roberts, Counselor to the Governor, Mark Rubin, Senior Advisor to the Governor, and Brian Shepard, Director of Policy, 15 May 2008, available through the Library of Virginia's Digital Collections, http://digitool1.lva.lib.va.us:8881/; Southern Environmental Law Center, letter to Rob Feagins, Virginia Department of Environmental Quality, 12 March 2008, 59–60, author's copy.

41. Straus, *Party and Procedure*, 261.

42. Email message from Vivian Thomson to Cindy Berndt, Virginia Department of Environmental Quality, 12 June 2008, author's copy.

43. Email message from Mark Rubin, Senior Advisor to the Governor, to Tim Kaine, 2 June 2008, available through the Library of Virginia's Digital Collections, http://digitool1.lva.lib.va.us:8881/; email exchanges among Mark Rubin, David Paylor, Preston Bryant, Brian Shepard, and Larry Roberts, 15 May 2008, available through the Library of Virginia's Digital Collections, http://digitool1.lva.lib.va.us:8881/.

44. Email message from Bruce Buckheit to David Paylor, 22 May 2008, email message from David Paylor to Preston Bryant, email message from Preston Bryant to Mark Rubin, 23 May 2008, available through the Library of Virginia's Digital Collections, http://digitool1.lva.lib.va.us:8881/.

45. Email messages between Governor Tim Kaine and Secretary of Natural Resources Preston Bryant, 22 May 2008, available through the Library of Virginia's Digital Collections, http://digitool1.lva.lib.va.us:8881/; email message from Mark Rubin to David Paylor and Preston Bryant, 21 May 2008, available through the Library of Virginia's Digital Collections, http://digitool1.lva.lib.va.us:8881/.

46. Email messages from Vivian Thomson to Cindy Berndt, Secretary to the State Air Pollution Control Board, 27 and 28 May 2008, author's copies; email message from David Paylor to Preston Bryant and Mark Rubin, 16 June 2008, available through the Library of Virginia's Digital Collections, http://digitool1.lva.lib.va.us:8881/.

47. Department of Environmental Quality, Dominion Virginia City Hybrid Energy Center, Public Comments, http://www.deq.state.va.us/Programs/Air/Permitting Compliance/Permitting/PowerPlants/DominionVirginiaCityHybridEnergyCenterT

EST/PublicComments.aspx; email messages from Vivian Thomson to Cindy Berndt and David Paylor, 28 May 2008 and 5 June 2008, author's copies.

48. Email message from Mark Rubin to Governor Tim Kaine, 2 June 2008, available through the Library of Virginia, available through the Library of Virginia's Digital Collections, http://digitool1.lva.lib.va.us:8881/; email message from David Paylor to Preston Bryant, 15 May 2008, available through the Library of Virginia's Digital Collections, http://digitool1.lva.lib.va.us:8881/.

49. Email message from Mark Rubin to Brian Shepard and Delacey Skinner, 5 June 2008, available through the Library of Virginia's Digital Collections, http://digitool1 .lva.lib.va.us:8881/; email message from Mark Rubin to David Paylor and Preston Bryant, 6 June 2008, available through the Library of Virginia's Digital Collections, http://digitool1.lva.lib.va.us:8881; letter from Governor Tim Kaine to State Air Pollution Control Board members, 10 June 2008, author's copy.

50. *Bristol Herald-Courier*, "Kaine Knee-Deep in the Muck," reproduced at thegreenmiles.blogspot.com/2008_06_01_archive.html; Glenn Hurowitz "Calamity Kaine: Virginia Gov, Possible Veep, Trembles at Big Coal," http://www .huffingtonpost.com/glenn-hurowitz/calamity-kaine-virginia-g_b_107478.html.

51. Virginia State Air Pollution Control Board, Public Hearing Meeting Minutes and Transcript, 24 June 2008 and 25 June 2008, 21, 95, 212, 266, author's copy.

52. Virginia Department of Environmental Quality, "Final Case-by-Case MACT Permit: Stationary Source Permit to Construct and Operate," 6, author's copy; Virginia Department of Environmental Quality, "Final Prevention of Deterioration Permit: Stationary Source Permit to Construct and Operate," 9, author's copy; Vivian Thomson, Memorandum to Cindy Berndt, "Information and Rationale Considered When Setting MACT and BACT Permit Limits for Dominion Power's Proposed Hybrid Energy Center in Virginia City, Virginia," author's copy.

53. Virginia State Air Pollution Control Board, Public Hearing Meeting Minutes and Transcript, 24 and 25 June 2008, 360.

54. Vivian Thomson, Memorandum to Cindy Berndt, Virginia Department of Environmental Quality, 30 June 2008.

55. Virginia State Air Pollution Control Board, Meeting Minutes, 25 June 2008, 135–137; Circuit Court for the City of Richmond, 10 August 2009 letter from Margaret Poles Spencer, Judge, to Cale Jaffe, Southern Environmental Law Center, et al., https://www.southernenvironment.org/uploads/pages/file/wise_county/wise _county_spencer_decision.pdf; Southern Environmental Law Center, Comments of Cale Jaffe, Senior Attorney, "Virginia State Air Pollution Control Board Public Meeting Re: Proposed Dominion Resources Virginia City Hybrid Energy Center, Wise, VA," 24 June 2008, 4, author's copy; Rex Springsteen, "New Permit for Coal-Fired Power Plant in Wise County Pleases Both Sides," Richmond-Times Dispatch,

3 September 2009, http://www.wsls.com/story/20814238/new-permit-for-coal-fired -power-plant-in-wise-co-pleases-both-sides; Staff report, "Amendment to Dominion Air Emissions Permit Approved," *TimesNews*, 2 September 2009, http://www .timesnews.net/News/2009/09/02/Amendment-to-Dominion-air-emissions-permit -approved.html.

56. Email message from Bruce Buckheit, former Air Pollution Control Board member, to Vivian Thomson, Hullie Moore, Richard Langford, and John Hanson, 7 March 2013, author's copy; Dominion, "Virginia City Hybrid Energy Center Joins the Fleet," https://www.youtube.com/watch?v=iF4vA6C-Hqs, at 3:32.

Chapter 3

1. Viney P. Aneja, "Characterization of Particulate Matter (PM_{10}) in Roda, Virginia," 1, undated, submitted to the Air Pollution Control Board in April 2009, author's copy; Sierra Club Scrapbook, "Big Coal Dust Victory in Virginia," 14 May 2009, http://sierraclub.typepad.com/scrapbook/2009/05/big-coal-dust-victory-in-virginia .html.

2. Viney P. Aneja, Characterization of Particulate Matter (PM_{10}) in Roda, Virginia, undated report submitted in April 2009 to the Virginia Air Pollution Control Board, 1, appendixes B and C, author's copy.

3. Ibid.

4. Code of Virginia § 10.1–1302, "Qualifications of Members of Board," http://law .lis.virginia.gov/vacode/title10.1/chapter13/section10.1-1302/.

5. Email message from David Paylor to Preston Bryant and Mark Rubin, 12 June 2008, available through the Library of Virginia's Digital Collections, http://digitool1 .lva.lib.va.us:8881/; email message from Paul Brockwell to Michael Kelly, 4 August 2008, available through the Library of Virginia's Digital Collections, http://digitool1 .lva.lib.va.us:8881/.

6. US Environmental Protection Agency, "Fine Particle (PM2.5) Designations," http://www.epa.gov/airquality/particlepollution/designations/faq.htm#0.

7. US Environmental Protection Agency, *Regulatory Impact Analysis for the Final Revisions*, 5–4, 5–5; Hamra et al., "Outdoor Particulate Matter Exposure," 906; Caiazzo et al., "Air Pollution and Early Deaths in the United States," 203; Lim et al., "A Comparative Risk Assessment," 2238; Michael Brauer, as quoted in Darryl Fears, "More Than 5 Million People Will Die From a Frightening Cause: Breathing," *Washington Post*, 12 February 2016, https://www.washingtonpost.com/news/energy -environment/wp/2016/02/12/more-than-5-million-people-will-die-from-a -frightening-cause-breathing/?utm_term=.e252145cd199.

8. Raz et el., "Autism Spectrum Disorder," 264; US Environmental Protection Agency, "President's Task Force," 2; Hubbard Brook, "Acid Rain," http://www.hubbardbrook .org/6-12_education/SubjectPages/AcidRainPage.htm; Chesapeake Bay Program, "Nutrients," http://www.chesapeakebay.net/issues/issue/nutrients#inline.

9. Reitze, "EPA's Fine Particulate Air Pollution Control Program," 10996–10997; US Environmental Protection Agency, "NAAQS Table," https://www.epa.gov/criteria -air-pollutants/naaqs-table.

10. US Environmental Protection Agency, "National Ambient Air Quality Standards," http://www.epa.gov/ttn/naaqs/criteria.html; 40 Code of Federal Regulations, Part 50 (1)(e), https://www.law.cornell.edu/cfr/text/40/50.1.

11. Pope et al., "Fine-Particulate Air Pollution and Life Expectancy in the United States," 379.

12. Karanasiou et al., "Assessment of Personal Exposure to Particulate Air Pollution," 796; L. Morawska et al., "Indoor Aerosols," 462; Brugge et al., "Developing Community-Level Policy and Practice," 93; Wallace and Ott, "Personal Exposure to Ultrafine Particles," 20.

13. US Environmental Protection Agency, "SO$_2$ NAAQS Designations Source-Oriented Monitoring Technical Assistance Document," December 2013, http:// www.epa.gov/airquality/sulfurdioxide/pdfs/SO2MonitoringTAD.pdf; US Environmental Protection Agency, "Guidance for Network Design," 2-19–2-22.

14. Scheffe et al., "The National Ambient Air Monitoring Strategy," 580.

15. Letter from David Paylor, Virginia Department of Environmental Quality, to Shawn Garvin, US Environmental Protection Agency, "Virginia Annual Air Quality Monitoring Network Review," 14 June 2013, maps at end of document (pages not numbered), http://www.epa.gov/ttnamti1/files/networkplans/VA2013Plan.pdf; Shenandoah National Park, "Monitoring—Air Quality," http://www.nps.gov/shen/ learn/nature/mon_air.htm; City of Alexandria, "Environmental Quality," http:// www.alexandriava.gov/AirQuality; US Environmental Protection Agency, "Fine Particulate Matter (PM2.5) Designations," http://www.epa.gov/pmdesignations/.

16. Virginia Department of Environmental Quality, *Air Quality and Air Pollution Control Policies of the Commonwealth of Virginia (October 2008)*, 2, 13–14, http://www .deq.virginia.gov/Portals/0/DEQ/LawsAndRegulations/2008_FinalAirQualityandAirP ollutionControlPoliciesReport.pdf.

17. Viney P. Aneja, "Characterization of Particulate Matter (PM$_{10}$) in Roda, Virginia," undated, submitted to the Air Pollution Control Board in April 2009, author's copy; Aneja et al., "Characterization of Particulate Matter (PM$_{10}$) Related to Surface Coal Mining Operations in Appalachia," 497; US Environmental Protection Agency, "National Trends in Particulate Matter Levels," http://www.epa.gov/airtrends/pm

.html; Viney Aneja, letter to State Air Pollution Control Board, 28 April 2010, 3, author's copy.

18. Virginia State Air Pollution Control Board, Meeting Minutes, 24 April 2009, https://www.townhall.virginia.gov/L/GetFile.cfm?File=C:\TownHall\docroot\Meeting\1\12579\Minutes_DEQ_12579_v3.pdf.

19. Sierra Club and Southern Appalachian Mountain Stewards, "Petition to the Virginia Air Pollution Control Board to Amend Existing Regulations," 16 November 2009, 4, author's copy.

20. Viney Aneja, Presentation to the State Air Pollution Control Board, November 2009, author's copy; Sierra Club and Southern Appalachian Mountain Stewards, "Petition to the Virginia Air Pollution Control Board," 4–5.

21. Sierra Club and Southern Appalachian Mountain Stewards, "Petition to the Virginia Air Pollution Control Board," 26.

22. Southern Appalachian Mountain Stewards and Sierra Club, "Petition to the Virginia Air Pollution Control Board, 9-13.

23. Virginia State Air Pollution Control Board, Meeting Minutes, 20 November 2009, http://townhall.virginia.gov/L/GetFile.cfm?File=C:\TownHall\docroot\Meeting\1\13676\Minutes_DEQ_13676_v2.pdf; Virginia State Air Pollution Control Board, Meeting Minutes, 3-4; 8 January 2010, https://www.townhall.virginia.gov/L/GetFile.cfm?File=C:\TownHall\docroot\Meeting\1\13864\Minutes_DEQ_13864_v4.pdf.

24. Agency for Toxic Substances and Disease Registry, "Letter Health Consultation: Summary of Roda Air Exposures, Roda, Virginia, March 2010," ii-iii, author's copy.

25. Email message from Vivian Thomson to David Paylor, 22 March 2010; Agency for Toxic Substances and Disease Registry, "Letter Health Consultation," ii; Lora Siegmann Werner, "Public Health Review of Ambient Air Monitoring Data Roda, Virginia: Presentation for Air Pollution Control Board," March 26 2010, 8, author's copy; Dwight Flammia, Virginia Department of Health, email message to author, 7 April 2010.

26. See, generally, Ezzati et al., "The Reversal of Fortunes."

27. The individuals, companies and amounts donated to McDonnell are: Richard Gilliam, $400,000 and Marvin Gilliam, $180,000 of Cumberland Resources; Consol, $357,010; Alpha, $225,000; Massey Coal, $80,000; and Cumberland, $52,500. Campaign donation data available through the Institute for Money in Politics. Searches referenced here are from the Virginia Public Access Project, http://www.vpap.org/candidates/5666/top_donors/?page=6&end_year=all&start_year=all.

28. Burnley, "How Will Virginia Regulate Uranium Mining?" 42.

29. Colleen McKaughan, Associate Director, US EPA Region 9, Air Division, personal interview, 7 August 2015.

30. All population values from the US Census's "State and County QuickFacts," http://quickfacts.census.gov/qfd/; US Environmental Protection Agency, "Fine Particulate Matter Concentrations Based on Monitored Air Quality from 2009 to 2011," http://www.epa.gov/pm/2012/20092011table.pdf.

31. Virginia State Air Pollution Control Board, Meeting Minutes, 18 March 2011, 2, https://www.townhall.virginia.gov/L/GetFile.cfm?File=C:\TownHall\docroot\ Meeting\1\16140\Minutes_DEQ_16140_v2.pdf; Department of Mines, Minerals and Energy, "Agency Summary," http://law.lis.virginia.gov/admincode/title4/ agency25/preface/; State Air Pollution Control Board, "Agency Summary," http:// law.lis.virginia.gov/admincode/title9/agency5/preface/.

32. Rhodes, *Environmental Justice in America*, 19.

33. Shrader-Frechette, *Environmental* Justice, 77; Leciejewski and Perkins, "Environmental Justice in Appalachia," 113.

34. Turner, "People of Color," 4; Walker, *Environmental* Justice, 126.

35. Gaventa, *Power and Powerlessness*, 260.

Chapter 4

1. Kirstin Downey, "Compromise Preserves Board's Permitting Clout," *Washington Post*, 20 March 2008, http://www.washingtonpost.com/wp-dyn/content/article/ 2008/03/18/AR2008031803909_pf.html; Virginia Department of Environmental Quality, "Citizen Board Legislation," 1; email messages between Shelton Miles and Preston Bryant, 29 January 2007, available through the Library of Virginia's Digital Collections, http://digitool1.lva.lib.va.us:8881/.

2. Robert G. Burnley, "Let's Not Gut Our Citizen Boards: Busting the Citizen Environmental Boards Myths," *Virginian-Pilot*, 3 February 2008, http://www.redorbit .com/news/science/1240647/lets_not_gut_our_citizen_boards_busting_the_citizen _environmental/.

3. Andrews, *Managing the Environment*, 141–142; Wilson, "The Study of Administration," 210.

4. See generally Stone, *Policy Paradox*; Williams and Matheny, *Democracy, Dialogue, and Environmental Disputes*; Croley, *Regulation and Public Interests*.

5. Virginia Department of Environmental Quality, transcript of public hearing on Virginia City Hybrid Energy Center proposed permits, 3 April 2008, 15, 17, 20, 22, 24, author's copy.

6. Former Air Board member and Chair Williams Hullihen Moore, personal interview, 2 August 2015.

7. Clarke Morrison, "Witness: TVA Violated Air Laws," *Asheville Citizen Times*, July 2008 (exact date unknown), author's copy; Bruce Barcott, "Changing All the Rules," *New York Times*, 4 April 2004, http://www.nytimes.com/2004/04/04/magazine/changing-all-the-rules.html; McGarity, "When Strong Enforcement Works Better Than Weak Regulation," 1282.

8. See Croley, *Regulation and the Public Interests*, chapter 3, for a description of key assumptions in the regulatory capture literature and for Croley's criticisms thereof.

9. Lodge, "Regulatory Capture Recaptured," 539; for a description of the public choice literature, see generally Croley, *Regulation and Public Interests*, chapters 1–3.

10. Carpenter and Moss, Introduction to *Reinventing Regulatory Capture*, 11–12; Carpenter, "Detecting and Measuring Capture," 63; see generally Dal Bó, "Regulatory Capture: A Review"; see generally Derthick and Quirk, *The Politics of Deregulation*; Quirk, "In Defense of the Politics of Ideas," 40.

11. Pautz and Rinfret, *Lilliputians of Environmental Regulation*, 89; Yeager, *The Limits of Law*, 43, 296, Croley, *Regulation and the Public Interests*, 304, 306.

12. For a description of iron triangle politics involving pesticides regulation, see generally Bosso, *Pesticides and Politics*. See Waterman et al., *Bureaucrats, Politics, and the Environment*, for an extended analysis of common "myths" regarding bureaucratic politics.

13. Nye, *The Future of Power*, 14; Kearns and Lukes, "In Conversation with Steven Lukes," 274; Yeager, *The Limits of Law*, 205; Pautz and Rinfret, *The Lilliputians of Environmental Regulation*, 87–89.

14. Albert Pollard Jr., former member of the Virginia House of Delegates, personal interview, 30 July 2015.

15. Konisky and Woods, "Measuring State Environmental Policy," 563; Carley and Miller, "Regulatory Stringency and Policy Drivers," 748; Berry et al., "Driving Energy: The Enactment and Ambitiousness," 312; Thomson and Arroyo, "Upside-Down Cooperative Federalism," 41–46.

16. Elazar, *American Federalism*, 118–122.

17. Dave Ress, "A Part-Time Legislature with Full-Time Rewards: Part I," *The Daily Press*, 18 November 2014, http://www.dailypress.com/news/politics/dp-nws-virginiaway-overview-20141116-story.html#page=1; Squire, "Measuring State Legislative Professionalism," 214–215 and 219–221; Rosenthal, "State Legislative Development," 172.

18. Tung et al., "Political Factors Affecting the Enactment of State-Level Clean Indoor Air Laws," e96.

19. Albert Pollard Jr., former member of the Virginia House of Delegates, personal interview, 30 July 2015; W. Tayloe Murphy Jr., former member, Virginia House of Delegates and former Virginia Secretary of Natural Resources, personal interview, 3 September 2015; Associated Press, "Energy Giant Dominion Exerts Strong Influence On Virginia Lawmakers," 28 February 2015, http://wjla.com/news/local/energy -giant-dominion-exerts-strong-influence-on-va-lawmakers-111893; *NewsLeader* editorial, "Dominion's Domination," 7 February 2015, http://www.newsleader.com/ story/opinion/editorials/2015/02/07/dominions-domination/23067035/.

20. Dave Ress, "Making Lucrative Connections at the State Capitol," *The Daily Press*, 22 November 2014, author's copy; Pollard, interview; Jerry McCarthy, personal interview and email correspondence, 18 August and 23 October 2015; Murphy, interview and email correspondence, 3 and 15 September 2015.

21. Thomson and Arroyo, "Upside-Down Cooperative Federalism," 54. Campaign finance data from the Virginia Public Access Project, www.vpap.org, "Donors from Energy, Natural Resources, 2001 through 2009" and "Donors from Electric Utilities, 2001 through 2009." In the amount of funding ($5,381,101) attributed to Dominion or its employees the following are included: Dominion ($4,929,372), Thomas F. Farrell II, now CEO of Dominion ($220,661), Thomas N. Chewning ($102,650), Formerly Chief Financial Officer of Dominion; Eva Tieg Hardy, former Executive Vice President at Dominion ($97,668); Paul D. Koonce, Executive Vice President at Dominion ($30,750).

22. See generally Schlozman et al., *The Unheavenly Chorus* and Flavin, "Campaign Finance Laws."

23. Virginia Political Access Project, "Top Donors," www.vpap.org; Patrick Wilson, "Foes of Dominion Power Are Mainly Outside Legislature," *The Virginian-Pilot*, 6 February 2015, http://hamptonroads.com/2015/02/foes-dominion-bill-are-mainly-outside-legislature; Jacob Geiger, "Governor Signs Bill to Freeze Dominion Rates, Suspend Reviews," *Richmond Times-Dispatch*, 24 February 2015, http://www .richmond.com/business/local/article_b356b0cb-473d-5cb0-ad1c-6c5a076d45c1. html. Campaign finance data from The National Institute on Money in State Politics, FollowTheMoney.orgFollowTheMoney.org.

24. R. H. Melton, "Mark Warner Prepares for Role in Fall While Looking Toward 2001 Bid," *Washington Post*, 12 September 1999, V04. The specific data used for the computations in these two paragraphs are as follows, for coal mining giving/energy and natural resources giving in 2001–2015: Virginia, $6.8 million/$23.9 million, West Virginia, $2.7 million/$6.0 million, and Kentucky, $1.6 million/$5.3 million. Analytical results from the Institute for Money in Politics, http://www .followthemoney.org/show-me?y=2015,2014,2013,2012,2011,2010,2009,2008,2007

,2006,2005,2004,2003,2002,2001&f-core=1&f-fc=2&d-ccb=95#[{2| (coal   mining donations, all states), http://www.followthemoney.org/show-me?y=2015,2014,2013 ,2012,2011,2010,2009,2008,2007,2006,2005,2004,2003,2002,2001&f-core=1&f -fc=2&d-ccg=5 (energy/natural resources donations, all states); US Energy Information Administration, "Virginia Net Electricity Generation By Source, April 2015," http://www.eia.gov/state/?sid=VA#tabs-4. Total contributions to Governor Kaine from energy and natural resources donors were $279,705. The energy and natural resources super-category includes a long list of important sectors, ranging from aluminum mining and processing to the electric utilities to the steel industry. Of the $279,705 donated to Mr. Kaine, companies and individuals donated the following amounts: Dominion, $55,000; James W. McGlothlin, Chairman of United Coal, $25,000 (William and Mary Raymond A. Mason School of Business, "About the McGlothlins," https://mason.wm.edu/mcglothlin_forum/james_mcglothlin/index .php); Alpha Natural Resources, $10,000; Virginia Coal Association, $10,000; Donald L. Ratliff, $10,000 (longtime coal industry employee and executive, West Virginia Press, "Alpha Natural Resources' Vice President to Chair VCEA," 1 July 2014, http:// wvpress.org/wvpa-sharing/state-news/alpha-natural-resources-vice-president-chair-vcea/); Eva Teig Hardy (Dominion executive), $7,500; Thomas E. Capps, $2,500 (Dominion CEO, Dominion, "Capps to Retire as Dominion CEO on December 31, 16 December 2005, http://dom.mediaroom.com/news?item=71145); Jewell Smokeless Coal, $2,500; James F. Stutts, $2,500 (Dominion executive, PR Newswire, "James F. Stutts to Retire as General Counsel of Dominion," 9 November 2010, http://www .prnewswire.com/news-releases/james-f-stutts-to-retire-as-general-counsel-of -dominion-106951948.html); E. Morgan Massey, $2,000 (Massey coal executive). All information from National Institute on Money in State Politics, "Show Me Energy and Natural Resources Contributions Donated between 1 January 2003 and 1 January 2010 to Kaine, Timothy M., in elections in Virginiahttp://www.followthemoney .org/show-me?s=VA&f-core=1&f-fc=1,2&c-t-eid=6209648&d-ccg=5&d-dte=2003-01 -01,2010-01-01#[{1|gro=d-eid. For Governor Warner the figures are: total energy and natural resources giving, $374,070, of which: Dominion, $130,000; coal company Amvest, $10,000; Virginia Coal Association, $10,000; Duke Energy, $7,500; Morgan Massey, $7,500; Pittston Coal, $5,346; coal company Cumberland Resources, $5,000; Jewell Smokeless Coal, $5,000. National Institute on Money in State Politics, "Show Me Energy and Natural Resources Contributions Donated between January 1, 1999 and January 1, 2006 Warner, Mark Robert in elections in Virginia," http://www .followthemoney.org/show-me?s=VA&f-core=1&f-fc=1,2&c-t-eid=12996544&d-ccg =5&d-dte=1999-01-01,2006-01-01#[{1|gro=d-eid.

25. US Energy Information Administration, "Coal Production and Number of Mines"; Foster and Glustrom, *Trends in US Coal Production*, 22; US Energy Information Administration, "US End Use Coal Consumption"; US Energy Information Administration, "Electricity: Detailed States Data," http://www.eia.gov/electricity/ data/state/, and "Electric Power Monthly, February 2016," tables 1.3B and 1.4B,-

http://www.eia.gov/electricity/monthly/current_year/february2016.pdf; Hank Hayes, "Report Indicates Manufacturing Could Replace Lost SW Va. Coal Jobs," *TimesNews*, 10 February 2015, http://www.timesnews.net/News/2015/02/10/Report-indicates -manufacturing-could-replace-lost-SW-Va-coal-jobs.html.

26. Ansolabehere et al., 2003, "Why Is There So Little Money in US Politics?" 112; Baumgartner et al., *Lobbying and Policy Change*, 208, 212; Schlozman et al., *The Unheavenly Chorus*, 591; Powell, *Legislative Politics and Policymaking*, 5, 202.

27. Powell, *Legislative Politics and Policymaking*, 210.

28. Powell, *Legislative Politics and Policymaking*, 210; Flavin, "Campaign Finance Laws," 81–84; Squire and Moncrief, *State Legislatures Today* (2015), 64.

29. Elazar, *American Federalism: A View from the States*, 112, 119–121.

30. See, e.g., Mondak and Canache, "Personality and Political Culture"; Miller et al., "Mapping the Genome," 304.

31. Elazar, *American Federalism*, 115–119, 136.

32. Elazar, *American Federalism*, 135–136; Miller et al., "Mapping the Genome," 306.

33. Virginia General Assembly, Joint Legislative Review and Audit Commission, *Interim Report: Review of the Department of Environmental Quality*, and *Review of the Department of Environmental Quality*, 1997.

34. Mead, "State Political Culture," 284–287; Mead," Welfare Caseload Change," 181.

Chapter 5

1. Yeager, *The Limits of Law*, 115, 161–162; Jones, *Clean* Air, 253; Andrews, *Managing the Environment*, 232.

2. Representative Harley O. Staggers, 116 *Congressional Record*, 19,204, as cited in Dwyer, "The Practice of Federalism," 1192.

3. For a description of some of these legal disputes, see generally Garrett, "Down-wind Ozone." The EPA summarizes federal actions taken to address interstate air pollution transport at https://www.epa.gov/airmarkets/interstate-air-pollution -transport.

4. See generally Dwyer, "The Practice of Federalism"; Dwyer points out that transportation agencies must comply with the provisions of a State Implementation Plan, 1196–1197; Marcia Spink, US Environmental Protection Agency Region 3, "Sanctions, Federal Implementation Plans (FIPS), and SIP Calls Under the Clean Air Act," PowerPoint presentation, 26 October 2010, https://www.epa.gov/apti/ video/Sanctions1110/MarciaPresentationSanctions&FIPs_FINAL_8_26_10.pdf;

Buckley, "Clean Air Post-Healthcare," 811–812; McCarthy et al., *Clean Air Act*, 4; Reitze, "Federalism and the Inspection and Maintenance Program," 1463.

5. For a list of California's air-quality legislation and regulatory activities, see California Air Resources Board, "Key Events in the History of Air Quality in California," http://www.arb.ca.gov/html/brochure/history.htm. Michael B. Marois and Shin Pei, "Brown's California Overtakes Brazil with Companies Leading the World," *Bloomberg Business*, 16 January 2015, http://www.bloomberg.com/news/articles/2015 -01-16/brown-s-california-overtakes-brazil-with-companies-leading-world; California Air Resources Board, "California Local Air District Directory," https://www.arb. ca.gov/capcoa/roster.htm; US Environmental Protection Agency, "Clean Air Act Grant: South Coast Air Quality Management District, Opportunity for Public Hearing," Federal Register, 18 March 2014, https://federalregister.gov/articles/ 2014/03/18/2014-05906/clean-air-act-grant-south-coast-air-quality-management -district-opportunity-for-public-hearing; Bay Area Air Quality Management District, "Approved Budget for Fiscal Year Ending 2016," 10; Indiana Department of Environmental Management, "An Introduction to the Indiana Department of Environmental Management," Office of Air Quality, Total Funding, www.in.gov/idem/files/ about_idem_101.ppt, slide 35; US Environmental Protection Agency Region 5, "Air Program Grant Funding Targets for Fiscal Year 2015," https://yosemite.epa.gov/r5/ r5ard.nsf/216ee3876e2b57c786256641005b8d76/bef870e65f58edd886257e2d0053b 547!OpenDocument.

6. For a description of state-federal struggles over inspection and maintenance programs, see generally Reitze, "Federalism and Inspection and Maintenance Programs Under the Clean Air Act"; US Environmental Protection Agency, "California Waivers and Authorizations," https://www3.epa.gov/otaq/cafr.htm.

7. Letter from Catherine Witherspoon, Executive Director, California Air Resources Board, 21 December 2005, http://www.arb.ca.gov/cc/docs/waiver.pdf; letter from Stephen L. Johnson, EPA Administrator, to California Governor Arnold Schwarzenegger, 19 December 2007, https://www3.epa.gov/otaq/climate/20071219-slj.pdf; US Environmental Protection Agency, "EPA and NHTSA Finalize Historic National Program to Reduce Greenhouse Gases and Improve Fuel Economy for Cars and Trucks," April 2010, https://www3.epa.gov/otaq/climate/regulations/420f10014.pdf; California Air Resources Board, "Clean Car Standards—Pavley, Assembly Bill 1493," http://www.arb.ca.gov/cc/ccms/ccms.htm.

8. For a description of the Clean Air Act's various cap-and-trade programs, see Burtraw and Szambelan, "US Emissions Trading Markets for SO2 and NOx" and US Environmental Protection Agency, "Clean Air Markets," https://www.epa.gov/ airmarkets. For a brief overview the Clean Air Act's various programs, see US Environmental Protection Agency, "The Plain English Guide to the Clean Air Act."

9. See generally Grumet, "Old West Justice" and US Environmental Protection Agency, "Interstate Air Pollution Transport," https://www.epa.gov/airmarkets/

interstate-air-pollution-transport; Randy Lee Loftis, "Texas OKs Taking Over Green-house Gas Permits from EPA," *Dallas Morning News*, 26 March 2014, http://thescoopblog.dallasnews.com/2014/03/texas-oks-taking-over-greenhouse-gas-permits-from-epa.html/; *Massachusetts v. Environmental Protection Agency*, 549 US 497 (2007), 20; US Environmental Protection Agency, "Endangerment and Cause or Contribute Findings for Greenhouse Gases under Section 202(a) of the Clean Air Act," https://www3.epa.gov/climatechange/endangerment/.

10. Carlson, "Ode to the Clean Air Act," 120.

11. Associated Press, "Supreme Court Puts Obama's Clean Power Plan on Hold," 9 February 2016, http://www.nytimes.com/aponline/2016/02/09/us/politics/ap-us-supreme-court-clean-air-lawsuits.html.

12. US Environmental Protection Agency, "Carbon Pollution Emission Guidelines for Existing Stationary Sources: Electric Utility Generating Units; Final Rule," Federal Register 80, no. 205 (23 October 2015): 64661–65120, 32 percent figure at 64665, projected emission reductions relative to baseline levels in 2030 at 64924, definition of Best System of Emission Reduction at 64717–64722; US Environmental Protection Agency, "Clean Power Plan by the Numbers," https://www2.epa.gov/cleanpowerplan/fact-sheet-clean-power-plan-numbers; US Environmental Protection Agency, *Inventory of US Greenhouse Gas Emissions and Sinks: 1990–2014*, ES-5; US Environmental Protection Agency, *Regulatory Impact Analysis for the Final Mercury and Air Toxics Standards*, ES-2; for an analysis of the forces behind the decrease in greenhouse-gas emissions in the United States, see generally Ramseur, "US Green-house Gas Emissions"; US Energy Information Administration, "US Energy-Related Carbon Dioxide Emissions, 2014," http://ww.eia/gov/environment/emissions/carbon/; Umweltbundesamt, "Die Treibhausgase," https://www.umweltbundesamt.de/themen/klima-energie/klimaschutz-energiepolitik-in-deutschland/treibhausgas-emissionen/die-treibhausgase.

13. United States Geological Service, "The Use of Historical Production Data to Pre-dict Future Coal Production Rates," 16 September 1997, http://pubs.usgs.gov/circ/c1147/historical.html; Virginia Department of Mines, Minerals and Energy and Virginia Tech, "Virginia Energy Patterns and Trends," https://www.energy.vt.edu/vept/coal/.

14. Energy Information Administration, "Coal Production and Number of Mines by State and Mine Type, 2014," https://www.eia.gov/coal/annual/pdf/table2.pdf; US Energy Information Administration, "Electricity: Detailed States Data," http://www.eia.gov/electricity/data/state/, and "Electric Power Monthly with Data for October 2015," 2015 data are year to date through October, tables 1.3B and 1.4B, http://www.eia.gov/electricity/monthly/pdf/epm.pdf; US Energy Information Administration, "Energy Consumption Estimates for Major Energy Sources in Physical Units, 1960–2013, Virginia," http://www.eia.gov/state/seds/data.cfm?incfile=/state/seds/sep_use/total/use_tot_VAa.html&sid=VA; US Energy Information Administration,

"Coal Consumption Estimates and Imports and Exports of Coal Coke, 2014," http://www.eia.gov/state/seds/sep_fuel/html/pdf/fuel_use_cl.pdf.

15. Nye, *The Future of Power*, 12.

16. See generally Crenson, *The Unpolitics of Air Pollution*.

17. This abbreviated summary of the "faces of power" literature of Robert Dahl, Peter Bachrach and Morton Baratz, and Steven Lukes is drawn from Nye, *The Future of Power*, 10–16; Gaventa, *Power and Powerlessness*, 23, 42.

18. All data represent the most recent available. US Energy Information Administration, "Coal Production and Number of Mines by State and Mine Type, 2013 and 2014," http://www.eia.gov/coal/annual/pdf/table1.pdf; US Energy Information Administration, "Coal Consumption Estimates and Imports and Exports of Coal Coke, 2014," http://www.eia.gov/state/seds/sep_fuel/html/pdf/fuel_use_cl.pdf; US Energy Information Administration, "2013 State carbon dioxide emissions by energy sector," http://www.eia.gov/environment/emissions/state/; US Energy Information Administration, "Coal Production and Number of Mines by State and Mine Type, 2013, and 2012," www.eia.gov/coal/annual/pdf/table1.pdf; US Energy Information Administration, "Electricity: Detailed States Data," http://www.eia.gov/electricity/data/state/, and "Electric Power Monthly with Data for October 2015," 2015 data are year to date through October, tables 1.3B and 1.4B, http://www.eia.gov/electricity/monthly/pdf/epm.pdf; Global Carbon Atlas, "Fossil Fuel Emissions," http://www.globalcarbonatlas.org/?q=en/emissions; US Environmental Protection Agency, "Clean Power Plan: State Specific Fact Sheets," https://www2.epa.gov/cleanpowerplantoolbox/clean-power-plan-state-specific-fact-sheets; US Environmental Protection Agency, "Air Markets Program Data," https://ampd.epa.gov/ampd/.

19. US Environmental Protection Agency, "Title IV: Acid Deposition Control," https://epa.gov/air/caa/caaa_overview.html; Cohen, *Washington at Work*, see generally chapter 6; State of West Virginia, "Legal Actions Against EPA," http://www.ago.wv.gov/publicresources/epa/Pages/default.aspx.

20. Yale University Project on Climate Communication and George Mason University Center for Climate Change Communication, "Politics and Global Warming," 4; Lazarus, "A Different Kind of 'Republican' Moment," 1010–1020; US House of Representatives, H. R. 2454, "American Clean Energy and Security Act of 2009," https://www.govtrack.us/congress/votes/111-2009/h477; US Senate Roll Call Votes, 108th Congress, 1st Session, S. Amdt, 2028 to S. 139, http://www.senate.gov/legislative/LIS/roll_call_lists/roll_call_vote_cfm.cfm?congress=108&session=1&vote=00420; Senate Joint Resolution 24, "A joint resolution providing for congressional disapproval under chapter 8 of title 5, United States Code, of a rule submitted by the Environmental Protection Agency relating to 'Carbon Pollution Emission Guidelines

for Existing Stationary Sources: Electric Utility Generating Units,'" 17 November 2015, vote results at https://www.opencongress.org/vote/2015/s/306.

21. "Historical Interactive Maps," http://www.270towin.com/news/2015/06/02/more-historical-interactive-maps-launched_89.html#.VfCIUHgk_dn. (As was noted in the introduction, the commonly used shorthand descriptions "red" and "blue" refer to whether the state's electoral votes have been awarded to a Republican or to a Democrat in a presidential election.)

22. Results for House of Representatives elections in 2014, 2012, 2010, and 2008, 2008, *New York Times*, http://www.270towin.com/2014-house-election, http://elections.nytimes.com/2012/results/house, http://elections.nytimes.com/2010/results/house, and http://elections.nytimes.com/2008/results/house/map .html; League of Conservation Voters, "National Environmental Scorecard," http://scorecard.lcv.org/.

23. Ballotopedia is the source of state legislature partisanship patterns for each state: Illinois, https://ballotpedia.org/Illinois_General_Assembly; Indiana, https://ballotpedia.org/Indiana_General_Assembly; Kentucky, https://ballotpedia .org/Kentucky_General_Assembly; Ohio, https://ballotpedia.org/Ohio_General _Assembly; Pennsylvania, https://ballotpedia.org/Pennsylvania_General_Assembly; Texas, https://ballotpedia.org/Texas_State_Legislature; and, Virginia, https:// ballotpedia.org/Virginia_General_Assembly. The National Governors' Association provides gubernatorial party affiliations for all current governors (http://www.nga .org/cms/governors/bios) and for past governors by state: Illinois (http://www.nga .org/cms/home/governors/past-governors-bios/page_illinois.html), Indiana (http:// www.nga.org/cms/home/governors/past-governors-bios/page_indiana.html), Kentucky (http://www.nga.org/cms/home/governors/past-governors-bios/page_kentucky .html), Ohio (http://www.nga.org/cms/home/governors/past-governors-bios/page _ohio.html), Pennsylvania (http://www.nga.org/cms/home/governors/past-governors -bios/page_pennsylvania.html), Texas (http://www.nga.org/cms/home/governors/ past-governors-bios/page_texas.html), Virginia (http://www.nga.org/cms/home/ governors/past-governors-bios/page_virginia.html).

24. Carley and Miller, "Regulatory Stringency and Policy Drivers," 748; Berry et al., "Driving Energy: The Enactment and Ambitiousness," 312; Konisky and Woods, "Measuring State Environmental Policy," 563; Thomson and Arroyo, "Upside-Down Cooperative Federalism," 41–46.

25. Shin and Webber, "Red States, Blue States," 397; Ansolabehere et al., "Purple America," 115–116.

26. Ansolabehere and Konisky, *Cheap and Clean*, 157–159; Yale University Project on Climate Change Communication," Americans Support An International Climate Agreement in Paris," http://environment.yale.edu/climate-communication/article/americans-support-international-climate-agreement-paris.

27. Yale University Project on Climate Change Communication, *A National Survey of Republicans and Republican-Leaning Independents on Energy and Climate Change*, 2 April 2013, http://environment.yale.edu/climate-communication/files/Republican _Views_on_Climate_Change.pdf; Yale University Project on Climate Change Communication, "Is Global Warming Human Caused? The Views of US Senators and Their Constituents," http://environment.yale.edu/climate-communication/ causation/; Yale University Project on Climate Communication, "Not All Republicans Think Alike About Global Warming," http://environment.yale.edu/climate -communication/article/not-all-republicans-think-alike-about-global-warming/; Oliver Milman, "First EPA Chief Accuses Republicans of Ignoring Science for Political Gain," *The Guardian*, 23 November 2015, https://www.theguardian.com/ environment/2015/nov/23/epa-william-ruckelshaus-republicans-climate-change; Alan Neuhauser, "61 Percent of Public Supports Clean Power Plan in States Suing to Stop It," *US News and World Report*, 2 November 2015, http://www.usnews.com/ news/blogs/data-mine/2015/11/02/61-percent-of-public-supports-clean-power -plan-in-states-suing-to-stop-it.

28. Kirk Goldsberry, "Mapping the Changing Face of the Lone Star State," FiveThirtyEight Politics, 4 November 2014, http://fivethirtyeight.com/features/mapping -the-changing-face-of-the-lone-star-state/; see generally Cooper and Knotts, "Partisan Change in Southern State Legislatures"; Ari Berman, "How the GOP Is Resegregating the South," *The Nation*, 31 January 2012, https://www.thenation.com/article/ how-gop-resegregating-south/; Robin Toner, "Democrats Maintain Hold on South," *New York Times*, 21 March 1987, http://www.nytimes.com/1987/03/21/us/ democrats-maintain-hold-on-south.html.

29. Cohen, *Washington at Work*, 16, 51.

30. Krosnick and MacInnis, "Does the American Public Support Legislation," 28; Rabe and Borick, "Climate Change and American Public Opinion," 9, 11; George Mason University Center for Climate Change Communication and Yale University Project on Climate Communication, "The Francis Effect," 18; Yeager et al., "Measuring Americans' Issue Priorities," 7; Yale Project on Climate Change Communication, "Americans Support Reducing Emissions from Coal," http://www.environment.yale. edu/climate-communication/article/americans-support-reducing-emissions-from -coal/ ; Yale Project on Climate Communication, "Climate Change in the American Mind: October 2015," http://climatecommunication.yale.edu/publications/more -americans-perceive-harm-from-global-warming-survey-finds/2/.

31. Gallup, "Topics in Depth: Environment," http://www.gallup.com/poll/1615/ environment.aspx; David Leonhardt, "Americans Are Again Getting More Worried About the Climate," *New York Times*, 16 June 2015, http://www.nytimes.com/ 2015/06/17/upshot/americans-are-again-getting-more-worried-about-the-climate. html; European Commission, "Special Eurobarometer," 5; Bruce Stokes, Richard Wike, and Jill Carle, "Concern About Climate Change and Its Consequences," *Pew*

Research Center, 5 November 2015, http://www.pewglobal.org/2015/11/05/1
-concern-about-climate-change-and-its-consequences/; Krosnick and MacInnis,
"Does the American Public Support Legislation," 34.

32. Bessie Schwartz, *Huffington Post*, 2 November 2015, "61% of the Public in
the States Suing to Stop the Clean Power Plan Actually Support the Policy," http://
www.huffingtonpost.com/bessie-schwarz/61-of-the-public-in-the-states-suing-to
-stop-the-clean-power-plan-actually-support-the-policy_b_8451928.html; Jon Krosnick, "Public Opinion on Climate Change: Opinions in the States," 13 November
2013, http://climatepublicopinion.stanford.edu/sample-page/opinions-in-the-states/
#infoSheets.

33. Yale University Project on Climate Change Communication, "Americans
Support CO_2 Limits on Existing Coal-Fired Power Plants," survey conducted in October 2014, http://environment.yale.edu/climate-communication/article/americans
-support-co2-limits-on-existing-coal-fired-power-plants; Yale University Project on
Climate Change Communication, "Estimated % of Adults Who Support Setting
Strict CO_2 Limits on Existing Coal-Fired Power Plants, 2014," https://environment.
yale.edu/poe/v2014/; see generally Howe et al., "Geographic Variation"; Mining History Association, "History of the Pennsylvania Anthracite Region," http://www
.mininghistoryassociation.org/ScrantonHistory.htm.

34. Daniel Cusick, "Wind Energy Industry Strives to Expand with Leased Turbines,"
E & E Daily, 24 December 2015, http://www.eenews.net/stories/1060029984; Erin
Jordan, "Iowa Wind Projects Get Incentives, Provide Financial Benefits," *The Gazette*,
13 July 2014, http://www.thegazette.com/subject/news/iowa-wind-projects-get
-incentives-provide-financial-benefits-20140713.

35. For the conditions under which policy makers are likely act when costs are concentrated and benefits are spread widely, see generally Arnold, *The Logic of Congressional Action*; Rabe and Borick, "Report of the Virginia Climate Change Survey," 6;
Watson Center for Public Policy, "Toplines," 4; Stanford University, "Public Opinion
on Global Warming in Virginia," https://pprggw.files.wordpress.com/2015/
04/stanford-climate-polling-virginia-2013.pdf; Leiserowitz et al., "Climate Change
in the Texan Mind," 3; Gerry Mullany, "Rick Perry on the Issues," *New York Times*,
4 June 2015, http://www.nytimes.com/2015/06/05/us/politics/rick-perry-on-the
-issues.html.

36. Burstein, *American Public Opinion*, 69–70, 177–180.

Chapter 6

1. Hamm and Hogan, "Campaign Finance Laws and Candidacy Decisions," 465.

2. National Conference of State Legislatures, "State Campaign Finance Laws:
An Overview," http://www.ncsl.org/research/elections-and-campaigns/campaign

-finance-an-overview.aspx, "State Limits on Contributions to Candidates, 2015–2016 Election Cycle," http://www.ncsl.org/Portals/1/documents/legismgt/elect/ContributionLimitstoCandidates2015-2016.pdf, and "Campaign Finance and the Supreme Courts," http://www.ncsl.org/research/elections-and-campaigns/campaign-finance-and-the-supreme-court.aspx; Hunker, "Elections Across the Pond," 1118.

3. US Energy Information Administration, "Power Sector Coal Demand Has Fallen in Almost Every State Since 2007," 28 April 2016, http://www.eia.gov/todayinenergy/detail.cfm?id=26012; National Institute for Money in State Politics, "Coal Mining Contributions Donated Between January 1, 2001 and December 1, 2015, to Candidates and Committees" within each individual state and for the nation as a whole, http://www.followthemoney.org/.

4. Energy Information Administration, "Coal Report, Coal Production by State and Mine Type, for the years 2002 through 2013, http://www.eia.gov/coal/annual/"; National Institute for Money in State Politics, "Coal Mining Contributions Donated Between January 1, 2001 and December 1, 2013, to Candidates and Committees" within each individual state and for the nation as a whole, http://www.followthemoney.org/; state-specific URLs available from the author). Ohio produced less coal than Virginia through 2007, but since 2008 Virginia has produced less coal than any other state analyzed here. US Energy Information Administration, *Annual Coal Report*, for 2002–2013 (www.eia.gov/coal/annual/).

5. US Energy Information Administration, "Coal Production and Number of Mines by State and Mine Type, 2014 and 2013," http://www.eia.gov/coal/annual/pdf/table1.pdf. The super-donors are R. B. Gilliam, Marvin Gilliam, and Clyde Stacy (Virginia), Wayne and Emeline Boich (Ohio), and Steven E. Chancellor (Indiana). All searches on National Institute for Money in State Politics, www.followthemoney.org, 12 January 2016.

6. National Institute for Money in State Politics, "Coal Mining Contributions Donated Between January 1, 2001 and December 1, 2015, to Candidates and Committees" and "Energy and Natural Resources Contributions Donated Between January 1, 2001 and December 1, 2015, to Candidates and Committees," within each individual state and for the nation as a whole, http://www.followthemoney.org/; Suzanne Goldenberg, "Rockefeller Family Tried and Failed to Get Exxon Mobil to Accept Climate Change," *The Guardian*, 27 March 2015, https://www.theguardian.com/environment/2015/mar/27/rockefeller-family-tried-and-failed-exxonmobil-accept-climate-change. In Texas the oil and natural gas industry super-donors were Sayed Anwar, Ray Lee Hunt, Trevor Rees Jones, Curtis Mewbourne, and T. Boone Pickens.

7. National Institute for Money in State Politics, "Electric Utility Contributions Donated Between January 1, 2001 and December 1, 2015, to Candidates and Committees" and "Energy and Natural Resources Contributions Donated Between January 1, 2001 and December 1, 2015, to Candidates and Committees," within each

individual state and for the nation as a whole, http://www.followthemoney.org/. The Institute's aggregation technique for the electric utilities misses Dominion Electric Power substantial contributions because Dominion is included under "Energy and Natural Resources" but not "Electric Utilities." These figures correct for that categorization error.

8. Baumgartner et al., *Lobbying and Policy Change*, 225, 237.

9. National Institute for Money in State Politics, "Electric Utility Contributions Donated Between January 1, 2001 and December 1, 2015, to Candidates and Committees" and "Energy and Natural Resources Contributions Donated Between January 1, 2001 and December 1, 2015, to Candidates and Committees," within each individual state and for the nation as a whole, http://www.followthemoney.org/; US Department of Energy, "'List of Covered Electric Utilities' Under the Public Utility Regulatory Policies Act of 1978 (PURPA)," August 2008, http://energy.gov/sites/prod/files/oeprod/DocumentsandMedia/PURPA_2008.pdf.

10. The exact contribution limits for each state as of 2016 were as follows: Category 1, Few or no limits. Virginia: No limits. Pennsylvania and Texas: No limits for individuals, political action committees (PACs), or state parties. Corporations and unions may not contribute directly to candidates. Category 2, Some contributions limited. Indiana: No limits on individuals, state parties, or PACs. Corporations and unions may not contribute more than $5,000 in aggregate to statewide candidates and $2,000 in aggregate to legislature candidates. Ohio: Limits on individual and PAC contributions of $12,532.52 per candidate. State parties may not contribute more than $706,823.95 per statewide candidate, $140,988.82 per state Senate candidate, and $70,181.10 per state House candidate. Corporations and unions may not contribute directly to candidates. Kentucky: State party contributions are unlimited, although there are limits on amount of party contributions that candidates may keep. Individuals, unions and PACs are limited to $1,000 per candidate. Candidates may not keep more than a certain amount donated by PACs. Corporations may not contribute directly to candidates. Category 3, All contributions limited. Illinois: Limits of $5,400 per candidate for individual contributions. State party contributions are not limited during general elections or if a candidate is not seeking election in a primary, but state parties are limited during primaries to $215,800 per statewide candidate, $134,900 per state Senate candidate, and $80,900 per state House candidate. Political Action Committees (PAC) are limited to $53,900 per candidate per election cycle. Unions and corporations are limited to $10,800 per candidate per election cycle. Statewide candidates are exempted from all contribution limits if they receive benefit or detriment from independent expenditures exceeding $250,000. Candidates and their immediate family members may make unlimited contributions to that candidate's campaign. Any candidate whose opponent is self-funded is exempted from contribution limits. See National Conference of State Legislatures, "Contribution Limits Overview," http://www.ncsl.org/research/elections-and-campaigns/campaign-contribution-limits-overview.aspx.

11. Former Virginia Delegate Albert Pollard, personal interview, 30 July 2015; Tokaji and Strause, *The New Soft Money*, 78–79.

12. Elazar, *American Federalism*, 112; Formisano, "The Concept of Political Culture," 406; see generally Putnam et al., *Making Democracy Work*.

13. Elazar, *American Federalism*, 126–131.

14. Elazar, *American Federalism*, 120–121.

15. Elazar, American Federalism, 141–142.

16. Elazar, *American Federalism*, 133.

17. Sharkansky, "The Utility of Elazar's Political Culture," 78–83; King, "Political Culture, Voter Registration, and Voter Turnout," 127; Miller et al., "Mapping the Genome," 304, 313; Heck et al., "State Political Culture, Higher Education Spending Indicators," 29, 32; Fisher, "State Political Culture and Support for Obama," 708; Mead, "State Political Culture and Welfare Reform," 286; Koven and Mausoloff, "The Influence of Political Culture on State Budgets," 72–74.

18. Lieske, "The Changing Regional Subcultures," 541–543.

19. Elazar, *American Federalism*, 120–121, 135–136; Sharkansky, "Utility of Elazar's Political Culture," 72. Sharkansky assigned the following scores to all possible combinations of Elazar's political cultures: M 1 MT 2 MI 3 IM 4 I 5 IT 6 TI 7 TM 8 T 9. Sharkansky then used Elazar's map of state-level subcultures provided in the 1966 edition of *American Federalism* (p. 79) to compute an average political culture score for each state by simply adding up all subculture scores for any given state and dividing by the total number of scores. Updated scores here were derived by applying Sharkansky's method to the 1984 edition of *American Federalism* (124–125), which differs somewhat from the map Elazar published in 1966.

20. Elazar, *American Federalism*, 115, 120–121; Lieske, "American State Cultures," appendix B.

21. Elazar, *American Federalism*, 136; Lieske, "Changing Regional Subcultures," appendix B; Bateman et al., "*Southern Politics* Revisited," 178; Gaddie and Wert, "Before KKV, V. O. Key, Jr.," 87; "belt" obtained by mapping percentages of African Americans, five classes, equal intervals, at US Census, "Census Data Mapper," http://datamapper.geo.census.gov/map.html.

22. National Council of State Governments, "Our State Legislatures," 2.

23. Squire and Moncrief, *State Legislatures Today*, 2015, table A-3; Squire, "Measuring State Legislative Professionalism," 220–221.

24. National Conference of State Legislatures, "Size of State Legislative Staff, 2009," http://www.ncsl.org/research/about-state-legislatures/staff-change-chart-1979-1988 -1996-2003-2009.aspx, and "Legislative Session Length," http://www.dailypress

.com/news/politics/dp-nws-virginiaway-overview-20141116-story.html. Staff data are available only through 2009.

25. Pennsylvania General Assembly, Joint State Government Commission, "Waste Tire Recycling and Reuse"; Pennsylvania General Assembly, Joint State Government Commission, "Report of the Task Force"; Texas Legislature, House Committee on Environmental Regulations, "Interim Report to the 84th Legislature"; Illinois General Assembly, Special Reports, http://www.ilga.gov/reports/specialreports.asp; Kentucky Legislative Research Commission, "LRC Reports," http://www.lrc.ky.gov/lrcpubs/research_reports.htm; Ohio Legislature, "Member Only Briefs," https://www.legislature.ohio.gov/publications/members-only-briefs; Indiana General Assembly, 2016 Session, "Publications," https://iga.in.gov/legislative/2016/publications/evaluation_report/; Virginia General Assembly, Joint Legislative Audit and Review Commission, http://jlarc.virginia.gov/reports.asp.

26. Squire and Moncrief, *State Legislatures Today*, 2010, 82–83, 255; Squire and Moncrief, *State Legislatures Today*, 2015, 72; National Conference of State Legislatures, "State Legislator Compensation," http://www.ncsl.org/research/about-state-legislatures/2015-state-legislator-compensation.aspx; Tom Loftus, "Salary, Expenses for Each Kentucky Legislator in 2013," 2 June 2014, *Courier-Journal*, http://www.courier-journal.com/story/politics-blog/2014/06/02/legislative-salaries/9858895/; University of Texas "Texas Politics: The Legislative Branch, Compensation," http://www.laits.utexas.edu/txp_media/html/leg/0205.html; Amelia Thomson-DeVeaux, "How Much Should State Legislators Get Paid?" FiveThirtyEight, 7 April 2016, http://fivethirtyeight.com/features/how-much-should-state-legislators-get-paid/; Dave Ress, "A Part-Time Legislature with Full-Time Rewards," Daily Press, 14 November 2014, http://www.dailypress.com/news/politics/dp-nws-virginiaway-overview-20141116-story.html.

27. Squire and Moncrief, *State Legislatures Today*, 2010, 77–78; Amelia Thomson-DeVeaux, "How Much Should State Legislators Get Paid?" FiveThirtyEight, y April 2016, http://fivethirtyeight.com/features/how-much-should-state-legislators-get-paid/.

28. The professionalism scores employed here were calculated as follows. Squire and Moncrief (2010) score state legislature professionalism on a descending scale ranging from 1.0 to 0.0, with 1.0 representing a legislature that is as professionalized as the US Congress. Here higher scores must signify decreasing professionalism, since higher scores in the system used here are associated with increased susceptibility to a climate of capitulation. Because the campaign finance and political culture indices in table 5.3 employ a roughly 1 to 10 scale, and the professionalism scale should be normalized to that scale, the professionalism scale extends from 1 (low susceptibility to a climate of capitulation) to 10 (high susceptibility to a climate of capitulation). The susceptibility scores displayed in table 5.5 were calculated as follows: (1 – Squire/Moncrief score) * 10.

29. Tom Eblen, "Is Kentucky a Southern State?" http://tomeblen.bloginky.com/
2008/08/28/is-kentucky-a-southern-state/; https://www.reddit.com/r/todayilearned/
comments/19sduk/til_kentucky_never_seceded_from_the_union_during/.

30. US Census, "Census Regions and Divisions of the United States," http://www2
.census.gov/geo/pdfs/maps-data/maps/reference/us_regdiv.pdf.

31. US Environmental Protection Agency, "Air Markets Program Data," https://
ampd.epa.gov/ampd/; US Energy Information Administration, "US Coal Consumption by End Use Sector, Census Division, and State, 2014 and 2013," https://www
.eia.gov/coal/annual/pdf/table26.pdf.

32. US Energy Information Administration, "Coal Production and Number of Mines
by State and Mine Type, 2014," https://www.eia.gov/coal/annual/pdf/table2.pdf.

33. National Institute on Money in State Politics, "Show Me Coal Mining
Contributions Between January 1, 2001 and December 31, 2013 to Candidates and
Committees in Alabama," "Show Me Coal Mining Contributions Between January 1,
2001 and December 31, 2013 to Candidates and Committees in Virginia" (www
.followthemoney.org); US Energy Information Administration, "Annual Coal
Report," for the years 2002 through 2012 (www.eia.gov/coal/annual/).

34. All campaign finance figures from the National Institute on Money in State Politics (www.followthemoney.org). Census data from US Census, "QuickFacts," http://
www.census.gov/quickfacts/.

35. Lieske, "American State Cultures," 123, appendix B, figures C1 and C2; Putnam,
"E Pluribus Unum," 137; Putnam, "Social Capital," figure 6.

36. Carter, "More Than Race," 149.

37. Maibach et al., "A National Survey of Republicans," 1; for a detailed description
of the North Carolina Clean Smokestacks case, see generally Andrews, "State Environmental Policy Innovation"; North Carolina State University Institute for Emerg-
ing Issues, "Civic Engagement Around EPA's Proposed Clean Power Plan," 2
April 2015, 3, https://iei.ncsu.edu/wp-content/uploads/2015/04/April2015_Env.pdf;
Samantha Page, "Solar Gets a Win in North Carolina, But Not For Homeowners,"
ClimateProgress, 1 May 2015, http://thinkprogress.org/climate/2015/05/01/3653810/
north-carolinas-solar-investment/; Terrence Henry, "How Denmark and Texas
Became Wind Energy Kings," National Public Radio, 18 December 2014, https://
stateimpact.npr.org/texas/2014/12/18/how-denmark-and-texas-became-wind-
energy-kings/; Roger Real Drouin, "How Conservative Texas Took the Lead in US
Wind Power," Environment360, 9 April 2015, http://e360.yale.edu/feature/how
_conservative_texas_took_the_lead_in_us_wind_power/2863/; Center for Climate
and Energy Solutions, "Florida Governor Signs Energy and Climate Change Bill,"
http://www.c2es.org/us-states-regions/news/2008/florida-governor-signs-energy
-climate-change-bill; Thomson, Sophisticated Interdependence, 14–15; The Southeast

Florida Regional Climate Change Compact, http://www.southeastflorida climatecompact.org/who-we-are/.

38. Ned Barnett, "NC Lets Sun Set on Solar Tax Credit," *News and Observer*, 10 October 2015, http://www.newsobserver.com/opinion/opn-columns-blogs/ned-barnett/ article38700429.html; Lori Montgomery, "On N.C.'s Outer Banks, Scary Climate-Change Predictions Prompt a Change of Forecast," *Washington Post*, https://www .washingtonpost.com/business/economy/ncs-outer-banks-got-a-scary-forecast -about-climate-change-so/2014/06/24/0042cf96-f6f3-11e3-a3a5-42be35962a52 _story.html; Tristram Korten, "Florida's Case of Climate Denial: A Case of Two Governors," *Miami Herald*, 27 December 2015, http://www.miamiherald.com/news/ local/environment/article51778500.html.

39. Coal use figures apply to the sixteen-state area covered by the Southern States Energy Board in "Southern States Regional Energy Profiles, 2014," 18, http://www .sseb.org/wp-content/uploads/2014/07/2014-Southern-States-Energy-Profiles _FINAL.pdf.

Chapter 7

1. Virginia Foundation for the Humanities, "Encyclopedia Virginia: Seal of the Commonwealth of Virginia," http://www.encyclopediavirginia.org/seal_of_the _commonwealth_of_virginia.

2. Kalman, "AHR Forum," 1052.

3. President's Committee, "Administrative Management in the Government of the United States," 5; Fesler, "The Brownlow Committee Fifty Years Later," 293.

4. Executive Office of the President, "Fiscal Year 2016 Budget Overview," EOP-3, https://www.whitehouse.gov/sites/default/files/docs/eop_fiscal_year_2016 _congressional_justification_0.pdf.

5. Patricia Sullivan, "How Two Accidental Virginia Activists Have (Almost) Closed GenOn Coal Plant," *Washington Post*, 23 September 2011, https://www .washingtonpost.com/local/how-two-accidental-virginia-activists-have-almost -closed-genon-coal-plant/2011/09/01/gIQABxA3zJ_story.html. In 2011 Ms. Chimento was named Alexandria's citizen of the year for her efforts to control Mirant's air pollution.

6. Capital News Service, "Head DEQ Official Accepted Dominion Gifts, Including Paid Trip to Master's Tourney," 15 March 2016, http://wtvr.com/2016/03/15/ head-deq-official-accepted-dominion-gifts-including-paid-trip-to-masters-tourney/.

7. US Environmental Protection Agency, "Clean Power Plan: State at a Glance, Virginia," https://ww.epa.gov/airquality/cpptoolbox/virginia.pdf.

8. US Energy Information Administration, "Coal Consumption by End Use Sector, Census Division, and State, 2014 and 2013," http://www.eia.gov/coal/annual/pdf/table26.pdf.

9. US Energy Information Administration, "Coal Consumption by End Use Sector, Census Division, and State, 2014 and 2013," http://www.eia.gov/coal/annual/pdf/table26.pdf; State of Maryland Department of the Environment, "Greenhouse Gas Emissions Reduction Act: Plan Update," first full page of text (pages unnumbered); Maryland Department of the Environment, "Governor Martin O'Malley Announces Legislation to Reduce Global Warming Pollution," 23 January 2009, http://www.mde.state.md.us/programs/PressRoom/Pages/1165.aspx; National Oceanic and Atmospheric Administration, "Shoreline Mileage," https://coast.noaa.gov/data/docs/states/shorelines.pdf; National Oceanic and Atmospheric Administration, "National Coastal Population Report: Population Trends from 1970 to 2020," 9, http://oceanservice.noaa.gov/facts/coastal-population-report.pdf ; US Energy Information Administration, "Iowa," http://www.eia.gov/state/?sid=IA#tabs-4 ; Devin Henry, "Why the EPA's Clean Power Plan Makes Even Green Minnesota a Little Nervous," 11 March 2015, https://www.minnpost.com/dc-dispatches/2015/03/why-epa-s-clean-power-plan-makes-even-green-minnesota-little-nervous.

10. *Massachusetts et al. v. EPA*, 549 U.S. 497 (2007); *Murray Energy Corporation, State of West Virginia v. EPA*, 2015 U.S. App. LEXIS 9573 (2015); Adam Liptak, "Justices Uphold Emission Limits on Big Industry," *New York Times*, 23 June 2014, http://www.nytimes.com/2014/06/24/us/justices-with-limits-let-epa-curb-power-plant-gases.html; Revesz and Lienke, *Struggling for Air*, 161; DeBellis, "In Defense of the Clean Power Plan," 255.

11. US Environmental Protection Agency, "Cross-State Air Pollution Rule," https://www3.epa.gov/crossstaterule/, costs cited here reflect CSAPR.

12. See generally Siikamäki et al., "The US Environmental Protection Agency's Acid Rain Program" and Wettestad, "Rescuing EU Emissions Trading: Mission Impossible?";Dallas Burtraw, "The Institutional Blind Spot in Environmental Economics," August 2012, Resources for the Future, 8, http://www.rff.org/files/sharepoint/WorkImages/Download/RFF-DP-12-41.pdf; Charles Driscoll: National Public Radio, "Questions Raised about Mercury 'Hot Spots' in the US," 19 January 2007, http://www.npr.org/templates/story/story.php?storyId=6921983; Gabriel Nelson, "Has Emissions Cap and Trade Created Toxic Hot Spots? A New Study Says No," *New York Times*, 31 March 2011, http://www.nytimes.com/gwire/2011/03/31/31greenwire-has-emissions-cap-and-trade-created-toxic-hotsp-4746.html; US Environmental Protection Agency, "Air Markets Program Data," https://ampd.epa.gov/ampd/.

13. Repetto, "Cap and Trade Contains Global Warming Better Than a Carbon Tax," 55. For an explanation of the complications in setting carbon taxes, see Williams, "Environmental Taxation."

14. US Congressional Budget Office, "Effects of a Carbon Tax," 2; Repetto, "Cap and Trade Contains Global Warming Better than a Carbon Tax," 56–58.

15. Emily Holden, "Local Groups Push Back on Utility's Carbon-Cutting Plan," ClimateWire, 27 January 2016; for the emissions increases projected from reliance on rate-based state plans, see US Energy Information Administration, "Effects of the Clean Power Plan," figure If1–1, http://www.eia.gov/forecasts/aeo/section_issues .cfm#cpp; US Department of Energy, "Effects of the Clean Power Plan," 20 June 2016, figure IF1–1, http://www.eia.gov/forecasts/aeo/section_issues.cfm#cpp.

16. Presidential Climate Action Project, "Emission Reductions Needed to Stabilize Climate," August 2011, 4, https://www.climatecommunication.org/wp-content/ uploads/2011/08/presidentialaction.pdf.

17. See generally Burger et al., "Legal Pathways to Reducing Greenhouse Gas Emissions Under Section 115 of the Clean Air Act."

18. Carter, "More Than Race,"149.

19. Gaventa, *Power and Powerlessness*, 42; Fisher, "State Political Culture and Support for Obama," 702.

20. Carter, "More Than Race," 149.

21. Joint Legislative Audit and Review Commission of the Virginia General Assembly, *Review of the Department of Environmental Quality*, v.

22. Virginia Department of Environmental Quality, "Commonwealth of Virginia: Clean Power Plan for Greenhouse Gases, Stakeholder Group Members," http://www .deq.virginia.gov/Portals/0/DEQ/Air/GHG/mbrlst.pdf.

23. Legal Information Institute, 42 U.S. Code § 7403, Research, investigation, training, and other activities, https://www.law.cornell.edu/uscode/text/42/7403.

24. US Environmental Protection Agency, Region 5, "Grants: Air Program Grant Funds for Fiscal Year 2015," https://yosemite.epa.gov/r5/r5ard.nsf/216ee3876e2b57 c786256641005b8d76/bef870e65f58edd886257e2d0053b547!OpenDocument; Jeff Whitlow, US Environmental Protection Agency, personal communication, 8 July 2016. The EPA also makes grants to state and local air-pollution-control agencies under Section 105 of the Clean Air Act for carrying out Clean Air Act programs but those grants require matching funds in the amount of 40 percent. In fiscal year 2016 Section 105 grants totaled $228 million. National Association of Clean Air Agencies, Testimony of S. William Becker, Executive Director, before the House Appropriations Committee, Subcommittee on Interior, Environment, and Related Agencies, 21 March 2016, 1, http://www.4cleanair.org/sites/default/files/resources/ NACAATestimony-House-FY17%20(2).pdf. Former DEQ Director Robert Burnley suggested using Virginia's Emergency Response Fund as a source for citizen research grants. Fund balances were provided by Valerie Thomson, Director of

Administration, Department of Environmental Quality, 29 February 2016. Statutory authority for use of the fund can be found at http://law.lis.virginia.gov/vacode/title10.1/chapter25/section10.1-2500/.

25. For overviews of the Federal Advisory Committee Act's implementation and authority, see generally Straus et al., "Restricting Membership," and Brown, "Fairly Balanced." Under part d of the Federal Advisory Committee Act, members can be compensated. US General Services Administration, "The Federal Advisory Committee Act," http://www.gsa.gov/portal/content/100916. Remuneration for travel expenses and per diem allowances for meeting days are standard, as indicated in the databases of advisory committee members: http://facadatabase.gov/datasets/. The EPA's various advisory committees are listed here: https://www.epa.gov/faca/all-federal-advisory-committees-epa.

26. Buckley, "Clean Air Post-Healthcare," 839.

27. Straus et al., "Restricting Membership," 311; see generally Conley, "Conflict of Interest and the EPA's Science Advisory Board" and US General Accounting Office, "EPA's Science Advisory Board Panels"; Haskell and Price, *State Environmental Management*, 258; Patricia Sullivan, "Anne Gorsuch Burford, 62, Dies; Reagan EPA Director," *Washington Post*, 22 July 2004, B06, http://www.washingtonpost.com/wp-dyn/articles/A3418-2004Jul21.html.

28. Booknotes, "Molly Ivins," C-SPAN, 26 April 1998, https://www.youtube.com/watch?v=fQyHF_iKPx8.

29. For overviews of *McCutcheon v. Federal Election Commission*, see Hartobey, "Money, Money, Money"; National Conference of State Legislatures, "Contribution Limits Overview," http://www.ncsl.org/research/elections-and-campaigns/campaign-contribution-limits-overview.aspx.

30. Alan Simpson, "Former Republican Senator Alan Simpson: Restore the Balance of Money in Politics," *Time*, 15 December 2015, http://time.com/4149277/republican-debate-money-and-politics/.

31. Tokaji and Strause, *The New Soft Money*, 82–83.

32. Governor Terry McAuliffe, "Governor Announces Actions to Stimulate Growth of Renewable Energy in the Commonwealth," 21 December 2015, https://governor.virginia.gov/newsroom/newsarticle?articleId=13729; National Institute on Money in State Politics, "Contributions to McAuliffe, Terence Richard (Terry), Between January 1, 2012 and December 1, 2015" http://www.followthemoney.org/show-me?f-core=1&f-fc=2&c-t-eid=1343597&d-ccg=5&d-dte=2012-01-01,2015-12-01#[{1|gro=d-eid. Overall electric utility campaign finance analysis documented in chapter 5. The Fact Checker, "McAuliffe's Claim of Not Taking Money from Dominion Doesn't Include Executives," *Washington Post*, 20 May 2009, http://www.washingtonpost.com/wp-dyn/content/article/2009/05/19/AR2009051903518.html;

Editorial Board, "Bob McDonnell's Indictment Shows the 'Virginia Way' Will Have to Change," *Washington Post*, 21 January 2014, https://www.washingtonpost.com/opinions/bob-mcdonnells-indictment-shows-the-virginia-way-will-have-to-change/2014/01/21/b00ea8b6-82e8-11e3-9dd4-e7278db80d86_story.html; Robert Barnes, "Supreme Court Overturns Corruption Conviction of Former Virginia Government McDonnell," *Washington Post*, 26 June 2016, https://www.washingtonpost.com/politics/supreme-court-rules-unanimously-in-favor-of-former-va-robert-f-mcdonnell-in-corruption-case/2016/06/27/38526a94-3c75-11e6-a66f-aa6c1883b6b1_story.html.

33. See generally Panagopoulis, *Public Financing*.

34. National Conference of State Legislatures, "Overview of State Laws on Public Financing," http://www.ncsl.org/research/elections-and-campaigns/public-financing-of-campaigns-overview.aspx.

35. Bachrach and Baratz, "Two Faces of Power," 949.

36. Crenson, *The Unpolitics of Air Pollution*, 130, 80.

37. Virginia State Air Pollution Control Board, Meeting Minutes for 27 January 2006, 1–2; Virginia General Assembly, "HB 1471: Mercury Emission Controls;" *Environmental Protection*, "Several States Adopting Mercury Rules Tougher than Federal Standard," 1 November 2006, https://eponline.com/articles/2006/11/01/several-states-adopting-mercury-rules-tougher-than-federal-standard.aspx?admgarea=News; *New Jersey v. EPA*, 517 F.3d 575.

38. Patrick Lee Plaisance, "High Profile: W. Tayloe Murphy, Jr.," *Daily Press*, 21 June 1999, http://articles.dailypress.com/1999-06-21/news/9906210009_1_murphy-virginia-marine-resources-commission-legislative/2.

39. California Air Resources Board, "Clean Car Standards—Pavley, Assembly Bill 1493," http://www.arb.ca.gov/cc/ccms/ccms.htm; Ka and Teske, "Ideology and Professionalism," 333.

40. Squire and Moncrief, *State Legislatures Today*, 2015, 64–65.

41. Squire and Moncrief, *State Legislatures Today*, 2010, 79–80 and 89–90; Amelia Thomson-DeVeaux, "How Much Should State Legislators Get Paid?" FiveThirtyEight, 7 April 2016, http://fivethirtyeight.com/features/how-much-should-state-legislators-get-paid/. A scatter plot of average age of state legislators as a function of ratings on the Squire Index of legislative professionalization is given in the appendix and is based on National Conference of State Legislatures, "Who We Elect: Legislators 2015, Average Age By Chamber, Revised," http://www.ncsl.org/research/about-state-legislatures/who-we-elect-an-interactive-graphic.aspx and Squire and Moncrief, *State Legislatures Today*, 2015, appendix A-3.

42. Maestas, "The Incentive to Listen," 454; Squire and Moncrief, *State Legislatures Today*, 1; Dave Ress, "Networking and Career Building in the Capitol," *The Daily Press*, 21 November 2014, http://www.dailypress.com/news/politics/dp-virginiaway -part-7--career-20141121-story.html.

43. Squire and Moncrief, *State Legislatures Today*, 2015, 18–19; Carey et al., 2006, 123.

44. Squire and Moncrief, State Legislatures Today (2015), 71ff; Pennsylvania General Assembly, Joint State Government Commission, "Truancy and School Dropout Prevention"; North Carolina General Assembly, "2013–14 Legislative Commissions, Non-Standing Committees, Interim Studies."

45. Rocky Mountain Institute, "Total Per Capita Electricity Use, 1960–2009," http://www.rmi.org/RFGraph-total_per_capita_eletricity_use; US Energy Information Administration, "Net Generation by Energy Source: Total," http://www.eia .gov/electricity/monthly/epm_table_grapher.cfm?t=epmt_1_01; US Census Bureau, "Monthly Population Estimates for the United States," http://factfinder.census .gov/faces/tableservices/jsf/pages/productview.xhtml?src=bkmk; Energy Information Administration, "U.S. Economy and Electricity Demand Growth Are Linked, But Relationship Is Changing," 22 March 2013, http://www.eia.go/todayinenergy/ detail.cmf?id=10491.

46. US Energy Information Administration, "US Electricity Flow 2014," https:// www.eia.gov/totalenergy/data/monthly/pdf/flow/electricity.pdf.

47. Borbely and Kreider, "Distributed Generation: An Introduction," 1; PBS NewsHour, "Gridlocked by the Power Grid: Why Hawaii's Solar Energy Industry Is at a Crossroads," 11 April 2015, http://www.pbs.org/newshour/bb/gridlocked-power -grid-hawaiis-solar-energy-industry-crossroads/; Edgar Meza, "Arizona Leads US in Per Capita Solar," 24 July 2013, *PV Magazine*, http://www.pv-magazine.com/news/ details/beitrag/arizona-leads-us-in-per-capita-solar_100012145/#axzz3xL2EoTsG; Environment Massachusetts, "Lighting the Way: What We Can Learn from America's Top 12 Solar States," July 2013, 6–7, http://environmentmassachusetts.org/sites/ environment/files/reports/Lighting_the_way_MA_scrn.pdf.

48. Diane Cardwell and Julianne Creswell, "Rooftop Solar Providers Face a Cloudier Future," *New York Times*, 10 February 2016, http://www.nytimes.com/2016/02/11/ business/energy-environment/rooftop-solar-providers-face-a-cloudier-future.html; Edison Electric Institute, "Disruptive Challenges: Financial Implications and Strategic Responses to a Changing Retail Electric Business," January 2013, http://www.eei/ org/ourissues/finance/documents/disruptivechallenges.pdf.

49. Dar Danielson, "Iowa Poised to Move Back Up in Wind Power Production Ranking," RadioIowa, 28 January 2015, www.radioiowa.com/2015/01/28/iowa-poised-to-move-back-up-in-wind-power-production-ranking/; Iowa Wind Energy Association, "Iowa Wind Energy Fact Sheet," undated, http://iowawindenerg.org/pdf/

Iowa-Wind-Fact-Sheet-05115.pdf; Melissa May, "Why Is Texas Changing Its Mind About Wind Power?" *America Tonight*, 7 May 2015, america.aljazeera.com/watch/shows/america-tonight/articles/2015/5/7/texas-wind-subdieis/html.

50. This figures was computed as follows. Carbon trading prices have been $13.18 per allowance in California (January 2016) and $7.50 per allowance in the Regional Greenhouse Gas Initiative (December 2015). Here the median of those two figures was used, $10.34. Ohio's emissions-reduction target under the Clean Power Plan varies from 67 million metric tons in 2030 to 80 million metric tons between 2022 and 2024. Typically, one allowance corresponds to one metric ton of carbon dioxide. Regional Greenhouse Gas Initiative, "Auction Results: Allowances Prices and Volumes (By Auction)," https://www.rggi.org/market/co2_auctions/results; Climate Policy Initiative, "California Carbon Dashboard," http://calcarbondash.org/; US Environmental Protection Agency, "Clean Power Plan: State at a Glance, Ohio," https://www3.epa.gov/airquality/cpptoolbox/ohio.pdf (short tons converted to megagrams for these computations).

51. Morrice and Colagiuri, "Coal Mining, Social Injustice and Health"; World Wildlife Fund, "Appalachian-Blue Ridge Forests," undated, http://www.worldwildlife.org/ecoregions/na0403.

52. Nolden, "Governing Community Energy," 543; Germany Renewable Energies Agency, "Renewable Energies: A Success Story," March 2015, https://www.unendlich-viel-energie.de/media/file/394.Flyer_Success_Mrz15_Web.pdf; Thomson, *Sophisticated Interdependence*, see generally pp. 47–71; Stefan Schultz, "Power Failures: Germany Rethinks Path to Green Future," *Der Spiegel*, 28 August 2012, http://www.spiegel.de/international/germany/problems-prompt-germany-to-rethink-energy-revolution-a-852815.html.

53. Schattschneider, *The Semi-Sovereign People*, 34–35; *New York Review of Books*, "Marilynne Robinson and President Obama," 15 November 2015, http://www.nybooks.com/articles/2015/11/05/president-obama-marilynne-robinson-conversation/.

Bibliography

Abt Associates, Inc. Assessing the Economic Impact of Dominion Virginia Power's Coal Fired Power Plant in Wise, Virginia. http://www.abtassociates.com/reports/Economic_Analysis_of_Wise_County_Coal_Plant_1-22-09.pdf

Andrews, Richard N. L. *Managing the Environment, Managing Ourselves*, second edition. Yale University Press, 2006.

Andrews, Richard N. L. State Environmental Policy Innovation: North Carolina's Clean Smokestacks Act. *Environmental Law* 43 (2013): 881–939.

Aneja, Viney, Aaron Isherwood, and Peter Morgan. Characterization of Particulate (PM_{10}) Related to Surface Coal Mining Operations in Appalachia. *Atmospheric Environment* 54 (July 2012): 496–501.

Anonymous. First Amendment—Freedom of Speech—Aggregate Contribution Limits—*McCutcheon v. FEC. Harvard Law Review* 128 (1) (November 2014): 201–210.

Ansolabehere, Stephen, John M. DeFigueiredo, and James M. Snyder Jr. Why Is There So Little Money in US Politics? *Journal of Economic Perspectives* 17 (1) (2003): 105–130.

Ansolabehere, Stephen, and David M. Konisky. *Cheap and Clean: How Americans Think About Energy in the Age of Global Warming*. MIT Press, 2014.

Ansolabehere, Stephen, Jonathan Rodden and James M. Snyder Jr. Purple America. *Journal of Economic Perspectives* 20 (2) (2006): 97–118.

Arbuckle, Matthew B. The Role and Implications of Citizen Environmental Boards in State-Level Policy-Making: Does Agency Structure Matter? PhD dissertation, University of Missouri, Columbia, 2013.

Arnold, R. Douglas. *The Logic of Congressional Action*. Yale University Press, 1990.

Bachrach, Peter, and Morton S. Baratz. Two Faces of Power. *American Political Science Review* 56 (4) (1962): 947–952.

Bateman, David A., Ira Katznelson, and John Lapinsky. *Southern Politics* Revisited: On V. O. Key's "South in the House." *Studies in American Political Development* 29 (October 2015): 154–184.

Baumert, Kevin A., Timothy Herzog, and Jonathan Pershing. *Navigating the Numbers: Greenhouse Gas Data and International Environmental Policy.* World Resources Institute, 2005. http://www.wri.org/sites/default/files/pdf/navigating_numbers.pdf.

Baumgartner, Frank R., Jeffrey M. Berry, Marie Hojnacki, David C. Kimball, and Beth L. Leech. *Lobbying and Policy Change: Who Wins, Who Loses, and Why.* University of Chicago Press, 2009.

Bay Area Air Quality Management District. Approved Budget for Fiscal Year Ending 2016. file:///Users/VET4Y/Downloads/BAAQMD%20Budget%202016.pdf.

Berry, Michael J., Frank N. Laird, and Christopher H. Stefes. Driving Energy: The Enactment and Ambitiousness of State Renewable Energy Policy. *Journal of Public Policy* 35 (2) (August 2015): 297–328.

Bolton, Alexander, Rachel Augustine Potter, and Sharece Thrower. Organizational Capacity, Regulatory Review, and the Limits of Political Control. *Journal of Law Economics and Organization* 32 (2) (2015): 1–30.

Borbely, Anne-Marie, and Jan F. Kreider. Distributed Generation: An Introduction. In *Distributed Generation: The Power Paradigm for the New Millennium*, ed. Anne-Marie Borbely and Jan F. Kreider. CRC Press, 2001.

Bosso, Christopher. *Pesticides and Politics: The Life Cycle of a Public Issue.* University of Pittsburg Press, 1987.

Brown, Mark B. Fairly Balanced: The Politics of Representation on Government Advisory Committees. *Political Science Quarterly* 61 (4) (December 2008): 547–560.

Brugge, Doug, Allison P. Patton, Alex Bob, Ellin Reisner, Lydia Lowe, and Oliver-John M. Bright. Developing Community-Level Policy and Practice to Reduce Traffic-Related Air Pollution Exposure. *Environmental Justice* 8 (3) (2015): 93–104.

Buckley, Sarah. Clean Air Post-Healthcare: The Federalism Limits of the Spending Power and the Future of Environmental Regulation. *Virginia Law Review* 101 (3) (May 2015): 807–848.

Burger, Michael, Ann E. Carlson, Michael P. Gerrard, Jayni Foley Hein, Jason A. Schwartz, and Keith J. Benes. Legal Pathways to Reducing Greenhouse Gas Emissions Under Section 115 of the Clean Air Act. Sabin Center for Climate Change Law, Columbia Law School, Emmett Institute for Climate Change and the Environment, University of California-Los Angeles School of Law, Institute for Policy Integrity, and New York University School of Law, 2016. https://web.law.columbia.edu/sites/default/files/microsites/climate-change/legal_pathways_to_reducing_ghg_emissions_under_section_115_of_the_caa.pdf

Burnley, Robert G. How Will Virginia Regulate Uranium Mining? *Virginia Lawyer* 60 (June-July 2011) 41–4. http://www.vsb.org/docs/valawyermagazine/vl0711-uranium .pdf.

Burstein, Paul. *American Public Opinion, Advocacy, and Policy in Congress: What the Public Wants and What It Gets*. Cambridge University Press, 2014.

Burtraw, Dallas, and Sarah Jo Szambelan. U.S. Emissions Trading Programs for SO2 and NOX. Resources for the Future, 2009. file:///Users/VET4Y/Desktop/Burtraw%20 Cap%20Trade%202009.pdf.

Caiazzo, Fabio, Akshay Ashok, Ian A. Waitz, Steve H.L. Yim, and Steven R.H. Barre. Air Pollution and Early Deaths in the United States: Part I, Quantifying the Impact of Major Sectors in 2005. *Atmospheric Environment* 79 (2013): 198–208.

Carey, John M., Richard G. Niemi, Lynda W. Powell, and Gary F. Moncrief. The Effects of Term Limits on State Legislatures: A New Survey of the 50 States. *Legislative Studies Quarterly* 31 (1) (February 2006): 104–131.

Carley, Sanya, and Chris J. Miller. Regulatory Stringency and Policy Drivers: A Reassessment of Renewable Portfolio Standards. *Policy Studies Journal* 40 (4) (2012): 730–735.

Carlson, Ann. An Ode to the Clean Air Act. *Journal of Land Use & Environmental Law* 30 (1) (Fall 2014): 119–141.

Carpenter, Daniel. Detecting and Measuring Capture. In *Reinventing Regulatory Capture: Special Interest Influence and How to Limit It*, ed. Daniel Carpenter and David A. Moss. Cambridge University Press, 2014.

Carpenter, Daniel, and David A. Moss. Introduction. In *Reinventing Regulatory Capture: Special Interest Influence and How to Limit It*, ed. Daniel Carpenter and David A. Moss. Cambridge University Press, 2014.

Carter, Dan. More Than Race: Conservatism in the South Since V. O. Key. In *Unlocking V. O. Key, Jr.: Southern Politics for the Twenty-First Century*, ed. Angie Maxwell and Todd G. Shields. University of Arkansas Press, 2011.

Chimento, Elizabeth, and Poul Hertel. Mirant Power Plant Emissions and Health Effects Report, 20 August 2003. Unpublished paper.

Cohen, Richard. *Washington at Work: Back Rooms and Clean Air*. Allyn and Bacon, 1995.

Conley, Joe G. Conflict of Interest and the EPA's Science Advisory Board. *Texas Law Review* 86 (2007): 165–189.

Cook, L. M., B. S. Grant, I. J. Saccheri, and J. Mallet. Selective Bird Predation on the Peppered Moth: The Last Experiment of Michael Majerus. *Biology Letters* 8 (2012): 609–612.

Cooper, Christopher A., and H. Gibbs Knotts. Partisan Change in Southern State Legislatures, 1953–2013. *Southern Cultures* 20 (2) (Summer 2014): 75–89.

Crenson, Matthew A. *The Unpolitics of Air Pollution: A Study of Non-Decisionmaking in the Cities.* Johns Hopkins University Press, 1971.

Croley, Steven P. *Regulation and Public Interests: The Possibility of Good Regulatory Government.* Princeton University Press, 2008.

Dal Bó, Ernesto. Regulatory Capture: A Review. *Oxford Review of Economic Policy* 22 (2) (2006): 203–225.

DeBellis, Eric Anthony. In Defense of the Clean Power Plan: Why Greenhouse Gas Regulation Under Section 111(d) Need Not, and Should Not, Stop at the Fenceline. *Ecology Law Quarterly* 42 (May 2015): 235–261.

Derthick, Martha. *Agency Under Stress: The Social Security Administration in American Government.* Brookings Institution, 1990.

Derthick, Martha. Compensatory Federalism. In *Greenhouse Governance: Addressing Climate Change in America*, ed. Barry Rabe. Brookings Institution, 2010.

Derthick, Martha, and Paul J. Quirk. *The Politics of Deregulation.* Brookings Institution, 1985.

Dewey, Scott Hamilton. *Don't Breathe the Air: Air Pollution and U.S. Environmental Politics, 1945–1970.* Texas A&M University Press, 2000.

Dwyer, John P. The Practice of Federalism Under the Clean Air Act. *Maryland Law Review* 54 (4) (1995): 1183–1225.

Elazar, Daniel Judah. *American Federalism: A View from the States.* Harper and Row, 1984.

Eshleman, Keith N., Robert D. Sabo, and Kathleen M. Kline. Surface Water Quality Is Improving Due to Declining Atmospheric N Deposition. *Environmental Science & Technology* 47 (21) (2013): 12193–12200.

European Commission. Special Eurobarometer 435: Climate Change. European Commission, 2015. http://ec.europa.eu/clima/citizens/support/docs/report_2015_en .pdf

European Environment Agency. *Annual European Union Greenhouse Gas Inventory 1990–2013 and Inventory Report* 2015. file:///C:/Users/Patrick%20Roach/Downloads/ Annual%20EU%20greenhouse%20gas%20inventory%202015%20-%20Full% 20report.pdf.

Ezzati, Majid, Ari B. Friedman, Sandeep C. Kulkarni, Christopher J. L. Murray. The Reversal of Fortunes: Trends in County Mortality and Cross-Country Mortality Disparities in the United States. *PLoS Medicine* 5 (4) (2008): 0557–0568.

Fesler, James W. The Brownlow Committee Fifty Years Later. *Public Administration Review* 47 (4) (July-August 1987): 291–296.

Fisher, Patrick. State Political Culture and Support for Obama in the 2008 Presidential Primaries. *Social Science Journal* 47 (2010): 699–709.

Flavin, Patrick. Campaign Finance Laws, Policy Outcomes, and Political Equality in the American States. *Political Research Quarterly* 68 (1) (2015): 77–88.

Formisano, Ronald P. The Concept of Political Culture. *Journal of Interdisciplinary History* 31 (3) (2001): 393–426.

Foster, Teresa, and Leslie Glustrom. Trends in US Coal Production: 1990–2012. Clean Energy Action, 2012. https://cleanenergyaction.files.wordpress.com/2013/10/coal_production_top_16_states.pdf

Gaddie, Ronald Keith, and Justin J. Wert. Before KKV, V. O. Key, Jr. In *Unlocking V. O. Key: Southern Politics for the Twenty-First Century*, ed. Angie Maxwell and Todd G. Shields. University of Arkansas Press, 2011.

Garrett, Theodore A. Downwind Ozone: Clearing the Air. *Natural Resources and Environment* 18 (3) (2004): 10–15.

Gaventa, John. *Power and Powerlessness: Quiescence and Rebellion in an Appalachian Valley*. Clarendon, 1980.

Gelpe, Marcia. Citizen Boards as Regulatory Agencies. *Urban Lawyer* 22 (3) (1990): 451–483.

George Mason University Center for Climate Change Communication and Yale University Project on Climate Communication. The Francis Effect: How Pope Francis Changed the Conversation About Global Warming. November 2015. http://climatepublicopinion.stanford.edu/wp-content/uploads/2013/04/Krosnick -May2010-Measuring-Americans-Issue-Priorities2.pdf

Germany, Umweltbundesamt. *Submission Under the United Nations Framework Convention on Climate Change and the Kyoto Protocol 2016: National Inventory Report for the German Greenhouse Gas Inventory 1990-2014*. https://www.umweltbundesamt.de/sites/default/files/medien/378/publikationen/climate_change_24_2016_submission_under_the_united_nations_framework_nir_2016.pdf

Grumet, Jason S. Old West Justice: Federalism and Clean Air Regulation 1970–1998. *Tulane Environmental Law Journal* 11 (1998): 375–413.

Hamm, Keith E., and Robert E. Hogan. Campaign Finance Laws and Candidacy Decisions in State Legislative Elections. *Political Research Quarterly* 61 (3) (2008): 458–467.

Hamra, Ghassan B., Neela Guha, Aaron Cohen, Francine Laden, Ole Raaschou-Nielsen, Jonathan M. Samet, Paolo Vineis, et al. Outdoor Particulate Matter

Exposure and Lung Cancer: A Systematic Review and Meta-Analysis. *Environmental Health Perspectives* 122 (9) (2014): 906–911.

Hansell, Tom. *The Electricity Fairy (DVD)*. Appalshop, 2010.

Hartobey, Patrick. Money, Money, Money: How the Supreme Court's Decision in *McCutcheon v. FEC* Could Impact Shareholders and Corporations. *Emory Law Corporate Governance and Accountability Review*, undated, http://law.emory.edu/ecgar/content/volume-1/issue-1/essays/money-money-money.html.

Haskell, Elizabeth H., and Victoria S. Price. *State Environmental Management: Case Studies of Nine States*. Praeger, 1973.

Heck, Ronald H., Wendy Lam, and Scott L. Thomas. State Political Culture, Higher Education Spending Indicators, and Undergraduate Graduation Outcomes. *Educational Policy* 28 (1) (2014): 3–39.

Hood, M. V., III , Quentin Kid, and Irwin L. Morris. *The Rational Southerner: Black Mobilization, Republican Growth, and the Partisan Transformation of the American South*. Oxford University Press, 2012.

Howe, Peter D., Matto Mildenberger, Jennifer R. Marlon, and Anthony Leiserowitz. Geographic Variation in Opinions on Climate Change at State and Local Scales in the USA. *Nature Climate Change* (5) (June 2015): 596–603.

Hunker, Kathleen. Elections Across the Pond: Comparing Campaign Finance Regimes in the United States and the United Kingdom. *Harvard Journal of Law & Public Policy* 36 (3) (2013): 1099–1137.

Hurley, Andrew. *Environmental Inequalities: Class, Race, and Industrial Pollution in Gary, Indiana, 1945–1980*. University of North Carolina Press, 1995.

International Energy Agency. Global Energy-Related Emissions of Carbon Dioxide Stalled in 2014, 13 March 2015. http://www.iea.org/newsroomandevents/news/2015/march/global-energy-related-emissions-of-carbon-dioxide-stalled-in-2014.html

Jastremsky, Wendy. Comment: Cracking Down on Coal: Pennsylvania Takes a Crack at Regulating Hazardous Mercury Emissions from Coal-Fired Power Plants with a State-Specific Rule that Is Stricter than the Federal Clean Air Mercury Rule. *Penn State Environmental Law Review* 16 (Winter 2008): 431–450.

Jones, Charles O. *Clean Air: The Policies and Politics of Pollution Control*. University of Pittsburgh Press, 1975.

Ka, Sangjoon, and Paul Teske. Ideology and Professionalism—Electricity Regulation and Deregulation Over Time in the American States. *American Politics Research* 30 (2002): 323–343.

Kalman, Laura. AHR Forum: The Debate Over the Constitutional Revolution of 1937. *American Historical Review* 110 (4) (2005): 1052–1080.

Karanasiou, Angeliki, Zavier Querol Mar Viana, Teresa Moreno, and Frank de Leeuw. Assessment of Personal Exposure to Particulate Air Pollution During Commuting in European Cities—Recommendations and Policy Implications. *Science of the Total Environment* 490 (August 2014): 785–797.

Kaswan, Alice. Decentralizing Cap-and-Trade? State Controls Within a Federal Greenhouse Gas Control Program. *Virginia Environmental Law Review* 28 (3) (2010): 337–401.

Kearns, Ian, and Steven Lukes. In Conversation with Steven Lukes. *Public Policy Research* 13 (4) (2006): 272–275.

King, James D. Political Culture, Voter Registration, and Voter Turnout Among the American States. *Publius* 24 (4) (1994): 115–127.

Konisky, David M., and Neal D. Woods. Measuring State Environmental Policy. *Review of Policy Research* 29 (4) (2012): 544–569.

Koven, Steven G., and Christopher Mausoloff. The Influence of Political Culture on State Budgets: Another Look at Elazar's Formulation. *American Review of Public Administration* 32 (1) (2002): 66–77.

Krosnick, Jonathan A. Public Opinion on Climate Change: Opinions in the States. Stanford University, 2013. http://climatepublicopinion.stanford.edu/sample-page/opinions-in-the-states/.

Krosnick, Jonathan A., and Bo MacInnis. Does the American Public Support Legislation to Reduce Greenhouse Gas Emissions? *Daedalus* 142 (winter 2013): 26–39.

Lazarus, Richard J. A Different Kind of "Republican" Moment in Environmental Law. *Minnesota Law Review* 87 (2003): 999–1035.

Leciejewski, Mary, and Harold A. Perkins. Environmental Justice in Appalachia: Procedural Inequities in the Mine Permitting Process in Southeast Ohio. *Environmental Justice* 8 (4) (2015): 111–116.

Leiserowitz, A., G. Feinberg, P. Howe, and S. Rosenthal. Climate Change in the Texan Mind. Yale University Project on Climate Change, 2013. http://environment.yale.edu/climate-communication/files/Texas_Climate_Change_Report.pdf.

Lewis, Ronald L. *Black Coal Miners in America*. University Press of Kentucky, 1987.

Lieske, Joel. The Changing Regional Subcultures of the American States and the Utility of a New Cultural Measure. *Political Research Quarterly* 63 (3) (2010): 538–552.

Lieske, Joel. American State Cultures: Testing a New Measure and Theory. *Publius* 42 (1) (2012): 108–113.

Lim, Stephen S., et al. A Comparative Risk Assessment of Burden of Disease and Injury Attributable to 67 Risk Factors and Risk Factor Clusters in 21 regions, 1990–2010: A Systematic Analysis for the Global Burden of Disease Study 2010. *The Lancet* 380 (December 15/22/29 2012), 2224–2260. http://www.ncbi.nlm.nih.gov/pmc/articles/PMC4156511/

Lodge, Martin. Regulatory Capture Recaptured. *Public Administration Review* 74 (4) (2014): 539–542.

Maestas, Cherie. The Incentive to Listen: Progressive Ambition, Resources, and Opinion Monitoring among State Legislators. *Journal of Politics* 65 (2003): 439–456.

Maibach, Edward, Connie Roser-Renouf, Emily Vraga, Brittany Bloodhart, Ashley Anderson, Neil Stenhouse, and Anthony Leiserowitz. A National Survey of Republicans and Republican-Leaning Independents on Energy and Climate Change, April 2, 2013. Yale University, 2013. http://environment.yale.edu/climate-communication/files/Republican_Views_on_Climate_Change.pdf.

Malhotra, Neil. Disentangling the Relationship between Legislative Professionalism and Government Spending. *Legislative Studies Quarterly* 33 (3) (2008): 387–414.

Maryland Department of the Environment. Greenhouse Gas Emissions Reduction Act: Plan Update 2015. http://www.mde.maryland.gov/programs/Marylander/Documents/ClimateUpdate2015.pdf

McCarthy, James E., Claudia Copeland, Larry Parker, and Linda-Jo Schierow. Clean Air Act: A Summary of the Act and Its Major Requirements. Washington, DC: Congressional Research Service, 2011. http://fpc.state.gov/documents/organization/155015.pdf.

McGarity, Thomas O. When Strong Enforcement Works Better Than Weak Regulation: The EPA/DOJ New Source Review Enforcement Initiative. *Maryland Law Review* 72 (4) (2013): 1204–1293.

Mead, Lawrence M. State Political Culture and Welfare Reform. *Policy Studies Journal* 32 (2) (2004): 272–296.

Mead, Lawrence M. Welfare Caseload Change: An Alternative Approach. *Policy Studies Journal* 31 (2) (2003): 163–185.

Meltz, Robert, and James E. McCarthy. The D.C. Circuit Rejects EPA's Mercury Rules: *New Jersey v. EPA*. Washington, DC: Congressional Research Service, 28 February 2008. http://assets.opencrs.com/rpts/RS22817_20080228.pdf

Miller, David Y., David C. Barker, and Christopher J. Carman. Mapping the Genome of American Political Subcultures: A Proposed Methodology and Pilot Study. *Publius* 36 (2) (2006): 303–315.

Moeller, James W. Clean Air v. Electric Reliability: The Case of the Potomac River Generation Station. *Washington and Lee Journal of Energy, Climate, and the Environment* 5 (December 2014): 27–91.

Mondak, Jeffery J., and Damarys Canache. Personality and Political Culture in the American States. *Political Research Quarterly* 67 (1) (2014): 26–41.

Morawska, L., A. Afshari, G. N. Bae, G. Buonanno, C. Y. H. Chao, O. Hanninen, W. Hofmann, et al. Indoor Aerosols: From Personal Exposure to Risk Assessment. *Indoor Air* 23 (2013): 462–487.

Morello-Frosch, Rachel, Manuel Pastor, and James Sadd. Environmental Justice and Southern California's "Riskscape": The Distribution of Air Toxics Exposures and Health Risks Among Diverse Communities. *Urban Affairs Review* 36 (4) (2001): 551–578.

Morrice, Emily, and Ruth Colagiuri. Coal Mining, Social Injustice and Health: A Universal Conflict of Power and Priorities. *Health & Place* 19 (2013): 714–779.

Moss, David A., and Daniel Carpenter. Conclusion: A Focus on Evidence and Prevention. In *Reinventing Regulatory Capture: Special Interest Influence and How to Limit It*, ed. Daniel Carpenter and David A. Moss. Cambridge University Press, 2014.

National Council of State Governments. "Our." *State Legislatures* (1948).

National Oceanic and Atmospheric Administration. National Coastal Population Report: Population Trends from 1970 to 2020. Washington, DC: NOAA, 2013. http://oceanservice.noaa.gov/facts/coastal-population-report.pdf

New York Times, Stanford University, and Resources for the Future. Poll on Global Warming. *New York Times*, 29 January 2015. http://www.nytimes.com/interactive/2015/01/29/us/politics/document-global-warming-poll.html

Nolden, Colin. Governing Community Energy—Feed-In Tariffs and the Development of Community Wind Energy Schemes in the United Kingdom and Germany. *Energy Policy* 63 (2013): 543–552.

North Carolina General Assembly. 2013–14 Legislative Commissions, Non-Standing Committees, Interim Studies. http://ncleg.net/documentsites/legislativepublications/Research%20Division/Commissions,%20Committees,%20Interim%20Studies%20Report/2013-2014%20Legislative%20Commissions%20Non-Standing%20Committees%20Interim%20Studies.pdf

Nye, Joseph S., Jr. *The Future of Power*. PublicAffairs, 2011.

Panagoupoulis, Costas. *Public Financing in American Elections*. Temple University Press, 2011.

Pautz, Michelle C., and Sara R. Rinfret. *The Lilliputians of Environmental Regulation: The Perspective of State Regulators*. Routledge, 2010.

Pennsylvania General Assembly, Joint State Government Commission. Report of the Task Force and Advisory Committee on Opioid Prescription Drug Proliferation. Harrisburg: Joint State Government Commission, 2015. http://jsg.legis.state.pa.us/resources/documents/ftp/publications/2015-412-HR659%20OPIOID%20REPORT%20FINAL%2006.23.15.pdf

Pennsylvania General Assembly, Joint State Government Commission. Truancy and School Dropout Prevention: Report of the Truancy Advisory Committee. Harrisburg: Joint State Goernment Commission, 2015. http://jsg.legis.state.pa.us/resources/documents/ftp/publications/2015-10-27%202015%20TAC%20Final%20Report%2010-27-15%203pm.pdf.

Pennsylvania General Assembly, Joint State Government Commission. Waste Tire Recycling and Reuse in Pennsylvania: An Analysis of the Industry, Markets, and State Use, Including Rubber Modified Asphalt. Harrisburg: Joint State Government Commission, 2007. http://jsg.legis.state.pa.us/resources/documents/ftp/publications/2007-29-Tire%20Report%20III.pdf

Pope, C. Arden, Majid Ezzati, and Douglas W. Dockery. Fine-Particulate Air Pollution and Life Expectancy in the United States. *New England Journal of Medicine* 360 (2009): 376–386.

Pope, C. Arden, Majid Ezzati, and Douglas W. Dockery. Fine Particulate Air Pollution and Life Expectancies in the United States: The Role of Influential Observations. *Journal of the Air & Waste Management Association* 63 (2) (2013): 129–132.

Powell, Lynda W. *Legislative Politics and Policy Making: The Influence of Campaign Contributions in State Legislatures: The Effects of Institutions and Politics.* University of Michigan Press, 2012.

President's Committee. Administrative Management in the Government of the United States. Washington: Government Printing Office, 1937. http://users.polisci.wisc.edu/kmayer/408/Report%20of%20the%20Presidents%20Committee.pdf

Putnam, Robert D. *E Pluribus Unum*: Diversity and Community in the Twenty-first Century: The 2006 Johan Skytte Prize Lecture. *Scandinavian Political Studies* 30 (2) (2007): 137–174.

Putnam, Robert D. Social Capital: Measurements and Consequences. OECD. www.oecd.org/innovation/research/1825848.pdf

Putnam, Robert D. with Robert Leonardi and Raffaella Nanetti. *Making Democracy Work: Civic Traditions in Modern Italy.* Princeton: Princeton University Press, 1993.

Quirk, Paul. In Defense of the Politics of Ideas. *Journal of Politics* 50 (1) (1988): 31–41.

Rabe, Barry. Contested Federalism and American Climate Policy. *Publius* 41 (3) (2011): 494–521.

Rabe, Barry, and Christopher Borick. *Climate Change and American Public Opinion: The National and State Perspectives.* University of Virginia: Miller Center of Public Affairs, 2008.

Rabe, Barry, and Christopher Borick. Report of the Virginia Climate Change Survey. http://web1.millercenter.org/panels/pdf/panel_2008_1021_borick.pdf

Ramseur, Jonathan L. *US Greenhouse Gas Emissions: Recent Trends and Factors.* Washington, DC: US Congressional Research Service, 2014., https://www.fas.org/sgp/crs/misc/R43795.pdf.

Raz, Raanan, Andrea L. Roberts, Kristen Lyall, Jaime E. Hart, Allan C. Just, Francine Laden, and Marc G. Weisskopf. Autism Spectrum Disorder and Particulate Matter Air Pollution before, during, and after Pregnancy: A Nested Case–Control Analysis within the Nurses' Health Study II Cohort. *Environmental Health Perspectives* 123 (3) (2015): 264–270.

Reitze, Arnold W., Jr. EPA's Fine Particulate Air Pollution Control Program. *Environmental Law Reporter* 44 (November 2014): 10996–11019.

Reitze, Arnold W., Jr. Federalism and the Inspection and Maintenance Program Under the Clean Air Act. *Pacific Law Journal* 27 (1996): 1461–1520.

Reitze, Arnold W., Jr. *Stationary Source Air Pollution Law.* Washington, DC: Environmental Law Institute, 2005.

Repetto, Robert. Cap and Trade Contains Global Warming Better Than a Carbon Tax. *Challenge* 56 (5) (2013): 31–61.

Revesz, Richard L., and Jack Lienke. *Struggling for Air: Power Plants and the "War on Coal."* Oxford University Press, 2016.

Rhodes, Edwardo Lao. *Environmental Justice in America: A New Paradigm.* Indiana University Press, 2003.

Rosenthal, Alan. State Legislative Development: Observations from Three Perspectives. *Legislative Studies Quarterly* 21 (2) (1996): 169–198.

Schattscheider, E. E. *The Semi-Sovereign People.* Holt, Rinehart and Winston, 1960.

Scheffe, Richard D., Paul A. Solomon, Rudolf Husar, Tim Hanley, Mark Schmidt, Michael Koerber, Michael Gilroy, et al. The National Ambient Air Monitoring Strategy: Rethinking the Role of National Networks. *Journal of the Air & Waste Management Association* 59 (May 2009): 579–590.

Schlozman, Kay Lehman, Sidney Verba, and Henry E. Brady. *The Unheavenly Chorus: Unequal Political Voice and the Broken Promise of American Democracy.* Princeton University Press, 2012.

Sharkansky, Ira. The Utility of Elazar's Political Culture: A Research Note. *Polity* 2 (1) (1969): 66–83.

Sierra Club and Appalachian Mountain Stewards Southern. Petition Virginia Air Pollution Control Board to Amend Existing Regulations. 16 November 2008. http://www.townhall.virginia.gov/l/ViewPetition.cfm?petitionid=97

Shin, Geiguen, and David Webber. Red States, Blue States: How Well Do the Recent National Election Labels Capture State Political and Policy Differences? *Social Science Journal* 51 (2014): 386–397.

Shrader-Frechette, K. S. *Environmental Justice: Creating Equity, Reclaiming Democracy.* Oxford University Press, 2002.

Siikamäki, Juha, Dallas Burtraw, Joseph Maher, and Clayton Munnings. The US Environmental Protection Agency's Acid Rain Program. Washington: Resources for the Future, 2012. http://www.rff.org/RFF/Documents/RFF-Bck-AcidRainProgram.pdf.

Squire, Peverill. Measuring State Legislative Professionalism: The Squire Index Revisited. *State Politics & Policy Quarterly* 7 (2) (2007): 211–227.

Squire, Peverill, and Gary Moncrief. *State Legislatures Today: Politics Under the Domes.* Pearson, 2010.

Squire, Peverill, and Gary Moncrief. *State Legislatures Today: Politics Under the Domes,* second edition. Rowman & Littlefield, 2015.

Stone, Deborah. *Policy Paradox: The Art of Political Decision Making.* Norton, 2002.

Straus, Jacob. *Party and Procedure in the US Congress.* Rowman and Littlefield, 2012.

Straus, Jacob R., Wendy R. Ginsberg, Amanda K. Mullan, and Jaclyn D. Petruzzelli. Restricting Membership: Assessing Agency Compliance and the Effects of Banning Federal Lobbyists from Executive Branch Advisory Committee Service. *Presidential Studies Quarterly* 45 (2) (2015): 310–344.

Tennesen, Michael. On a Clear Day. *National Parks*, November-December 1997: 26–29.

Texas Legislature and House Committee on Environmental Regulations. Interim Report to the 84th Legislature, December 2014. http://www.lrl.state.tx.us/scanned/interim/83/en89.pdf.

Thomson, Vivian E. *Sophisticated Interdependence in Climate Policy: Federalism in the United States, Brazil, and Germany.* Anthem, 2014.

Thomson, Vivian E., and Vicki Arroyo. Upside-Down Cooperative Federalism: Climate Change Policymaking and the States. *Virginia Environmental Law Journal* 29 (1) (2011): 1–61.

Tokaji, Daniel P., and Renata E. B. Strause. The New Soft Money: Outside Spending in Congressional Elections. Moritz College of Law, Ohio State University, 2012. http://moritzlaw.osu.edu/thenewsoftmoney/wp-content/uploads/sites/57/2014/06/the-new-soft-money-WEB.pdf.

Tollefson, Jeff. America's Top Climate Cop. *Nature* 473 (May 19, 2011): 268–270.

Tung, Gregory Jackson, Jon S. Vernick, Elizabeth A. Stuart, and Daniel W. Webster. Political Factors Affecting the Enactment of State-Level Clean Indoor Air Laws. *American Journal of Public Health* 104 (6) (2014): e92–e97.

Turner, William H. People of Color in the Green Future of Central Appalachia. Berea College, 2010. http://www.appalachiantransition.org/wp-content/uploads/2014/05/Bill-Turner-Essay-FINAL.pdf.

United Nations Framework Convention on Climate Change. Intended Nationally Determined Contributions: United States. Bonn: United Nations Framework Convention on Climate Change, 31 March 2015. http://www4.unfccc.int/submissions/INDC/Published%20Documents/United%20States%20of%20America/1/U.S.%20Cover%20Note%20INDC%20and%20Accompanying%20Information.pdf

US Congressional Budget Office. Effects of a Carbon Tax on the Economy and the Environment. Washington, DC: Congressional Budget Office, May 2013. https://www.cbo.gov/sites/default/files/113th-congress-2013-2014/reports/Carbon_One-Column.pdf

US Department of Energy. Special Environmental Analysis for Actions Taken Under US Department of Energy Emergency Orders Regarding Operation of the Potomac River Generating Station in Alexandria, Virginia, November 2006. http://energy.gov/nepa/downloads/sea-04-special-environmental-analysis

US Energy Information Administration. Coal Production and Number of Mines by State and Mine Type, 2013 and 2012. http://www.eia.gov/coal/annual/pdf/table1.pdf

US Energy Information Administration. State Energy-Related Carbon Dioxide Emissions by Year, 2000–2011. http://www.eia.gov/environment/emissions/state/analysis/pdf/table1.pdf

US Energy Information Administration. State Carbon Dioxide Emissions by Energy Sectors, 2013. http://www.eia.gov/environment/emissions/state/

US Energy Information Administration. US End Use Coal Consumption By End Use Sector, Census Division, and State, 2014 and 2013. http://www.eia.gov/coal/annual/pdf/table26.pdf

US Environmental Protection Agency. Costs and Benefits of Reducing Lead in Gasoline: Final Regulatory Impact Analysis. 1985.

US Environmental Protection Agency. *Emission Facts: The History of Reducing Tailpipe Emissions*, May 1999. http://www.epa.gov/otaq/consumer/f99017.pdf

US Environmental Protection Agency. Environmental Justice State Guidance: How to Incorporate Equity and Justice Into Your State Clean Power Planning Approach. Washington, DC: US EPA, January 2016. http://www.eesi.org/files/EJ-State -Guidance-Final-v5-jan-15-2016.pdf

US Environmental Protection Agency. Guidance for Network Design and Optimum Site Exposure for PM2. 5 and PM10. Washington, DC: US EPA, 1997. http://www .epa.gov/ttnamti1/files/ambient/pm25/network/r-99-022.pdf

US Environmental Protection Agency. Inventory of US Greenhouse Gas Emissions and Sinks: 1990–2014, April 2016. https://www3.epa.gov/climatechange/ Downloads/ghgemissions/US-GHG-Inventory-2016-Chapter-Executive-Summary .pdf and https://www3.epa.gov/climatechange/Downloads/ghgemissions/US-GHG -Inventory-2016-Chapter-3-Energy.pdf.

US Environmental Protection Agency. National Emissions Inventory (NEI) Air Pol- lutant Emissions Trends Data and Estimation Procedures. http://www.epa.gov/ ttnchie1/trends/

US Environmental Protection Agency. The Plain English Guide to the Clean Air Act. 2007. https://www.epa.gov/sites/production/files/2015-08/documents/peg.pdf

US Environmental Protection Agency. President's Task Force on Environmental Health Risks and Safety Risks to Children, May 2012. http://www.epa.gov/ childrenstaskforce/federal_asthma_disparities_action_plan.pdf

US Environmental Protection Agency. 2012 *Progress Report: Clean Air Interstate Rule, Acid Rain Program, and Former NO_x Budget Trading Program.* http://www.epa.gov/sites/ production/files/2015-08/documents/arpcair12_02.pdf

US Environmental Protection Agency. *Regulatory Impact Analysis for the Clean Power Plan Final Rule.* Washington: US EPA, 23 October 2015, http://www.epa.gov/sites/ production/files/2015-08/documents/cpp-final-rule-ria.pdf

US Environmental Protection Agency. *Regulatory Impact Analysis for the Final Mercury and Air Toxics Standards.* 2011. www3.epa.gov/ttnecas1/regdata/RIAs/ matsriafinalpdf.

US Environmental Protection Agency. *Regulatory Impact Analysis for the Final Revi- sions to the National Ambient Air Quality Standards for Particulate Matter.* 2012.

US General Accounting Office. EPA's Science Advisory Board Panels: Improved Poli- cies and Procedures Needed to Ensure Independence and Balance. Washington, DC: GAO, June 2001. http://www.gao.gov/new.items/d01536.pdf

Virginia Department of Environmental Quality. Citizen Board Legislation: House Bill 3113/Senate Bill 1403, November 2007. http://www.deq.virginia.gov/Portals/0/DEQ/LawsAndRegulations/HB_3113_Report_Final_111607.pdf

Virginia General Assembly. HB 1471, Mercury Emission Controls; Prohibits Air Pollution Control Board from Imposing, 2006 Session. http://lis.virginia.gov/cgi-bin/legp604.exe?061+sum+HB1471

Virginia General Assembly. VA HB 1332, 2008, Regular Session. https://legiscan.com/VA/bill/HB1332/2008

Virginia General Assembly, Joint Legislative and Audit Review Commission. Interim Report: Review of the Department of Environmental Quality, 1996 session. http://jlarc.virginia.gov/pdfs/reports/Rpt184.pdf

Virginia General Assembly, Joint Legislative and Audit Review Commission. Review of the Department of Environmental Quality, 1997. http://jlarc.virginia.gov/pdfs/reports/Rpt197.pdf

Walker, Gordon. *Environmental Justice: Concepts, Evidence and Politics*. Routledge, 2012.

Wallace, Lance, and Wayne Ott. Personal Exposure to Ultrafine Particles. *Journal of Exposure Science & Environmental Epidemiology* 21 (1) (2011): 20–30.

Waterman, Richard W., and Kenneth J. Meier. Principal-Agent Models: An Expansion? *Journal of Public Administration: Research and Theory* 8 (1998): 173–202.

Waterman, Richard W., Amelia A. Rouse, and Robert L. Wright. *Bureaucrats, Politics, and the Environment*. University of Pittsburgh Press, 2004.

Watson Center for Public Policy. Toplines: Virginia Environmental Attitudes Survey 2010. Newport News, Virginia: Christopher Newport University, 2010. http://cnu.edu/cpp/pdf/finaltoplines2010.pdf

Wettestad, Jørgen. Rescuing EU Emissions Trading: Mission Impossible? *Global Environmental Politics* 14 (2) (2014): 64–81.

Williams, Bruce A., and Albert R. Matheny. *Democracy, Dialogue, and Environmental Disputes: The Contested Languages of Social Regulation*. Yale University Press, 1995.

Williams, Roberton C. Environmental Taxation. Washington, DC: Resources for the Future, June 2016. http://www.rff.org/files/document/file/RFF-DP-16-24.pdf

Wilson, Woodrow. The Study of Administration. *Political Science Quarterly* 2 (2) (1887): 197–222.

Woodin, S. J. Environmental Effects of Air Pollution in Britain. *Journal of Applied Ecology* 26 (1989): 749–761.

Yale University Project on Climate Communication and George Mason University Center for Climate Change Communication. Politics and Global Warming: Democrats, Republicans, Independents, and the Tea Party. New Haven: Yale University, 2011. http://environment.yale.edu/climate-communication/files/PoliticsGlobalWarming2011.pdf

Yeager, David Scott, Samuel B. Larson, and Jon A. Krosnick. Measuring Americans' Issue Priorities: A New Version of the Most Important Problem Question Reveals More Concern About the Environment and Global Warming. Stanford University, 2013. http://climatepublicopinion.stanford.edu/wp-content/uploads/2013/04/Krosnick-May2010-Measuring-Americans-Issue-Priorities2.pdf.

Yeager, Peter Cleary. The Limits of Law: The Public Regulation of Private Pollution. Cambridge University Press, 1992.

Index